REBEL

WITH A CAUSE

REBEL

WITH A CAUSE

THE TRUE STORY OF JERRY TARKANIAN

DANNY TARKANIAN

CHAMPION
PRESS

Left: NCAA Awarding the 1990 National Championship
trophy to Jerry Tarkanian (JT) and Rebel Players

For information about special discounts for bulk purchases or author interviews,
appearances, and speaking engagements please contact the author at:

>   Twitter: @DannyTarkanian
>   Facebook: http://www.facebook.com/dannytarkanian

First Edition

ISBN hardcover: 978-1-946875-54-9
ISBN paperback: 978-1-946875-55-6
ISBN ebook: 978-1-946875-56-3

Edited by Christina Debusk
Designed by Rodney Miles
All images © the author unless noted

Image this page: UNLV Players, David Butler and Moses Scurry, celebrating with Jerry Tarkanian in closing seconds of 1990 National Championship game

CONTENTS

FOREWORD

COACHING BASKETBALL for over 40 years has given me the opportunity to coach under, coach with and compete against some of the greatest basketball coaches of all-time. Our Duke teams had two epic battles against Coach Jerry Tarkanian and his powerful UNLV teams. We tasted defeat in one and victory in the other, but after both I had tremendous respect for Jerry and his players.

Coach Tarkanian is arguably the best defensive coach in college basketball history and certainly one of its greatest coaches. His teams applied relentless pressure defense, causing havoc to opposing teams, many times leaving them helpless. This was accomplished by the incredible intensity and work ethic his players exhibited.

I do not believe a coach can get his players to play with that level of intensity and effort unless a special bond exists between the players and the coaches. Watching Jerry's teams play, it was clear he had a unique and special relationship with his players. Their love for one another, their coaches and the university were obvious.

Coach Tarkanian has left a lasting and enduring impact on college athletics, one that will be appreciated by coaches and players alike for many years to come.

Mike Krzyzewski
Head Basketball Coach
Duke University

PREFACE

AS A BOY I played the miniature 45 record over and over until I memorized every word - "Three in a row, it has never been done before and it may never be done again, but in March of 1966, Riverside City College basketball team won its third consecutive California State Junior College Championship. There were many hurdles along the way, many a close call..."

I never knew those words would one day represent the beginning of one of the most exciting, celebrated and controversial careers in all of sports.

And I was fortunate to be a part of it all.

As a youngster, I accompanied my father to work, into the dark, cramped campus gymnasiums that housed California's unheralded junior college basketball teams. I often had the gym to myself. I'd shoot long range jumpers, dreaming of making a last-second, game-winning shot, causing the crowd to roar with delight.

I accompanied my father and his teams to most away games. As the team's ball boy, I'd bring towels and drinks to the players and share in the excitement each win created. On one occasion, Mom had an argument with Dad and decided to teach him a lesson. She had the entire family stay home and not attend the game.

When the team was losing at halftime, she grabbed all four of us kids, threw us in the car and drove to the game. She said we needed to be there to support the team.

In college, I was the starting point guard for UNLV's (University of Nevada, Las Vegas) first number-one ranked basketball team in school history. We played in front of sell-out crowds, on national TV, against the country's best programs. We helped rejuvenate my father's UNLV program into a basketball juggernaut.

As an adult, I worked alongside my father in his last coaching job at Fresno State. I experienced the highs and lows that accompanied each win and loss. I was also his attorney and defended him at his last NCAA (National Collegiate Athletic Association) hearing and, in doing so, I witnessed firsthand the malevolent process I had heard about since childhood.

At the time Dad started his college coaching career, the basketball world was filled with legendary coaches like John Wooden of UCLA (University of California, Los Angeles), Adolph Rupp of University of Kentucky, and Dean Smith of Chapel Hill in North Carolina.

My father was perhaps the least likely of his peers to ever join this illustrious group at the top of the college basketball world. Dad was not a good athlete, he didn't attend a great university, he wasn't part of a great sports program and he didn't play for a great coach. In fact, Dad never had a real coaching mentor. There was no early indication that he would one day reach the pinnacle of college sports.

For this unassuming man from humble beginnings, it was even more unlikely that he would become one of the most controversial coaches in the history of college basketball. Who would have imagined that this droopy-eyed, first generation Armenian-American with a modest educational background, whose only interest was instructing young kids in the art of basketball, would one day square off in heated debates against pillars of the broadcast world such as Mike Wallace of *60 Minutes* and Ted Koppel of *Nightline*?

There was nothing to indicate that articles from the most powerful newspapers in the country—*The New York Times*, the *Los Angeles Times* and *the Washington Post*—would heatedly debate his actions and often negatively portray his character, motives and personality. This, however, was my father's destiny.

Dad defended his actions and courageously spoke out against the hypocrisy of the NCAA. He was ridiculed and maligned for his honesty. It wasn't until many years after his career ended that facts came to light about actions of the NCAA (through investigations at other schools) which substantiated the truth of his previous protestations and uncovered the unjustified persecution of my father by the NCAA. How did this come about?

Dad had the courage and perseverance to stand up and challenge the most powerful, vindictive, immoral—and some say racist—organization in all of sports. For over 30 years, he fought a full-fledged war against the NCAA and its tyrannical dictator, Walter Byers.

Dad fought through four outrageous investigations spanning more than 15 years. There were six Committee on Infractions hearings, four probations, two Congressional investigations and a journey through the American judicial system, all the way to the United States Supreme Court.

Through it all, my father took over one losing program after another; programs with no winning tradition, horrendous facilities, and meager resources. Each time, he turned them into the most successful program in their school's history.

In 1973, Dad took over a struggling UNLV program which had finished 13-15 the previous year. By the end of his tenure, his UNLV teams won an amazing 509 games and lost only 105. His last ten teams averaged 31 wins a season.

In Dad's first 24 years in major college basketball, he coached 15 teams to the Sweet 16, seven to the Final 8, and four to the Final Four, with one team winning the 1990 National Championship. When he was forced to resign at UNLV, he had the highest winning percentage in college basketball history at .834%, with 630 wins.

Most amazing is the fact that Dad accomplished all of this while being constantly harassed, maligned and investigated by the NCAA. Disparaging stories were leaked to the media.

NCAA investigators persuaded recruits not to join his teams. His players were suspended at the most inopportune times for the most ridiculous reasons. And each time his program reached national prominence, they were unfairly placed on probation.

Then, when he finally reached the pinnacle of his profession, the national championship, pressure from the NCAA forced his career to prematurely end. No coach has ever endured so much persecution and, yet, he refused to buckle under the pressure or to back down.

In spite of it all, my father, Jerry Tarkanian, amassed one of the greatest coaching records of all-time; he influenced an entire generation of young players without regard to race and ethnicity; he developed the run-and-gun offense and innovative defensive strategies that changed the way college basketball is played; and, he forever altered the way college sports is regulated.

In early April 2014, while watching another scintillating Final Four played in front of nearly 80,000 people and millions more watching on TV, I couldn't help but reflect upon those wonderful memories of the UNLV Runnin' Rebels and the towel-chewing coach who towered over the college basketball world more than 20 years earlier. Apparently, I wasn't the only one.

The rock band *The Killers* was performing between the two games. The band's lead singer, Brandon Flowers, strolled onstage wearing a UNLV letterman's jacket adorned on the back with the names of the starters from the Rebels' record-setting 1990 National Championship Team. Above the names were the words "Never Forget." I am always amazed and touched when I am reminded of how many people were affected by my father's lifework.

Dad is a simple, uncomplicated man who always had one devout interest: to coach college basketball. Aside from his family and basketball, he cared about nothing else. Even his family didn't always get his full attention, such as when he sheepishly admitted he didn't know the color of Mom's eyes after 35 years of marriage.

After winning the national championship and achieving the highest winning percentage in college basketball history, and after creating the most powerful juggernaut of his time, my father, at the young age of 60, had his dreams and aspirations taken away. In doing so, he lost the one thing he loved most in life.

After a tortuous battle with the most powerful organization in amateur athletics, he lost. He lost not only his job, but also his reputation. Furthermore, his amazing accomplishments have been largely ignored, or minimized.

Today, I looked into my 84-year old father's eyes and wondered what he was thinking. In the twilight of his life, does he feel a sense of satisfaction for the crucial help he provided so many poor inner-city kids, as well as the love they still have for him? Has the happiness and excitement his teams brought to so many people, or the personal fulfillment from being one of the greatest in his profession, subsided? Or, is he filled with sadness of what could have been; what should have been?

Further, I wonder if he regrets fighting for what was right, fighting to pave the way for other coaches and players that came after him, knowing that his career was cut short because he had the courage to fight an unfair system.

I decided to write this book about my father's coaching career to provide a much truer, more honest and complete account of what can and really does happen in the world of big-time college athletics under the NCAA. I have done this with the sincere hope that what happened to my father cannot, and will not, ever happen again.

Danny Tarkanian

Tarkanian family reunion at Bass Lake just outside of Fresno

PROLOGUE:
LIGHTS DIM ON THE WORLD'S MOST FAMOUS STREET

HIS BODY LAY motionless and his deep, dark, sunken eyes were in a blank stare. Jerry Tarkanian was resting in the hospital room with a large tube inserted in his throat in an effort to keep him alive. The gregarious, people-loving personality had disappeared.

Jerry was surrounded by his family; his wife Lois and four children, Pam, Jodie, George and Danny. His 11 grandchildren were nervously trying to keep busy in the waiting room.

Danny reached over, kissed him on his forehead and whispered, "You are the greatest father, ever". Jodie was holding his hand trying to keep back the tears. Pam, who couldn't hold the tears back, moved to the back of the room where George was. They both cried.

The sound of a walker dragging slowly on the floor was growing louder and louder. Suddenly, Irwin and Susan Molasky, UNLV's biggest boosters during the Tarkanian years, entered the cramped room. Showing fragilities themselves, Irwin and Susan said they had to see Coach one more time.

They told him how much he meant to their lives and that the greatest thrills they had was traveling with the Runnin' Rebel. They told him Las Vegas was never the same after he left. Susan got up, kissed him on the cheek and her and Irwin slowly walked away.

As each hour passed, more drugs were inserted into the fluid-filled bags hovering over Jerry, their liquids slowly dripping through the lines and into his body, trying desperately to pull him through one more time.

Former Rebel greats Freddy Banks, Moses Scurry and Eldridge Hudson slowly meandered into the room. They stayed for hours, hugging Lois and telling her they had to be with Coach at this time.

He meant so much to them; he was like family to them. Each one thanked Coach for giving them a chance in life and for having such an impact in developing the person they were.

Late that night, Danny was the only person in the room. His phone rang. It was Melvin Ely, Fresno State's greatest player. Melvin was in Japan and his wife told him Coach was in the hospital. He asked Danny to place the phone next to Coach's ear.

"Thank you, Coach," Melvin said. "You took a troubled young kid from Harvey, Illinois, brought me to Fresno and made me the man I am today. Without you, I would have died in the streets of Harvey."

Later that evening, Mike Toney, who looked and acted like one of those Vegas mobsters you would see on TV, entered the room. He was one of Jerry's best friends and always made him laugh.

Mike sat down and bent over the motionless Tark. He started telling old stories and laughing hysterically at them. He would say, "Remember Tark, remember?" and tell another story and burst into laughter.

Danny swore his father's eyes lit up after one such story. Mike jumped out of the chair and said, "See, Coach loves my stories." Mike stayed for hours telling one story after another until the early morning hours.

That morning, Jodie called everyone together in the waiting room. She told the family what they had all expected to hear. The doctors said there was no hope for recovery. It was time to turn off the machines. Adults and kids alike started crying and hugging one another.

As the preparations began, Danny received a call from Coach Calipari, who said he was in church saying a prayer for Tark. Tark loved Cal, said he was a great coach and even better person. Honest, not phony. Tark hated phonies.

The time had come. Several of the children went into the room to watch the final seconds of their father's life. Others couldn't stand to watch him pass so, instead, waited outside the door. Banks, Scurry and Hudson had come back to the hospital to be with their Coach, their family, for his final minutes.

At 9:05 a.m. on February 11, 2015, Jerry Tarkanian took his last breath and passed from this earth.

Close to one hundred former players attended the funeral for the man they called "Coach," "Friend" and "Second Father." Former coaches, fans and friends filled the church, all paying their final respects to a man they deeply loved.

Long Beach State, UNLV and Fresno State all held ceremonies before their games honoring their greatest Coach.

The city of Las Vegas bestowed its ultimate honor. The Strip, the most famous street in the world, dimmed its lights in honor of Coach Tarkanian, a distinction shared with only six other people, two of whom were President Reagan and President Kennedy.

JT as an infant

CHAPTER 1:
ARMENIAN GENOCIDE

T HE HOLOCAUST is a term now defined in dictionaries as "the systemic extermination of nearly 6-million Jews during World War II." Most people, upon learning of the extermination camps as they were liberated by Allied troops, were aghast that such atrocities could even be conceived, let alone executed.

As horrifying as the atrocities were in Nazi concentration camps, and as shocked as the world became upon learning the truth about the systematic extermination of an entire race of people just because their religious views were different, this was *not* the first time in history that such a wholesale massacre of an entire race, based on religious beliefs, had ever taken place. In fact, it wasn't even the first time in the 20th Century!

During World War I, the Ottoman Empire, for centuries one of the most powerful monarchies in the world, was falling into economic ruin and aligned itself with Germany with the hope of regaining world-power status. At the same time the Empire was reorganizing its armies and economy, a political group known as the "Young Turks" launched a campaign designed to bring the Ottoman's back into line with Sharia (Islamic) Law and clearly divide the population into Muslims and "Infidels."

While armies fought in trenches across Europe and Africa and were otherwise occupied, the Young Turks began rounding up Armenian Christians, confiscating their property and executing the educated—the students, scholars, administrators and political leaders—on the spot.

Women, children and the elderly were "deported," often to Syria, where tens-of-thousands of them were stripped naked then forced to march barefoot across hundreds of miles of scorching desert. Those who stopped to rest or fell behind were murdered. The remainder were taken far out into the desert and abandoned to die slowly.

By 1915, several concentration camps had been established, but most of these served only to gather Armenians and load them into trucks, trains and boats. Hundreds were loaded on barges and rowboats and towed far into the Black Sea. The boats were then sunk, leaving the women, children and elderly Armenians to drown.

Of all the ways used by these death-squads to carry out the extermination of the Armenian Christians, burning seemed to be their favorite. To make the point that this was a "religious-cleansing," they usually crammed the Armenian populations of small towns and villages into their Christian churches before setting them ablaze.

This Armenian Holocaust was the first time in the 20th Century that a large-scale extermination of an entire race of people, based on their religious beliefs, was attempted. In fact, words did not exist to clearly portray the extent of the brutality so, in describing the mass-killings of Christians in Turkey during World War I, Raphael Lemkin coined the word "genocide." It was first used together with the word Armenian, as in the "Armenian Genocide," which is now how the period from 1914-1918 in Turkey has become known.

It was in this violent and hateful territory that a Christian Armenian girl by the name of Haigouhie was born. It was around the turn of the 20th century and this young girl would later become the mother of Jerry Tarkanian.

CHAPTER 2:

MALATYA

"Some people just can't see beyond the color of a person's skin or their religious choices. It is wrong to judge people just because they are different, but here they do. And all we can do is prepare for the worst and hope for the best."

—Jerry's grandmother, to his mother

"SHHH! KEEP QUIET, sweet Haigouhie," the mother cautioned her daughter as she placed her upon the back of a horse. The child was, of course, delighted and had let out a giggle, causing her mother to chide her. "Maghrib will be over soon and the Turks will return. We must be gone by then."

The mother knew that if she was caught teaching her children to ride horses, she could be executed on the spot. But she also knew that learning to ride might one day save their lives, so she taught them all, secretly, during the Islamic evening prayer sessions. She would take them to the large barn, close the doors and instruct them, while her older children kept watch for Turks.

Her husband Mickael Effendi Tarkhanian—like Tarkanian, but with an "h" in the middle—was a village leader and he often heard news before most others. He warned her that he had heard about Turkish death-squads which had rounded up educated or influential Armenians in Constantinople and other large cities. As the city's

Treasurer, and with a nice home, horses and farmland, Mickael knew he and his family would be targets.

It was not just a rumor. The Turks had already executed hundreds and deported thousands more just because they were Armenian, Christian or Jew. The violence had not yet seeped into their village, except for random and isolated incidents, but Mickael warned his wife that they must be prepared for the Turks would soon turn their attention to the smaller towns and villages.

Malatya, the small, predominantly Islamic village within the Ottoman Empire, was not unlike many similar farming villages in 1915 in a land that would soon become Turkey. The primary agricultural product of the region was the splendid harvest of apricots and cherries, as well as livestock: goats, cattle and horses.

Beneath the calm surface of this friendly farming community boiled a volcano of ethnic and religious conflict that would soon explode and leave behind an unprecedented wake of death and destruction.

This village had a significant Christian Armenian population which had, over the years, created peaceful relations with the Islamic Turks in the area. Children played with other children regardless of race, religion or ethnicity, and many warm friendships were formed across ethnic lines. But all this soon came to a shameful end when the Turkish death squads descended upon the town.

Young Haigouhie Tarkhanian, whom her mother called "Rose," was just fourteen-years-old when she had her final horseback riding lesson, after which she watched in confusion as her mother sewed precious coins into the hem of her slip. "If ever I give you this slip to wear," her mother explained slowly and carefully, "tell only the people I send you to about this money."

"What people?" Rose asked.

"The people who have offered to help us, to take care of you, if things go badly for us here."

"But *you* take care of me, Mama. Where will you be?"

"And I will always take care of you, my Sweet," her mother said, giving the child a hug. "But if something were to happen to me...or your father…and we could no longer be here for you, then you know where to go right? You and your brother, Levon?"

"Yes, ma'am," Rose replied dutifully, "Go north, across the hills as we did last spring, when we visited our friends. I will follow the trail you showed us. But why, Mama? Why?"

"Oh, my Rose, "that is the question on all our minds," her mother said while stroking the little girl's hair. "Many Turks hate us simply because we are different."

"Different?" Rose asked.

"Armenian people come from a different place and we worship at a different church."

"Why should that make people hate us?"

"It shouldn't, but it does. Some people just can't see beyond the color of a person's skin, or their religion. It is wrong to judge people just because they are different, but here they do. And all we can do is prepare for the worst and hope for the best. But you, Rose, you must promise to always get to know someone and to know what is in their hearts before you judge them. And never, ever judge others because of the color of their skin or the church they go to. Promise?"

"Yes, Mama. I promise."

They shared a warm hug before Rose snuggled into her bed for the night. Her mother closed the door and turned to her husband Mickael for comfort.

"I am afraid," she said as she took his hand and held it tightly.

"And there is much to fear," he responded. "We have done all we can do and now we must place our faith in God."

The morning brought a messenger to the Tarkhanian house with news that the Turkish Army would soon reach town. Mickael had a terrible sense of foreboding as he prepared to go to the town square and greet the arriving soldiers.

Mickael's eldest son Mehran had recently graduated from medical school in Lebanon and he accompanied Mickael. Mehran often helped his father with projects and paperwork, so it was not unusual for them to be seen together. What *was* unusual though was to find 200 Turkish soldiers, part of the so-called Special Organization *Teşkilat-ı Mahsusa*, gathered in the town square.

As Mickael and Mehran approached, the officers were speaking with the Ayatollah of the Islamic mosque. The Ayatollah saw the Tarkhanians approaching and pointed to them with an evil sneer on his face.

"There," he said, "is the infidel who is the treasurer in village affairs. He offends Allah by speaking directly to Turks as if he were an equal. And beside him walks his eldest son who has outraged Allah by studying medicine at the university. Only those who walk with grace in the presence of Allah are permitted higher studies. These men are both contemptible Armenian pigs!"

The Turkish officer looked at the Tarkhanians with undisguised contempt and ordered his men to seize Mickael and Mehran and arrest them, forcing them into a prison camp. Rose's mother soon learned of the arrests and the next day made arrangements to get food to her husband and her son for she knew they would not get enough to eat in prison. Each day thereafter, she prepared a plate of food for them and had a younger son take it to a friendly guard who, with a bribe, gave it to the two men.

For a few days, the son was able to get food to his father and brother. Then one day the guard would not take the plate. When the young boy kept persisting, the guard grabbed the plate, turned it upside down and let the food fall on the ground as he gestured, "Gone, gone." The boy ran quickly home to tell his mother. She knew what that meant. Her husband and son were dead.

A Turkish officer drew his curved sword while soldiers forced Mehran to his knees and made him lower his head, as if in prayer. Mickael was held and forced to watch as the officer drew back his sword and cut off Mehran's head, letting it roll onto the dirt. The father's devastation and anguish at seeing his eldest son killed was short-lived as the Turkish officer stepped over to Mickael and, with a single stroke of the sword, sent his head rolling into the dirt as well.

Word of the executions spread rapidly throughout the Armenian community. When his wife learned of it moments later, she quickly put Rose into the slip with the coins and ran to the barn with the little girl and her younger brother, Levon.

"Mama, I am scared," Rose said.

"We are all frightened, sweet Rose, but we must not let that stop us from doing what needs to be done! You and your brother remember where the trail is that leads over the mountains?"

Levon and Rose nodded their heads as their mother placed them on the back of the horse. Behind them, in the village square, they heard the soldiers gathering all the Armenians into their Christian church. The mother hugged her children for the last time and slapped the horse's rump. It bolted from the barn's rear entry and ran into the hills, carrying her children safely away.

When the siblings reached a nearby hilltop, they looked back and watched in transfixed horror as the rest of the Armenian villagers were herded into their church, which was then set afire by the Turks. As far as they knew, all of the town's people—their mother, entire family, and their friends...everyone they had ever known and loved—were burned to death in just a few short minutes. With tears in their eyes, they continued the journey as their mother had instructed.

The Armenian Genocide continued through 1918, with the Turks murdering more than 1.5 million Armenian Christians. From an Armenian population of nearly 2 million people at the start of World War I, less than 400,000 survived the slaughter. Levon and Rose were two, due to the bravery and kindness of a compassionate Turkish family who hid them in their basement while Turks continued to murder all Armenian Christians.

Little is known about the period of time between when Rose left her home on horseback and when she met her future husband, George Tarkanian, another Armenian who had escaped this genocide and made it to America. George saw a picture of Rose and immediately said he wanted to marry her. So, he communicated with people in Lebanon and a marriage was arranged, as was often the custom in those days.

After the wedding, the Tarkanians took a ship back to America to begin a new family and a new life. They never forgot the violent persecution of their childhood, feeling hatred and scorn from others simply because they were different. They taught their children never to judge people by the church they attended or the color of their skin but, rather, by their character and integrity alone.

Previous: JT with sister Alice, mother Rose, and father George at family's grocery store in Euclid, OH

JT and sister Alice

CHAPTER 3:
LOVE OF SPORTS

"You'll never amount to anything studying sports. Get a job being a barber. There's low overhead and you can make good money."

—Vahan Davidian, Jerry's stepfather

FTER ARRIVING in America, George and Rose Tarkanian settled in a small Armenian community in Euclid, Ohio, a suburb of Cleveland, near some of George's relatives. Their first child, born in 1928, was a girl they named Alice. On August 8, 1930, their first son was born.

Rose wanted to name her son Gregory, after St. Gregory, the Patron Saint of the Armenian Church who had led Armenia to become the world's first Christian nation. But Rose's English was so broken that the nurse at the hospital thought she was saying "Jerry;" so that is the name written on his birth certificate.

After escaping the death-squads in Turkey, the Tarkanian's arrived in America just in time for the Stock Market Crash of 1929 and the Great Depression that followed. With so many businesses closing, jobs were hard to find for most people. George, however, worked three different jobs to support his family.

George's family owned a grocery store and his first job of each workday was to buy produce and other perishables for the family store. Jerry remembered getting up while it was still dark outside, having breakfast with his father, and then going with him to select the produce.

After George bought grocery items for the store, he would make rounds, delivering ice to homes and local businesses before working the evening shift at the Chrysler automobile plant. Jerry never forgot the lunch pail his father carried to Chrysler as he had to leave his family again each evening. He absolutely refused for the rest of his life to ever use a lunch pail himself. He hated what it represented.

George was known in the Armenian community as a hardworking man with high integrity. His amazing work ethic made a significant impression on Jerry.

George and Rose also passed to their children stories of their childhood and their escapes from death at the hands of Turkish death-squads while many from their family were killed, raped and tortured. These stories were not shared simply to frighten the children or to make them appreciate their safe lives in America, but rather to prepare them to face any challenge, any threat. No matter how poor the odds, they would always fight to survive—and fight to win. More importantly, they learned to fight for justice and equality among all people.

Jerry and his sister Alice saw ethnic and racial discrimination in America in its schools and towns, and in in the headlines across the United States. But not against Armenians, so much, as against blacks. They did not understand why they were forbidden to drink from certain water fountains or forced to ride in the back of a bus. It was a lack of basic human dignity, the fact that an entire race of people was hated simply because of the color of their skin.

As Jerry grew older and began school, he developed a love of sports and nurtured a keen competitive spirit. He didn't just want to play, he wanted to *win*! When he was eight or nine, he took his favorite basketball to bed each night and dreamed about winning "the big game."

A family friend, Aroosiag Jamgochian, said, "All through Jerry's school years, he spent every spare moment at the gym or on the field, playing, watching, learning…and always with the greatest enthusiasm."

Jerry loved watching professional sports and became a huge fan of the Cleveland Indians baseball team and the Cleveland Browns football team. There was a time when he could recite any statistic for any player on either of those teams.

While he spent nearly all his free time watching or playing sports, as Jerry entered adolescence, he found he was not keeping up with all the other boys as far as height and weight. So, to stay competitive he had to look harder to find an "edge." In basketball, for example, he could not out-jump the taller boys, so he worked on his ball handling and speed. He became good at stealing the ball and driving to the basket for layups. Even though he may not have been as big or as tall as some of the other boys, he was always good at finding an edge.

This same knack for finding his own personal strengths to remain competitive against bigger or stronger competitors was a skill he passed along to his closest friends, his teammates. By showing other boys how to gain an edge, how to press their strengths while protecting their weaknesses, Jerry found a new love and a new way to approach sports even if he was not tall enough or big enough or strong enough to *play* professional basketball, football or baseball. He could coach!

Much like the stereotypical "jock," Jerry did not have much use for academics, or school in general. His parents were often frustrated by his less-than-average report cards, but George and Rose also knew that their son loved sports and they always encouraged him to pursue his dreams.

They were, however, less tolerant of the pranks and jokes he and his friends played on each other and on other classmates, teachers and faculty, many of which resulted in a "parent-teacher conference."

When Jerry was ten, his brother Myron was born. Shortly thereafter, George was diagnosed with tuberculosis and, within a year, passed away. This left Jerry, the elder son, "the man of the family" at only eleven years of age.

As America geared up for and prepared to enter World War II, the Tarkanians were struggling to survive in Ohio. Fortunately, being in an Armenian community was helpful to Rose and the children as there was always family or friends to help out, if needed.

Armenians are notoriously loyal to one another and Jerry explained this loyalty in one of his many humorous quips. A Las Vegas reporter jokingly asked Coach Tarkanian if he kept a marginally talented Bryan Emerzian on his national championship team because Bryan was Armenian. Jerry quickly responded, "No, I keep Bryan on the team because *I'm* Armenian."

Despite assistance from the Armenian community, Rose felt her children needed the help of a father. So, a few years later, she married another Armenian immigrant named Vahan Davidian.

Like Rose, Vahan was born in the Ottoman Empire just before the turn of the century and had many family murdered by Turks, barely escaping with his life. He also found a new life in America in the Cleveland area and was traditional in his views on raising children. He felt boys needed to learn a trade skill and develop a career plan that would get them into the workforce as soon as they were finished with school.

For Vahan, sports was not considered a viable career choice. So, he and young Jerry disagreed frequently when the discussion turned to the future.

"You'll never amount to anything studying sports," Vahan once said when he saw Jerry stretched out on the floor reading the sports pages of the newspaper. "You should get a job being a barber. There's low overhead and you can make good money. Vahan even tried persuading Rose to push her son toward a more conventional nine-to-five job, but Rose had seen Jerry's enthusiasm for sports and she knew his dream was to play or coach basketball. She always encouraged her children to follow their dreams, so she did not pressure Jerry.

Shortly after the end of World War II, Rose and Vahan decided the family needed a fresh start in California. There were several strong Armenian communities in Southern California. Plus, Vahan had family living there, so they packed up and headed for the West Coast. Vahan refused to drive, so Rose drove 300 miles every day by herself. As Jerry would jokingly say years later, "most of the time on the wrong side of the road."

As members of the Armenian culture, when the Davidians reached California, they were welcomed into many homes of friends and relatives until they finally found their own place. Eventually, they settled in Pasadena, California. Rose woke each morning and gazed upon the picturesque San Gabriel Mountains and often exclaimed, "God Bless America."

For a kid from Ohio who was embodied by a love of sports, moving to Pasadena in the late 1940s was like a dream come true. Pasadena High School and Pasadena Junior College were both on the same campus, so students could finish high school and move right on to a two-year college in the same place. While this provided a rich learning environment for the students, for athletes in team sports it also provided a unique venue to develop skills on the high school level that could then be refined in junior college.

An incredible group of athletes were on campus during those years and Jerry made friends with all of them. They included Dick Williams, who played and managed Major League Baseball, winning two World Series; Bobby Lillis, who managed the Houston Astros; Lee Walls, one of Jerry's closest friends who played 12 years in Major League Baseball; Irv Noren, enshrined in the National Baseball Hall of Fame as a baseball player and a coach; Dick Davis, a champion golfer who won the U.S. Open; Hugh Stewart, who became a professional tennis player; and Harry Hugasian, an All-American in football at Stanford who subsequently played for the Chicago Bears in the NFL (National Football League). Jerry fit right in with this crowd and he loved every thrilling moment of it.

After he graduated from Pasadena High School, Jerry enrolled in Pasadena City College and played basketball for the Lancers. Since academics had never been a priority for him, it took him four years to graduate.

Upon graduation, Fresno State recruited Jerry, his best friend Dale Arambel (who was also a basketball player), and three of their friends who played football. Excited about the prospect of getting a Division-I basketball scholarship and being able to play with four long-time friends, he packed his bags and moved to Fresno.

Little did Jerry know that his life was about to change in so many ways. He became more focused on his dream of coaching basketball and eventually found a whole new appreciation for square dancing!

JT as player (#34) on Pasadena City College basketball team

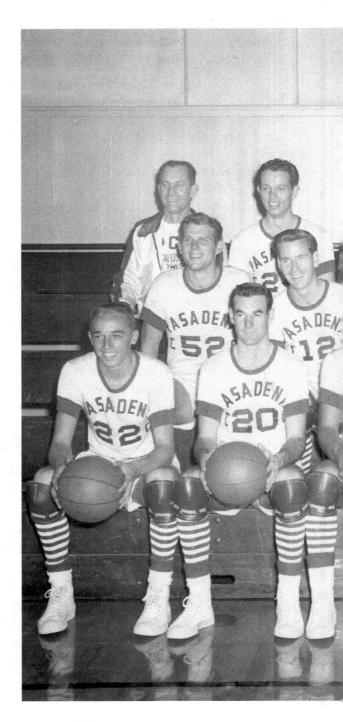

CHAPTER 4:

JERRY FINDS HIS GIRL

"No, I will not go out with you," she said, and turned and walked away.

—Lois, at her first meeting with Jerry

AS WITH MOST schools, Fresno State offered many non-academic activities besides sports, such as the chess club or the science club. Of course, Jerry and his athletic buddies had little time for any of these. If it wasn't a class or sports, it was a waste of time, they figured. One such group that year was the Square Dance Club.

The square dancers wanted to put on a dance demonstration for the freshman class to possibly gain new members. School administrators approved this demonstration for when the classes ate lunch. The dancers worked hard planning the event and was ready to begin.

Jerry and a few of his friends, including Darryl Rogers, the school's star football player who later coached the Detroit Lions, decided to have a little fun during the square dance demonstration.

Music was being played over the PA system and Jerry, Darryl and their friends knew where the circuit breakers were. Every time the dancers would get into the demonstration, one of the jocks would shut off the power by pulling a plug for a moment, throwing the whole dance into chaos.

The perpetrators thought it was hilarious. For the majority of the people there, including the students who had rehearsed for weeks to do the show, it was a disaster. Jerry and his friends were cited for causing the disruption and ordered to appear before Student Court for their penalty.

Fresno State had, at the time, a system of student jurisprudence, whereby students charged with certain misbehaviors would appear before the court and before their accusers. Each side would present its case and the student judges would hear the evidence and the explanations. Then the judges would decide what corrective or punitive action, if any, was appropriate.

This was not the first time Jerry and his cohorts in crime had appeared before the court. Each time, it was for pranks or practical jokes played around campus. Usually, since they were all-star athletes, these offenses generally cost them a simple slap on the wrist, so to speak. But this time, there was a new judge to consider!

Lois Huter was a sophomore at Fresno State and, in her extended family, the first to go to college. This was not a barrier she took lightly as she had heard her mother and father arguing about it for weeks before the final decision was made. Her father said it was a waste of money because "girls only ended up getting married anyway." The family had little money and they were working a small farm outside of Fresno.

Neither Lois' mother nor father graduated from high school. Her father joined the Navy at 17 and fought in World War II and the Korean conflict. Her mother, Josephine, dropped out of the eighth grade to stay home and care for her younger brothers and sisters while her own mother, Agnes, worked two jobs to get her family through the Great Depression.

Agnes was an intelligent woman and always regretted not being able to continue her education. As a result, she was ardently insistent that Lois be given the opportunities she missed. In the end, Lois' mother carried the winning vote and Lois was provided $250 for her four years of college and all the fresh fruit and vegetables she could eat.

Jerry and Lois Tarkanian wedding reception

Because Lois wanted to live up to her mother's expectations, she dedicated herself to school. She set a frenetic, nearly impossible schedule for herself, taking a full load of classes and working 35 hours a week to earn money for her expenses.

Lois had been selected "Freshman Woman of the Year" and was involved with student government, the women's honor society and student court. She was also a reporter on the student newspaper staff. When not involved with any of the above, Lois could usually be found at the library, doing research or homework.

This was a far, far cry from the college life Jerry and his friends were enjoying and Lois certainly did not appreciate their cavalier attitude toward the student court proceedings.

Lois found the boys quite charming as she listened to their excuses for their misbehavior, but she was also insistent that they receive an appropriate consequence for their actions. She decided that it was time these boys learn a lesson and they were not going to come away with a mere slap on the wrist this time.

After the charges had been read and both sides presented arguments, the court took a short break before the judges would decide the penalty for the athletes. During this break, Lois heard heavy footsteps coming down the hallway toward her and, when she turned, she found herself looking at a slightly out-of-breath Jerry Tarkanian.

"Hello, Lois," he began. "Say, if you don't have any plans on Friday night, maybe you and I could get together?"

"You're asking me out?" she responded in amazement. "Are you trying to influence my vote for the square dance incident?" His face looked surprised, almost shocked, as he listened to her.

"No...I'm not," he stammered. "I just think you are nice...and smart. I was hoping we could go out sometime?"

"No, I will not go out with you," she said as she turned and walked away, leaving Jerry stunned.

Shortly afterward, the court members met in private to decide what should be done with those who disrupted the square dancing. Three of the four student judges felt that the incident was nothing more than a childish prank and undeserving of any serious consequences. Yet, Lois was concerned that, by letting the athletes off unpunished, it would send the wrong message to both the Square Dance Club and the student body. She suggested that the boys receive a punishment that would create a positive contribution to the aggrieved.

After a short discussion, Lois convinced the others that the appropriate punishment was, for the remainder of the 1952-53 school year, each time a student election was held, Jerry and his co-conspirators would have to set up and take down the voting booths.

Jerry felt it was a harsh punishment for what was nothing more than a practical joke. Despite the severity, which was all due to Lois, he still wanted to date her.

In the coming weeks, he asked her out several more times and she continued to turn him down. Irrespective of the continual rejections, there was something about that girl that kept her on Jerry's mind and in his thoughts. He knew he was going to have his work cut out for him if he were to succeed in getting that date.

Lois, who was 18, had seriously dated only one boy (an art major) since coming to college and Jerry was very different from the types she was usually attracted to. Some of her friends encouraged her to go out with him while others argued against it.

Some even pointed out that he was Armenian and there was still a lot of prejudice in Fresno toward Armenians. When Lois first began college, the top sororities did not pledge Armenians. Armenians were also not allowed to live in Fig Gardens, the most desired residential area of Fresno.

Fresno State was a fairly small campus and it was hard to keep secrets for long. Lois knew people were talking about Jerry's frustrated attempts to woo her. It was almost funny, the confident school jock and the bookworm. They were so unalike, it seemed.

Lois was asked about her intentions with Jerry so often, she finally came up with a response that closed the discussion for most folks. She simply told them that she and he had not been properly introduced!

Surely, no one could expect her to take seriously the pleadings of a man with whom she was not even formally acquainted. Well, the "proper introduction" excuse worked for only so long.

One of Lois' girlfriends was dating a roommate of Jerry's, Sid Craig. When Sid heard Lois saying that she and Jerry had never been properly introduced, he arranged it!

Unlike Jerry's other roommates, though a cheerleader and quite a disciplined athlete, Sid was the only one who was not on any school athletic team. In fact, after college, Sid would go on to own Arthur Murray's dance studios before he and wife Jenny created their own revolutionary weight loss system called "The Jenny Craig Program."

After the formal introduction, Lois was *still* not convinced and continued to turn Jerry down. She had heard a lot about him, much of which was not good, and was concerned about the rumors of the "wild parties" he and his roommates would throw. One of her closest friends, Sally O'Neal, was dating Fritz Lauritzen, one of Jerry's closest friends, so Sally had been to a few of these parties.

Sally finally convinced Lois that the parties were not so wild and the boys were just being boys. Sally told her that she really liked Jerry and that the image many people had of him was just not correct.

After months of persistence, Jerry was finally rewarded with a "yes" to his offer of a date. And soon, Jerry and Lois became an item around campus.

Jerry had been sold on Lois from the very beginning, which is why he never gave up on asking her out, even though she always turned him down. There was something about her. He loved her ambition and loyalty.

He also loved her competitiveness and often said that Lois was the most competitive person he ever met. Years later, she extended that competitiveness into the sports world.

When their son Danny was in 5th grade, he was playing in an outdoor playground league in Huntington Beach, California, and Jerry was the coach. One weekend, Jerry went out of town and asked Lois to fill in for him. Late in a close game, the officials made a bad call against her team. Lois stormed onto the court yelling at the official until he finally threw her out of the game…*and off the playground!*

After Danny graduated from high school, he attended Dixie Junior College in St. George, Utah, a small, quiet religious town. While playing in the regional finals, he fouled out on a questionable call late in the game and his team ended up losing in the final seconds. The town folks in St. George still talk about Lois chasing those two officials to their cars, a high heel in each hand.

In another instance, after an emotional loss at UNLV, in a game that contained several bad calls, Lois also chased those officials to their locker room and waited patiently for them to reappear. Finally, security had to come and escort the officials to their cars.

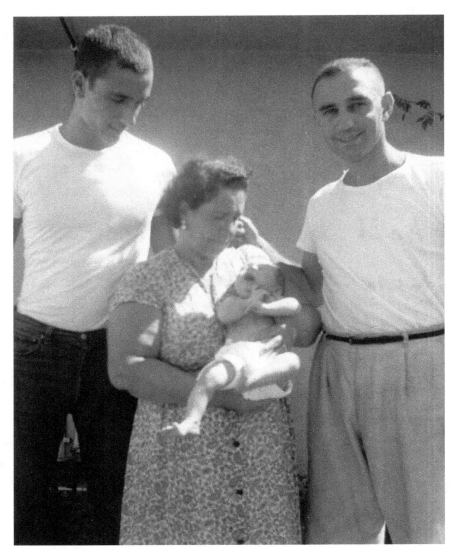

JT with brother, Myron, and mother, Rose, holding the Tarkanians' first child Pam in Redlands, California

CHAPTER 5:

COACHING TARK'S WAY

"He could feel the cut of those words, sharp as a sword, when he read the signs: 'Whites Only.'"

—Excerpt about Jerry and his first year of coaching

IN JUNE of 1950, the newly formed United Nations was tested when North Korea invaded South Korea. Twenty-one countries furnished troops and supplies to defend South Korea, with the United States providing nearly 90% of the soldiers.

All across America, calls were made to young men to enlist in the military to defend, for the first time, against "Communist Expansion." To gain a sufficient number of troops for the Korean War, Congress reinstituted the military draft which had been suspended after World War II.

Jerry was a scholarship athlete and could easily have taken the student deferment, as most of his peers did. But with his mother's terrifying childhood memories and barely escaping Turkey with her life, Rose became one of the most patriotic Americans ever. She passed that love of her new country on to her children, so when Jerry became of age, not only did he register for the draft, he *enlisted* in the Army Reserve.

As a soldier in the Army Reserve, Jerry was assigned as a military policeman and trained in the mountains around Fresno. He was proud to be able to serve his country while still maintaining his grades and competing in college athletics. He took his duty seriously and quickly rose to the rank of Sergeant.

Only one thing can motivate a young man more than patriotism and that would be a pretty woman. One summer, when Jerry and Lois began dating, Jerry had to go in for his Reserve training. Since his unit was out in the mountains, he didn't think anyone would miss him if he made a short trip.

Jerry snuck out of camp and went down to Fresno to see Lois. It was all going great until he got back and found out that he'd been caught! They demoted him to the lowest private rank and made him pull KP duty (which stands for "kitchen police" or "kitchen patrol") for the remainder of his tour. But for the love of his woman, Jerry thought it was a pretty fair trade, and Lois thought it was quite romantic.

Lois went to a few basketball games to watch Jerry play and learn about the game. He was not a starter and played infrequently, but she noticed how much he loved the sport. "He was like a little boy," she said, "always talking about the abilities of players and discussing plays. He'd follow the coaches around for hours, just listening to them and learning their coaching techniques."

Once a writer asked Lois what she thought of Jerry's playing ability and she remarked, "For a basketball player, he's a little slow, and short."

Jerry just laughed and said, "Sounds like a good scouting report to me!"

When basketball season ended, Jerry had his evenings free from practices so he was able to spend more time with Lois...when *she* was available.

Because he was on such a tight budget, one thing always bothered him though. Whenever they would go out, he'd order coffee, which cost five cents. Lois didn't drink coffee, so she ordered hot chocolate. And that cost a quarter!

Often, a date for them was going to a baseball game or school play. Lois was in a presentation of George Bernard Shaw's *The Lady's' Not For Burning*. She played the second lead and Jerry came to watch her perform. He was very impressed with her acting and she was equally as impressed that he sat through the entire play and actually seemed to enjoy it.

Of course, Jerry also spent a lot of time with his athletic friends. He lived with nine guys in a three-bedroom house. None of them had any money, but they learned that being broke college students had its creative side. They were always looking for inexpensive ways to deal with everyday things like eating, drinking and watching the World Series.

On many occasions, Jerry and his friend Harry Gaykian would go into a diner and order a cup of hot water. With a little catsup, salt and a handful of saltine crackers (also furnished gratis), they pretended they had tomato soup. And it was free!

On another occasion, one of Jerry's roommates had a job driving a meat delivery truck to area businesses. When food became especially scarce at the house, he turned the refrigeration off in the truck and let the meat spoil. The owner of the company would instruct him to dispose of the deteriorating meat, so he brought it back to the house, to the delight of his roommates who enjoyed an unprecedented smorgasbord. Now, about seeing the World Series…

One summer, when television sets were just coming into the market, stores would often let customers try the television out for a day or so before they bought it. During the World Series, Jerry brought a television home for one of these "tryouts." After a couple of days, the salesman called requesting it be returned. When no one returned his call, he went to the house and banged on the door, but no one answered. Jerry and his friends were inside laughing up a storm. Only after the World Series ended was the television returned.

Jerry drove a beat-up car in college, and he felt lucky to have that car, even though it only started after it was moving. This meant, if he wanted to go someplace, he had to push it down the hill he parked on, run beside it and jump in so he could jam it into gear and pop the clutch.

Jerry needed to find a job to help pay for his expenses, so he started looking around campus. The one he found was one of the biggest breaks of his career. He was hired, for $50 per month, to work in the football office under head coach Clark Van Galder. Jerry soon came to idolize this man.

Jerry did everything he could for and with Van Galder. They watched game films, shared meals and Jerry even attended team and staff meetings. He was soaking up everything like a sponge.

The most important thing Jerry learned from being around Coach Van Galder was that it was very important to be a *friend* to your players. Van Galder believed that, until you got to know them as individuals, you could not effectively motivate nor coach them to their highest potential. Jerry saw this and saw it worked, though other coaches did not share this same philosophy.

Coach Van Galder knew that most of his players, Jerry included, had little money. So, he would invite them all over from time to time to talk football and have a good, hot meal. They would also go to local high school games to scout talent and spend an inexpensive evening watching the game.

On Thanksgiving, Van Galder even took a turkey to Jerry's house to share with all his roommates. It was quite common for Van Galder to reach into his own wallet if an emergency came up and pay for a necessity of one of his players. Jerry knew Van Galder genuinely cared about his players——every one of them!

More and more, Jerry found himself drawn to coaching. He still loved to *play,* but the challenges of coaching were so complex, and yet so simple. He found coaching totally fascinating, regardless of whether it was football or basketball. It was an art form unto itself and Jerry dedicated himself to becoming a master.

While techniques and plays change continually, what Jerry learned from coach Van Galder was the very *essence of coaching.* The heart and soul of every championship team begins with the coach getting to know each player well enough to know what motivates them. Then he has to reach inside that player and pull out the very best performance from him every single game by keeping him motivated and enthusiastic.

Just before the season tipped off in 1954, Edison's basketball coach had an unfortunate nervous breakdown and the school replaced him with Ellis Carrasco, the football coach. Carrasco knew little about basketball, but he was a close friend of Clark Van Galder, who recommended Jerry. Carrasco asked Jerry to help as an assistant coach, so Jerry did his student teaching as an assistant basketball coach at Edison High School.

Carrasco focused on discipline and Jerry did the rest of the coaching. Edison High had an outstanding season and went undefeated. Then they won the city and county championships. The last game of the year was for the Valley Championship and would be played at Taft High School.

Edison's team included mostly black players while Taft's was all white. Competition between mixed races on the court was deemed appropriate in Taft at the time, but practice sessions were another matter.

With its multi-racial team, Edison was not allowed to practice in segregated Taft. Instead, they practiced at nearby Bakersfield High.

The team also couldn't eat its pre-game meal in Taft because the restaurants wouldn't serve the black players. Edison was even "encouraged" not to have its student body attend the game because most of them were black and that would cause a problem in Taft.

Jerry felt the bitter sting of this blatant racial discrimination and remembered well the lessons his mother had taught him. He could feel the cut of those words, sharp as a sword, when he read the signs: "Whites Only." A nonjudgmental man, Jerry never forgot the humiliation his players had to face on that basketball trip.

To make matters worse, Taft won the game by a single point...in overtime...on a *very* questionable call. Jerry knew there was no point arguing with the referees, so the team quietly headed to their bus for the ride home. It was their only loss of the season.

Ellis Carrasco was named Coach of the Year and, after the season ended, recommended Jerry for the coaching job at San Joaquin Memorial High School. Jerry was excited about his first head coaching opportunity, but was beginning to have second thoughts.

What was giving him concern was the predominant coaching philosophy at that time. When Jerry decided to become a coach, he started reading books and learning the philosophy of basketball coaching. No matter what the source, the message kept coming back to him that a coach was never supposed to get close to his players. That really bothered Jerry.

Jerry wanted to adopt Coach Van Galder's style of coaching that involved developing a close personal relationship with each player. There was no "one-size-fits-all" situation. He knew that each player had different ways of playing, different strengths and weaknesses mentally, emotionally and physically.

To motivate each player, to dig deep inside and get the very best performance, Jerry would have to know that player well enough to know if he was dealing with personal or family problems. He had to know exactly what buttons to push to get that player excited, even passionate, about the next game.

After a movie date with Lois, Jerry poured out his concerns about coaching. She told him he had already shown what a good coach he could be at Edison and he should keep doing it his way. That helped Jerry make his final decision.

Jerry Tarkanian was not only going to coach, but he was going to coach *his* way, similar to Coach Van Galder, developing close, personal relationships with his players.

It was right then and there, sitting in the warm evening breeze and talking about the future, that Lois said she began to fall in love with him, finding a connection with his sincerity, his concern and his caring.

And Jerry knew that, without Lois and her encouragement and support, he might just as well have become a barber.

CHAPTER 6:

TARK STARTS HIS COACHING CAREER

"Lois, it isn't every day that Idaho State plays Fresno State."

**—Jerry, explaining to Lois why they attended
a football game on their wedding night**

THE DAYS AT FRESNO State drifted by easily in the mid-50's.
Jerry immersed himself in studying coaching and was becoming
more and more excited about his new job at San Joaquin
Memorial High School. His pursuit of Lois also became more intense.

Lois continued her activities in student government as president of
Tokalon, the upper division women's honor society, and the
Journalism Society. She was also first attendant to the campus queen.
Lois finished her units early and was hired by the local school district
as a first-grade teacher.

More and more, she and Jerry became a supportive twosome. After
graduation they decided it was time to get married and start a family.
Soon, problems presented themselves.

Armenian ladies had convinced Jerry's mother that, by marrying an
"odar" (a non-Armenian), Jerry would be marrying into trouble. The
ladies told her it was what they had seen over and over again. The odar
would turn the son against his mother.

On Lois' side of the family, her parents were farmers, workers of
the land. They put stock in hard work and physical labor as the way to

feed a family. They did not understand coaching and did not see any possible future for someone who did not get their hands dirty.

Lois' father even told Jerry that perhaps he could get a job similar to his other son-in-law, who was driving a Hormel truck. He argued that "there was good pay and security there."

Many people also pointed out to Lois the prejudice towards Armenians which existed at that time. One of Lois' co-teachers said she might as well marry a "black man." Lois brushed off those concerns easily.

She and Jerry had already been dating for a long time and she had seen the looks she occasionally got from passers-by when she was with him. It did not bother her. Jerry and Lois just put their heads down and got married.

There was one problem at the wedding. Jerry's young niece Georgette was to be the flower girl. The little girl was adorable and made it through rehearsals without a hitch. But when the day of the ceremony arrived and the procession down the aisle was to begin, Georgette was frightened by the crowd and refused to move.

Since she was supposed to be the first person in the procession, the entire ceremony came to a halt. After three or four verses of "Here Comes the Bride," Lois was instructed to begin the procession without the flower girl, which she did.

Jerry's sister Alice was hurt that Georgette was not in the procession and felt the incident was a sign that her brother should not be marrying an odar. Fortunately, the reception went more smoothly.

Jerry was only able to get a few days off for the honeymoon, so Lois was hoping they could perhaps go up into the mountains. He had other ideas.

Football season was going strong by November of 1955 and Fresno State was playing a nationally ranked Idaho State football team. It was a rare chance for little Fresno State to take on a national powerhouse, and a rare chance for Jerry to see his buddies play on that level. So rare, in fact, that it warranted obtaining two tickets, even if they were on their honeymoon!

"Lois, it isn't every day that Idaho State plays Fresno State," he explained when he showed her the tickets. Lois never let him live that statement down! He later acknowledged, "It certainly was not a smart decision on my part."

At San Joaquin Memorial High School, Jerry began to work on defenses and offensive strategies that would one day carry him to the top of the NCAA basketball standings. Part of his job requirement was also to teach algebra, something he knew nothing about. So Jerry improvised, as he always did so well!

Every day before class, he met with his best student, Dave Vanascene, who gave him the lessons he would use for the class. With a little help, Jerry managed to get by as a teacher. He did much better as a coach.

In his first season coaching at Memorial, they beat heavily favored Edison in one of the greatest upsets of its time in Fresno. Fifty-four years later, seven members from that team attended Jerry's 80th birthday party. It brought tears to his eyes.

By the end of the season, Lois was pregnant, but she never missed a game or cruising through all the newspapers, looking for articles and quotes and putting them into large scrap books. She would do this for every year Jerry coached and now has a small room dedicated to these precious books.

Their first baby was born on May 17, 1957, a little girl named Pamela. Jerry doted over Pamela and he and Lois had a long summer with their new baby girl, enjoying every moment of it. Jerry sometimes joined his new daughter in a small rubber pool in the side yard.

Two years later, Jerry took over Antelope Valley High School's basketball program, where he experienced his only losing season as a coach.

In an effort to save money, Antelope Valley decided to close the gym in the evening and on weekends. Jerry went before the school board and convinced the members to reverse the decision.

Although he left Antelope Valley after one year, the following season, the team made it to the CIF (California Interscholastic Federation) playoffs, partly because the players were able to get additional practice time in the gym.

While coaches typically talk about offenses, defenses and ball handling, Jerry was learning that an important aspect of coaching was overcoming obstacles *off* the court as well. As with his on-court coaching wizardry, he learned to face up to, and overcome, the many challenges off the court. He realized it was all part of the game.

One off-the-court consideration was raising a family. Their little girl Pam was still a toddler when Lois and Jerry learned that Lois was pregnant again. She had another little girl on February 3, 1960. This one they named Josephine.

In the summer of 1959, Jerry took a new job and revived a dormant Redlands High School program. In his second year, he went 18-4 and was battling traditional power Ramona High School for the league title. It was a very close game in a very hot gym.

All the coaches were emotionally charged, yelling out instructions and directing the action from the sidelines. During the game, Jerry's mouth became dry from yelling. Every chance he had, he would run to a nearby water fountain to get a drink; however, the water barely trickled from the fountain, making it tough to wet his mouth.

With the game in overtime, he borrowed a towel and headed to the water fountain, where he used that towel to soak up the trickle of water. Thereafter, every time his mouth got dry, he simply sucked on the towel for moisture.

His Redlands squad won the game *and* the championship, so Jerry decided to continue the practice of sucking on a water-soaked towel, adopting it as his "good-luck charm." For the rest of his career, the team trainer folded a damp towel and placed it on a clean dry towel under his chair.

This simple and necessary act in the championship game created an iconic trademark that, to this day, people still associate with Coach Tarkanian. As the years went by, thousands of photographs and videos were taken of "Tark's Towel." Images of this strange, droopy-eyed man munching on a towel during stressful game moments became a media and fan favorite.

The towel—which had to be wet, folded a specific way and placed in a specific spot beneath his seat—joined a growing legion of superstitions and game-related rituals. For instance, next to his chair on the game floor was the so-called 'ghost seat.' No one was allowed to sit next to him; the chair always remained empty.

Another superstition Jerry had was that he never wore the same tie after a loss. It went into the trash. And if the team lost a game on the road, they never stayed at the same hotel again.

Once, he even exchanged his expensive Rolex watch for a cheaper one because he lost the first and only game in which he had worn the watch.

Lois also told of the time she reached for his toothpaste on the bathroom sink, when he almost knocked off her hand to keep her from touching it. Turns out that lucky toothpaste had to last him the rest of the season.

After his surprising conference championship win at Redlands in 1961, Jerry received an offer to be head coach at RCC (Riverside City College). He loved his Redlands High School coaching job, but he couldn't pass up the opportunity to pursue his dream of coaching at the collegiate level, even if it was only a two-year school.

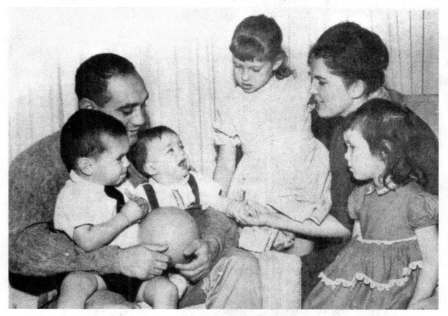

JT and Lois Tarkanian, with Pam, Jodie, George, and Danny (all their kids) when Jerry was selected Father of the Year in Riverside

CHAPTER 7:

TARK'S COLLEGE OPPORTUNITY

"Never put a kid so far in a hole he can't dig his way out of it."

—Bill Noble, Riverside City College President

D URING THE CHRISTMAS holidays in 1961, Jerry paced the halls at Redlands Memorial Hospital awaiting the birth of his third child. While he dearly loved his girls, among people of Armenian heritage, there is traditionally a very special bond between a father and his oldest son. And he was hoping for that first-born son!

When the nurse came out of the delivery room, she gave him the news he'd been waiting for. Lois fondly remembers hearing Jerry running down the hall, his many keys clanging together at his side, screaming excitedly, "It's a boy! It's a boy! It's a boy!" They named him Danny.

Immediately after Danny's birth, Jerry boarded a bus with his RCC basketball team for a seven-hour trip to St. George, Utah, to participate in the Dixie Junior College Tournament. On the way, the team stopped at the Thunderbird Hotel in Las Vegas for a quick bite to eat.

When the players entered the restaurant, the manager approached Jerry and told him that while he and his white players could eat there, his black players were not welcome and had to leave. Jerry, again, felt the sting of racial prejudice toward his players. Enraged, he quickly directed the entire team back to the bus and vowed never to step foot in that hotel again.

RCC finished dead last (seventh place) in the Dixie tournament, losing three straight games. Despite the most embarrassing stretch in his entire coaching career, Jerry was elated. He had his *first son* waiting for him at home.

Eighteen months later, on July 23, 1963, Lois gave birth to their second son and her last child, George, named after Jerry's father.

In trying to build a winning team at RCC, Jerry had his work cut out for him. The school was a member of the toughest junior college league in Southern California, the Eastern Conference, which was dominated by traditional power, Fullerton City College.

RCC had not beaten the Fullerton Hornets in 12 years. Actually, RCC had a tough time beating *anyone*, having finished last in the league the previous two seasons.

RCC finished the season an anemic 14-13, but the Tigers did manage to beat Fullerton, ending its 25-game losing streak. Jerry's brother Myron had warned him not to take the job. He said it was suicidal and would end his coaching career, but Jerry wouldn't listen.

Entering his second season, Jerry made a decision that dramatically impacted his coaching career. He really liked a high school player named Bobby Rule, but Rule's coach told him he was wasting his time, that Rule wasn't good enough to play at RCC.

Jerry ignored the advice and signed Rule anyway. He turned out to be the most dominating player in California junior college history.

RCC started the season with four straight wins before losing to San Diego City College in overtime. Rule was ejected from the game for punching an official. Jerry was furious and planned to suspend him for several games. When he arrived on campus Monday morning, Riverside's president Bill Noble told him he was going to impose the penalty himself, a mere two-game suspension.

Afterward, Noble imparted on a surprised Jerry a piece of wisdom that he never forgot and came to use frequently over the years: "Never put a kid so far in a hole that he can't dig his way out of it."

San Diego City College beat RCC a second time in one of the games Rule was suspended. It was the last regular season game Riverside would lose for more than two years.

RCC destroyed the powerful USC (University of Southern California) freshman team by 29 points. After the game, the Trojans began to actively recruit Rule. Each week, a USC assistant coach gave Jerry $50 to give to Rule, with instructions to deduct the money if he didn't go to class.

The USC recruiting effort was all for naught as the entire Trojan coaching staff lost their jobs before Rule graduated. Nevertheless, Jerry learned early how major college sports operated within the NCAA.

In league play, RCC destroyed one conference opponent after another. Local reporter Claude Anderson wrote, "The current RCC five might well be the best...in Eastern Conference history...their [Riverside's] defense...tighter than a Scotsman on a pension."

The Tigers finished league season 18-0, the best mark in league history, winning by an average of 36 points per game. Jerry Tarkanian was named Coach of the Year.

Riverside entered the state tournament as California's number one ranked team. In the first round, they faced the second-ranked team, Fresno City College. The RCC Tigers jumped out to a quick lead and kept it for most of the game, then Bobby Rule fouled out. Without him, RCC lost the game in the final seconds of overtime, 79-78.

RCC finished the season 32-3, the best record in school history.

Jerry Tarkanian began his third year at RCC with a talented and experienced team. Returning were two future NBA players, Bobby Rule and Roosevelt Lee. Tommy Crowder, Tom Quast and Randy Hoxie completed the starting roster, along with Tommy Ferraro and Sam Knight, who were reserve guards, giving RCC the best backcourt in the state.

RCC gelled into an unstoppable powerhouse, *destroying* one team after another. The Tigers didn't even have a close game, beating opponents by an average of 24 points. One opposing coach acknowledged, "We have two chances to beat Riverside: slim and none."

Each time RCC took the court, they put on a magnificent show of talent, effort and cohesiveness. One local columnist wrote, "It's the greatest show in town, every time the Tigers perform."

Bobby Rule was an absolute monster on the court. He averaged 25 points per game and was en route to becoming the leading scorer in conference history. It looked like it would be the easiest championship ever, until tragedy struck.

Bobby Rule and Tommy Crowder were passengers in a car that collided with another vehicle. Their car overturned four times and flew some 60 feet in the air before coming to a stop 100 feet from the collision site.

Miraculously, Crowder was only slightly hurt, but Rule was critically injured. He lost more than two pints of blood and was rushed to the hospital, where he clung to life in intensive care.

For the second year in a row, RCC entered the state tournament ranked number one and its first-round opponent, San Francisco City College, was ranked number two. It was questionable whether Bobby Rule would be able to play for the Tigers. He was still recovering from the accident.

More than 2,000 Riverside fans followed their beloved Tigers to Walnut Creek, California, for the state playoffs. The gym's capacity was only 2,600 and several coaches remarked that RCC's cheering section was the greatest they had ever seen for a junior college basketball game.

More than 40 years later, Ron Shaffer, who covered the team for the *Press-Enterprise,* recalled, "When they came in, the place exploded. I've never been involved with anything that exciting in my life and that includes 33 years at the *Washington Post* and a war in Vietnam."

Shaffer reported that, during the first game of the tournament, a Pierce player was shooting free throws when Riverside's players, in street clothes, walked in the side door. "As if by unseen command, 2,200 fans stood and screamed," Shaffer said, "and the poor Pierce player was so startled he tripped over the free throw line."

The rabid RCC fans awaited the appearance of one very important person: Bobby Rule. Despite the seriousness of his injury and not having practiced in weeks, Rule was determined to play in the state playoffs.

He ended up playing one of the worst games of his career, making only one basket and scoring only seven points. But his presence helped bolster his team as the Tigers scratched and clawed their way through the game.

San Francisco had a four-point lead with 3:57 left to play when the Tigers' Randy Hoxie hit a long jump shot, then stole a pass and drove in for the tying lay-in[1]. Hoxie was the most unlikely of stars as he was not recruited out of high school and just walked on to Riverside's team. He was a back-up for most of the year, but worked so hard that he earned the starting job by year's end.

Hoxie harbored a special affection for Coach Tarkanian, later naming his only son "Tark." Sadly, Hoxie died at a very young age. Years later, at a Riverside reunion, Jerry had the opportunity to meet Tark. It was an emotional and special moment in Jerry's life.

Riverside got the ball back with 59 seconds remaining and the score tied. Jerry ordered his team into a delay game for the last shot.

Everyone knew the ball was going to Rule. As the clock wound down, three Ram players surrounded him. Tommy Ferraro dribbled the ball at the top of the key, but couldn't find an opening to Rule. With time running out, Ferraro drove the lane and threw up a 12-foot-high arched shot that fell softly through the net.

Once the buzzer sounded, delirious Tiger fans stormed the court and raised Ferraro on their shoulders, carrying him off in wild jubilation.

Riverside destroyed Pierce in the semifinals. On the following night, it made history by becoming the first California junior college

---

[1] A type of shot in basketball in which a player jumps and shoots or releases the ball so that it lands directly over the rim, allowing it to fall into the basket. . . The lay-in is similar to the layup in that a player will typically drive to or begin the move under or in front of the basket. The key difference is that the layup uses the backboard to bank in the shot, whereas the lay-in does not use the backboard at all. — https://www.sportingcharts.com/dictionary/nba/lay-in.aspx

team to finish the season undefeated when they beat Hancock 78 to 71. Rule had 27 points in the championship game and was named the tournament's MVP (Most Valuable Player).

RCC had just completed the greatest season in California junior college history with a 35-0 record. Future Lakers Coach Bill Sharman declared that the Tiger team was "the greatest junior college team I have ever seen."

After the season ended, Bobby Rule had scholarship offers from several big-time college programs, but rumors were running rampant around campus that Jerry was going to be taking a job at Fresno State, a NCAA Division-I school. Rule decided to sit out the next season and not attend any four-year college, hoping that Jerry would land the job.

Despite Jerry's record-breaking success at RCC, Fresno State hired Ed Gregory, claiming they didn't want to hire an alumnus. Many speculated it was really because they didn't want to hire an Armenian, with prejudices against them still strong in the Central Valley of California.

When the Fresno job failed to materialize, Bobby Rule turned down offers from bigger programs to attend Colorado State University (CSU) because this school promised to hire Jerry the following year. That didn't happen, either.

Rule ended up having a great career in basketball. He was drafted by the Seattle Supersonics and made the All-Rookie and All-Star teams. As a rookie, he scored 47 points against the Lakers and, two years later, scored 49 against Wilt Chamberlain and the Philadelphia 76ers.

The RCC basketball team began the 1964-65 season having won 35 straight games and 61 of its last 62. The consensus was that the upcoming season was going to be very difficult. The Tigers had lost *every* player from their state championship team and was picked to finish fourth in their own conference.

Jerry quickly realized how difficult it was going to be. His championship team had been big, athletic and unbreakable in their man-to-man defense. In pre-season practice, however, he realized his players couldn't defend anyone effectively in man-to-man, so he switched to a 1-2-2 zone defense.

By emphasizing every minute detail so his players could maximize their quickness, Jerry perfected the 1-2-2 better than any coach in the history of college basketball. He relied upon it for the next ten years.

Instead of forcing players to adapt to *his* coaching style, Jerry would take the talent and skills of any team he coached and alter the way he coached to better utilize the talents of its players, whatever those talents might be.

In the fourth game of the season, USC's freshman team beat Riverside 68-51, breaking the Tigers' 38-game winning streak. In front of a boisterous sell-out crowd at Fullerton City College, Riverside's 42-game conference winning streak came to an end when Fullerton shot 68% in the second half, upending the Tigers.

This loss created a tie in the league standings between Fullerton and RCC. It also meant that the conference championship and a berth to the state playoffs would be determined by Riverside's final home game of the year against Fullerton.

Fans for both schools came out in force. The fire marshals closed the gym an hour and fifteen minutes before game time, but not before the largest crowd in RCC's history—2,800 people—crammed into its 2,500-seat gymnasium.

Three thousand additional fans were turned away, some of whom kicked in panels to the side door and crowded around the holes to watch the classic unfold.

Fullerton's Walt Simon kept the game close, scoring 23 points in the first half. When Simon fouled out late in the game, the Tigers pulled away to clinch the win. Jerry was so happy when Simon fouled out that he remarked, "I was ready to kiss everyone in the crowd."

In the state playoffs, the Tigers cruised to the championship game against the Fresno City College Rams. Even though the game was played in Northern California, Riverside fans outnumbered Fresno's 4-to-1.

Fresno was in control for most of the game, but RCC kept it close and clawed back to force overtime. Steve Barber's field goal and free throw in the closing seconds sealed the win for the Tigers.

Riverside finished its rebuilding year 31-5, putting the team in possession of its second consecutive California State Junior College Championship.

JT celebrating with his players after winning 3rd straight California State Junior College championship

CHAPTER 8:

GREATEST JUNIOR COLLEGE DYNASTY EVER

"Tarkanian is destined to success… with this sincere, dedicated coach who not only recruits—he teaches, guides and creates…he burns with dedication to constructively shape the life of boys… the most important part of Jerry's success…perhaps is why his players are called the most dedicated on the court. They try harder because of the deep respect, the warmth they feel for their coach."

—The *L.A. Times*

JERRY CONSIDERED his 1965-66 Riverside team the best junior college team he ever coached. It was led by future professionals 7'0" center Larry Bunce and 6'4" point guard Lucky Smith. Steve Barber, Jim Gardner, Larry Bonzoumet, Curtis Cooper and Joe Stephens made up the rest of the "Splendid Seven" as they were called.

The Splendid Seven began the season 16-0 before being upset 83-82 by Long Beach City College, led by future NBA great Mack Calvin. Long Beach's shooting performance was so spectacular that Ron Shaffer of the *Press-Enterprise* wrote, "The Lakers would have had a hard time beating Long Beach tonight."

Nevertheless, RCC had three chances at the end of regulation play to win the game, but they came up a point short. The players were despondent after the loss. Larry Bonzoumet described what happened next:

Coach was coming off his 2nd consecutive Junior College championship. It was my freshmen year, and we had already grown used to winning and possibly were even becoming a little complacent. The team was down after the loss, but no one could have predicted Coach's reaction. He gathered us in the locker room and while we stood and watched, Tark kicked thru a steel mesh locker door and said "...damn it, I am tired of LOSING!" Our final record that year was 34-1.

RCC was on a quest to create history by becoming the first team to win three straight California Junior College State Championships.

Ron Shaffer wrote, "Each year about this time, a plague known as 'tournamania' sweeps through fans of the Riverside City College basketball team. The symptoms of this affliction are extra-wide eyes, occasional froth at the mouth, extreme nervousness, insomnia and a general dereliction of duty."

The 1966 State Championship field was considered the toughest ever. "Tarkanian's Terrors" opened the tournament by beating Vallejo by 41 points, followed by a 47-point win over Hancock. Afterward, the Hancock coach mused, "You could divide that Riverside team in half and they'd play each other in the state finals."

In the final round, RCC faced the San Francisco Rams, who had lost only one game all year. The Tigers won by 30 points. After the game, two thousand screaming Tiger fans stormed the court chanting, "We're Number One!" and "Three in a Row!"

San Francisco's coach declared, "I've never seen a team play better... In my 11 years of coaching this is by far the worst beating I've ever taken."

Eddie Lopez of the *Fresno Bee* reported, "Most of the coaches at the tournament said [RCC] could beat half of the four-year schools."

Ron Shaffer declared RCC "the greatest junior college basketball dynasty ever known." In five short years at the collegiate level, Jerry had built the greatest junior college basketball dynasty ever known.

The primary reason for his success was his ability to relate to and motivate the inner-city kids who dominated college basketball during his tenure. Jerry took players other coaches couldn't coach and wouldn't touch, and molded them into a finely tuned, cohesive unit that competed and played harder than any of its opponents.

Jerry was able to relate with the inner-city kids because of the lessons he learned in his childhood. He admitted he was a poor student with little interest in school. Until he met Lois, his only interests were sports and partying. It took him six years to graduate from college. With Lois's influence, he received his master's degree from the University of Redlands in two years, with an A-average.

Instead of turning his back on recruits with poor academic records, Jerry welcomed them into his program. He understood that, with the right guidance, many of these players could succeed academically *just as he had* with Lois's guidance.

He preached to his players the importance of a college degree and the urgency to do well. He didn't want them to have to return to school years later to get an education, perhaps with a wife and children, and no scholarship.

Jerry understood kids who had troubled pasts. During his youth, he hung out with crazy guys and often got into trouble himself. He was fortunate his own youthful misdeeds did not prevent him from pursuing his chosen career.

Jerry understood that most of these kids were not bad people and, if given a second chance, they would succeed. These kids were from poor neighborhoods fraught with drugs and crime. Many had little or no parental guidance, so it was only natural they would get into trouble. After all, it was Oscar Wilde who once said, "Every saint has a past and every sinner a future."

Most college programs would not touch these kids. Former Kansas Assistant Coach Matt Doughty once told Jerry's son Danny, "Please don't take this the wrong way, but we just don't recruit the same kids your dad does. We *couldn't* coach them."

Early in his career, Jerry learned not to prejudge his players but, rather, to try and understand their difficulties.

In his third year at RCC, one of Jerry's hardest working players, Randy Hoxie, had three straight bad practices. Jerry ripped into him for his lack of effort and, the next day, Hoxie came into his office and apologized.

"Coach, I'm sorry for practicing so badly, but I hadn't eaten anything in three days. I have had to drink hot water each night so that the pains wouldn't keep me awake. However, I had a good meal today and I promise to have a great practice."

Years later, Jerry recalled how terrible he felt about chastising Hoxie so strongly.

Sadly, Hoxie signed a pro baseball contract rather than a letter of intent from one of the major basketball programs that were strongly recruiting him. His family needed the signing bonus. He was sent to a team in the Deep South, fought the racism there towards blacks, but couldn't stand it and left. He died before the age of 30.

Jerry understood that before he could ask his players to sacrifice so much, to play as hard as he required them to play, he and the other coaches had to develop a close, caring relationship. His office door was always open to his players. If they had a problem or just wanted to talk, he was always available. He required his assistants to be available as well.

One of Jerry's favorite lines was that he would "never hire an assistant coach who owned a set of golf clubs or a fishing pole." He didn't want assistants taking vacations. He wanted them available for his players. Jerry knew if his players truly believed the coaches cared about them, they would play their hearts out.

Joe Hendrickson of the *L.A. Times* wrote: "Tarkanian is destined to success… with this sincere, dedicated coach who not only recruits— he teaches, guides and creates…he burns with dedication to constructively shape the life of boys…the most important part of Jerry's success…perhaps is why his players are called the most dedicated on the court. They try harder because of the deep respect, the warmth they feel for their coach."

With Lois by his side, Jerry mentored, counseled and supported his players in a structure not unlike a large, open family. And it had a lasting impact on the players he coached.

One of the greatest baseball players of his time was Darrell Evans. He had 414 career home runs and won the World Series with the Detroit Tigers. At a recent reunion, Evans declared, "The best times of my life was playing basketball for Coach Tarkanian."

Because of Jerry's steadfast belief in giving guidance, support and loyalty to his players, there are countless success stories, not only of the players, but their children as well.

Joe Barnes was 23-years-old and washing dishes in Detroit before he came to Riverside. Jerry made a deal with the RCC president that if Barnes received his master's degree, Riverside would hire him as a professor. When Jerry took the Pasadena City College job, he made its president agree to the same deal. Barnes received his master's degree at Whittier and was a chemistry professor at PCC for more than 30 years!

Sam Knight and Tommy Crowder were from Cleveland. They traveled to Riverside on a bus without a suitcase, just a plastic bag filled with clothes. During the trip, the bus stopped in Oklahoma City. Because they were black, no one served them food. So, they bought crackers and candy bars at a vending machine and that was their meal for the rest of the journey.

When Knight and Crowder finally arrived in Riverside, Jerry picked them up at the bus station and took them to his home. As tough as the bus ride was, it was not nearly as frightening as what happened next. Knight told the story:

> *When we arrived at Coach Tark's house, we went around the back to the guest house. Out of nowhere, a large German shepherd named Ace started barking wildly. We were scared to death, frantically looking for a place to hide. Coach said, "Don't worry, he won't bite you." We said, "Coach, in Cleveland, we call them police dogs."*

After they made peace with Ace, Jerry got Knight and Crowder jobs busing tables in the school cafeteria. The lady running the cafeteria told him they were the two best workers she ever had.

Lois also got Knight his first full-time job at a school for deaf children, where he worked before later being elected to the Rubidoux County School Board. Two of his sons played football at USC and another played at Colorado. One was the high school Player of the Year and another made it to the NFL. His daughter graduated from one of the top schools in the nation, the University of California, San Diego.

Crowder received his master's degree from Cal State Haywood. His son graduated from West Point, received his master's degree from Harvard University and currently works on Wall Street. His daughter graduated from U. C. Berkeley and worked on Governor Schwarzenegger's staff. At a recent RCC reunion, she told Jerry, "You know, growing up I knew more about you than I did my grandparents. We owe everything to you."

While at Riverside, Jerry was working the clock at a city league game for extra money when he noticed Lucky Smith playing. After the game, he had pizza and beer with some of the players and told Smith he should go to college. Smith said he couldn't afford it because he had a wife and two kids. At the time, he worked for the Postal Service.

Jerry persisted until Smith's wife consented, agreeing to sell their house to pay for her husband's college. Smith led RCC to the state championship and went on to play professionally for the Milwaukee Bucks. After his playing career ended, he made millions of dollars in the computer business.

These true success stories associated with Coach Tarkanian and his basketball players are plentiful. They are stories of young men who, some argued, should never have attended college but, when finally given a chance, excelled and achieved great success.

The lives *those men* have touched now number in the thousands. These were men who would never have left the ghetto had it not been for a small Armenian coach who saw their potential and pointed them in the right direction.

Martin Luther King may have had "a dream," but it was through people like Jerry Tarkanian that positive changes were made toward racial equality. He took a chance on kids no one else would even consider and, time and time again, his gamble paid huge dividends, both for the individual athletes and for the teams.

CHAPTER 9:

TARK RETURNS HOME

"No man had ever been able to handle my boy, myself included, until Mr. Tarkanian took him in... I would move to the ends of the earth to have my son play for Mr. Tarkanian."

—**George Trapp, Sr.**

AFTER THE 1965-66 season ended with RCC winning an unprecedented third-straight state championship, Jerry's dream job opened up. It was the head coaching position of the USC Trojans.

Despite Jerry's dominating success on the basketball court, and his living just an hour from campus, the Trojans hired former USC player and Santa Anita Junior College Coach Bob Boyd. It was a huge disappointment to Jerry.

For months, Pasadena City College President Armen Sarafian tried to persuade Jerry to accept the head coaching position at PCC. Sarafian sweetened the deal with a higher salary and fewer teaching requirements and even had former classmates from Pasadena call to lobby him into acceptance. Despite all of Sarafian's enticements, Jerry decided to remain at RCC.

When he told Lois of his decision, she told him he needed to tell Sarafian in person. So, he drove to Pasadena to meet with him.

When he arrived, Sarafian wouldn't take no for an answer. He pressed Jerry, reminding him of how much it would have meant to his mother Rose to have her son coaching in Pasadena. Jerry loved his mother and would do anything for her; Sarafian had hit the sweet spot. He relented and accepted the job at PCC.

JT and his team traveling on bus to game

Pasadena was renowned for its football program. Located near USC's campus, the Trojans placed many of its star football athletes at PCC in an effort to foster their eligibility.

Periodically, their coaches came by campus and dropped off cases of beer for PCC professors who had USC football players in their classes. That's how it worked back then. With USC's assistance, PCC built a powerhouse football program which played for the national championship in the 1966 Junior Rose Bowl.

Pasadena's basketball program, on the other hand, was in dismal shape. It often drew only a handful of fans to its games, had never won a league championship, had only one winning season in the past 11 years and was 6-22 the previous year.

Tark on bench with another coach and president of Pasadena City College, Armen Sarafian, who was very special to JT

Sarafian was undaunted. He boasted to the *Star-News*, "I'm sure that Pasadena will win the Western State Conference basketball title and go to the state playoffs… furthermore, I think we will win the state title."

Accompanying Jerry from RCC to Pasadena was John Q. Trapp. The new coach at Riverside asked Jerry to take John with him because he knew he couldn't handle John himself.

John had been raised in the projects in Detroit and had trouble making friends, particularly with white people. He attended and left four different schools before arriving at Riverside and, according to an *L.A. Times* article by Shay Glick, the coach at his last school warned Jerry to "forget that big guy, he'll only cause trouble."

When Jerry met John, he told him, "This is your last chance. However, if you straighten out, you will get a scholarship to a four-year college and have an opportunity to do something great with your life."

Jerry then told John that he and Lois had a dinner date that evening. He asked John to babysit his four children, the oldest being ten. This must have shocked John, who had previously spent nights in jail.

It was the first time a white person had ever trusted John with anything, much less with their children. He eventually became the Tarkanian's regular babysitter.

John is arguably the toughest kid Jerry ever coached. He was also the meanest looking with a menacing, deep, dark, penetrating stare.

One day during the school year, President Sarafian ran into the coach's office in a panic. He said students were rioting on campus and stuck a communist flag into the campus ground. The athletic director said he wanted to go outside and rip it out of the ground, but Sarafian said no. "That is just what they want, someone from the school to incite a riot."

Jerry told Sarafian he would have John go and get it. Sarafian replied, "Do you think John would do that?"

John was eager to help. He waded through the crowd looking for the flag. Meanwhile, Jerry and the athletic director stood on a hill franticly pointing to it. John kept pushing people aside until he found it and, when he did, he pulled the flag out of the ground and broke the staff in two.

Upon seeing this, one of the protestors grabbed John, who picked the protestor up and threw him into the crowd. The demonstration ended forthwith. Several of the television stations broadcast the event. For over a month, neither John nor Jerry could pay for a meal in town.

After Jerry's first season, Bradley University sent PCC a tough kid nicknamed "Crazy" Crusheff. Early in his stay, Crusheff decked Pasadena's best returning player, Sam Robinson, in a pick-up game.

After the game, in a moment of unvarnished machismo, Crusheff asked who the toughest person in town was. One of the players responded, "That would be John Q. Trapp." Crusheff searched all over town looking for John.

Like many players over the years, Crusheff stayed in the Tarkanian's guesthouse. One night, Jerry, his assistant Andy Gillmore and Crusheff went to a summer league game. After the game, Jerry went out with some coaches and had some drinks. He asked Gillmore to take Crusheff back to the house.

When they arrived, Ace, the Tarkanian's German Shepherd, sprinted from the front porch and chased them back into the car. They locked the doors in terror. Gilmore decided to call Willie Betts, knowing Betts had stayed in the guesthouse and was familiar with the dog. When Betts arrived, Ace likewise tore into him, chasing him back to the car as well.

In desperation, Gillmore called John. When John arrived and got out of his car, Ace sprinted toward him, snarling and scowling. John grabbed Ace by the neck, slapped him across the face and ordered him to sit. Ace obliged. The next day, Crusheff told Jerry, "I want nothing to do with that Trapp fellow! He is the baddest man I ever met!"

"No man had ever been able to handle my boy," John's father said, "myself included, until Mr. Tarkanian took him in. When I saw what he had done for John, I decided to move the family to California." Mr. Trapp later told *Sports Illustrated*, "I would move to the ends of the earth to have my son play for Mr. Tarkanian."

After graduating from Pasadena, John received a full scholarship to UNLV before playing several years in the NBA. Once he finished his professional career, Jerry hired him as a manager for UNLV's basketball team so he could go back to school and get his college degree.

Joining John in the frontcourt was Sam Robinson and "Sweet" Willie Betts. The Tarkanian family had a special relationship with the

Robinson family. Their mother Ester was the Tarkanian's primary babysitter.

Sam not only played for Jerry at Pasadena, but followed him to Long Beach State. Sam's younger brother Jackie later became Jerry's first recruit at UNLV. Their youngest son Angelo was like a brother to the Tarkanian's son Danny and, in fact, almost became his brother.

When Ester was dying of cancer some years later, she asked Jerry and Lois to adopt Angelo, to which they were honored and touched. They started adoption proceedings, but stopped when one of Angelo's sisters requested custody instead. Jerry delivered the eulogy at Ester's funeral.

Willie Betts transferred to PCC after flunking out of school at Bradley. Bradley's coaching staff sent him to Pasadena to give him one last chance.

The Tarkanians took Betts under their wing to help him succeed. Lois, caring for four young children of her own, tutored him until his grades improved. Jerry was there whenever Betts needed, offering him advice to help him through his difficulties.

"I had a lot of personal problems and I talked to Mr. Tarkanian about anything that bothered me," Betts professed. "You could go to him. He was something like a father."

PCC lost the third game of the 1966-67 basketball season to Imperial Valley, 88-84. They wouldn't lose again the rest of the year, winning 33 straight games…and Pasadena's first state championship.

In the championship, Pasadena beat Long Beach City College, led by Mack Calvin, 89-79. Don Pickard of the *Independent Star-News* wrote, "After the game, men who had played for Tarkanian at RCC in years past came over, one after another, to shake hands and congratulate Tarkanian."

The previous year, after RCC's third straight championship and with the players celebrating on the court, John Trapp, who was ineligible at the time, grabbed Jerry and said, "I just wanted to tell you that I'm going to play for you next year and we are going to win this again, and I'm going to be the MVP!"

Characteristically, John did not smile when he said it. And, as promised, they won it again and John was named the MVP of the state tournament.

After his fourth straight state championship, Jerry received a deluge of coaching accolades. In a *Sports Illustrated* article titled "The Pied Piper from Pasadena," Joe Jares wrote, "Tarkanian is a Pied Piper of Negro youngsters, not only because he is the best junior college coach in California, and maybe in the country, but also because he and his wife Lois take a genuine interest in the players' welfare."

"There can't be much doubt... that Pasadena has one of America's finest young basketball coaches," reported the *Independent Star-News*, adding, "Tarkanian is one of the few coaches in the West, who is capable of matching Johnny Wooden, someday."

After his first year, Sarafian gave Jerry a raise, paying him more than Bob Boyd made coaching the USC Trojans. He also appointed him director of the student union, which meant he didn't have to teach any classes. Jerry's only responsibility was supervising the student union, which included the bookstore.

Amusingly, when Jerry was a student at PCC, he and friends lifted books from the bookstore and sold them, taking the cash to bet on horses at Santa Anita. Bookstore Manager Earl Holder always tried to catch them and, fifteen years later, in a peculiar twist of fate, Jerry was his boss.

Jerry couldn't have had a more supportive school president than Sarafian. On one occasion, Sarafian had a meeting with staff and professors and told them that if they really wanted to learn how to teach, they should go watch Coach Tarkanian's practices.

Even after Jerry left PCC, Sarafian remained his biggest fan, until his last breath. In 1989, sitting in the stands watching UNLV win the Big West championship, Sarafian had a heart attack and died. His death was heartbreaking to Jerry, who thought of him as a father figure.

JT celebrating Calif State Junior College championship with John Trapp and other Lancer players

PCC began the 1967-68 season ranked number one in the state. John Trapp had graduated, but his brother George replaced him. In the third game of the season, Hancock snapped PCC's 35-game winning streak, destroying the Lancers by 20 points. It was Jerry's worst loss in six years.

After the setback, Jerry had a few games to prepare for their toughest test yet, USC's top-ranked freshman team. The Freshman Trojans had four high school All-Americans, including Dana Padgett (the Utah Jazz, Houston Rockets, New Jersey Nets and Memphis Grizzlies).

In the locker room before the game, Jerry had all the players form a close circle. He questioned each of his starters, beginning with Henry Saunders. "Henry, you went to high school right down the road from USC. Did they recruit you?"

"No!" Saunders responded.

"Instead they went to Florida to sign a center," Jerry concluded.

He finished by looking at George Trapp. "George, you destroyed Padgett in the high school state championship game. Were you named Player of the State?"

"No." George said.

"That's right, they gave it to Padgett, instead."

By the time Jerry finished, the players were sky high. He knew exactly which buttons to push with each one to get them pumped up for their best game ever.

George led the team onto the court for warmups, a ball in each hand. Racing toward the basket, he leapt into the air and dunked one ball after the other. It was the first time Jerry had ever seen a player do that.

By game time, the gym was electrified as the Lancers humiliated the best freshman team in the country, handing USC a 22-point loss. PCC never looked back, winning 26 straight games.

In the semifinals of the State playoffs, PCC avenged its earlier loss by destroying Hancock. "I've never had a team so keyed up for a game as we were for this one," Jerry told the media. "They couldn't even talk before the game."

For weeks, rumors persisted that Jerry was going to accept a Division-I coaching job at Long Beach State. He tried to downplay the story, but he could tell it affected his players. He tried to reassure them and get them to focus on the playoffs.

In the finals, Pasadena faced Cerritos College. The game was held in Cerritos' gym, where the Falcons had not lost all year. PCC led for most of the game, with the Cerritos scoring a late basket to force overtime and ultimately prevail with a score of 69-68. Jerry's only two losses in state tournament play were one-point, overtime defeats.

CHAPTER 10:

TARK AT THE MAJOR COLLEGE LEVEL

"When I first got here, our recruiting budget was less than some athletic departments spend on stamps."

—Jerry Tarkanian, about Long Beach State

L ONG BEACH STATE was founded in 1949, when two old apartment buildings were converted into the school's campus. In its first year, 25 courses were taught by 13 faculty members.

Over the years, Long Beach State blossomed. The school relocated to a spacious 323-acre site located three miles from the Pacific Ocean. Its enrollment exploded and, by 1968, there were 27,000 students. In 1972, the school finally acquired university status.

While the university itself was growing and building, its athletic programs languished in mediocracy in the small-college division of the NCAA. In a move to bolster its fledging athletic program, the school decided to leave this division and join Division-I, the most competitive level in the NCAA.

To compete at this top level, Long Beach State's outstanding athletic director, Fred Miller, hired some of the country's top young coaches.

Later named coach of the United States Olympic Swim Team, Dan Gambril was hired as the school's swim coach. Ted Banks, who became one of the most celebrated track coaches in collegiate history, winning several national championships at the University of Texas at El Paso, was hired as the school's track coach. Jim Stangeland was hired as the school's football coach and was the most successful in school history. Miller's most important hire was the school's basketball coach.

Long Beach State had experienced little success in this sport. In its first 18 years of competition in the small college division, the program had only six winning seasons, had never won a league championship and had not won a game outside of the State of California in eight years, losing 18 straight times. The team had just finished its third consecutive losing season when Fred Miller offered Jerry his first major college job.

Jerry had been happy at PCC and loved the school's president. He always thought he would retire in Pasadena, though his dream was to coach at the major college level. He was 38 years old and if he was going to make a move up the sports ladder, he had to act upon this opportunity.

Jerry accepted the head coaching position at Long Beach State with full awareness of the obstacles facing him. He knew it was a small college program with little money and resources, so he accepted a $5,000 per year pay cut.

He didn't tell Lois about the cut, so when she opened the first month's check, she thought he was getting paid semi-monthly. Jerry let her believe that for as long as he could.

Miller said, "In all my years as an athletic director, Jerry was the only one who took a cut in pay from his previous job. His transfer from Pasadena City College to an 18-year-old State College, with few resources, was an act of courage."

In fact, the entire budget for the basketball program was $3,000 annually. It was so small that, to scout and recruit, the coaching staff used money earned in summer camps and savings from the players' tennis shoes allowance.

Jerry noted, "For most long-distance recruiting, we rely merely on the words of friends. We don't have the budget or the staff to travel around the country checking out prospects." He even joked, "When I first got here, our recruiting budget was less than some athletic departments spend on stamps."

While most basketball programs at the time provided 20 to 25 scholarships to its players, Long Beach State provided only eight. Worse yet, an out-of-state scholarship cost the program one-and-two-thirds scholarships, making it cost prohibitive to recruit most out-of-state players.

The 49ers played their basketball games in a small, antiquated gym that seated just 2,385 people. The team had to share the gym with the physical education department and all other indoor sports, including the school's nationally acclaimed volleyball team.

On many occasions, the basketball players had no facilities in which to practice and train. Jerry didn't even have his own office and had to share one with another coach. The basketball program didn't have its own secretary. It had to share one with another program as well.

These were not the kind of facilities that impressed top recruits who visited other campuses such as UCLA, just 30 miles away. The Bruins played in the spacious 12,829 seat Pauley Pavilion.

Despite these obstacles, under Jerry Tarkanian, Long Beach State's basketball program would embark upon a euphoric ride to the top echelon of college basketball. No one could have foreseen this incredible, meteoric rise – or the trouble it would bring.

Jerry knew he was not going to get the great high school players, the ones recruited by programs such as UCLA, North Carolina or Kentucky. So, he decided to recruit the great junior college players, some of whom had troubled pasts. His initial teams at Long Beach State were composed predominantly of these types of players.

Over the years, as his programs grew more successful, Jerry was able to sign a few great high school players. But he always retained his affinity for junior college players and four-year transfers.

Years after his retirement, Jerry remained loyal to junior college players. Although apolitical by nature, he became a big Sarah Palin fan when he learned she had attended a junior college in Idaho. "She would be the first JUCO transfer to make it to the White House!" he explained with excitement.

Jerry's close ties to the junior college ranks proved to be a tremendous advantage. In each of his first three seasons, Long Beach State signed the California Junior College Player of the Year. His first year brought Sam Robinson, who had been his star at Pasadena.

Robinson was a two-time Los Angeles City Player of the Year in high school. In his first season in junior college, he led PCC to the state championship and, in his second season, he was named the State's MVP.

Sam was recruited by more than 75 colleges across the country. Few, if any, thought he would choose Long Beach State. But the Tarkanians were very close to his mother, Ester.

When Sam announced he was following Jerry to Long Beach State, Ester told the press, "He is going to Long Beach to play for a coach he so dearly loves…I never said anything to Sam, but I have prayed that he would get to stay with a coach he loves so much… I have never met anyone like Coach Tarkanian and his wife. I enjoy just being in his presence. This is the happiest day of my life."

Three additional California junior college transfers joined Robinson in the starting line-up that first year: Ray Gritton, Shawn Johnson, and Arthur "Sleepy" Montgomery (later Amen Rahh).

Amen was typical of the type of kids Jerry was often *criticized* for recruiting. He was a mean, tough kid from one of L.A.'s roughest neighborhoods and an equally poor student. On his official visit, he walked through the student union and told Jerry he was going to love this place because "many of these guys were paying me protection money in Compton."

There were not a lot of offers from Division-1 schools for this kid, but Jerry could see through the tough-guy act and saw the heart of a champion beating within. Amen wound up being an incredible asset for the 49ers program.

In the late 1960s, Long Beach State's campus was on the verge of rioting, as were many other college campuses across America. The administration scheduled an anti-rioting rally and asked Jerry and the assistant football coach, a former Marine, to speak. Jerry asked Amen to join them.

"If we want to help the students on campus, then we should stay out of trouble and not let *anyone* tell us what to do," Amen told the crowd. "There's been a great deal of separation among blacks and whites. We want to bring them together so they will respect each other." Amen's remarks, more than anyone else's that day, helped prevent a nasty riot on campus.

"Before I came to Long Beach State, my only interest was basketball," Amen stated in a local newspaper article. "I didn't care a thing about studies. When I came down here, a few people told me I would never graduate. Now I want to be a high school principal or a college administrator. Basketball is my first love, but my degree is the most important thing to me."

When Amen graduated, he was on the Dean's list with a 3.25 grade point average and appointed dean of the Department of Black Studies at Long Beach State. A respected faculty member for more than 30 years in the California school system, Amen was also elected to the Compton City Council and School Board.

"If there is a college coach in America who treats black players better, I would like to meet him," Amen challenged when talking about Coach Tark. "This man is totally dedicated, and totally concerned about his players' welfare. He will go to bat for any of them..."

In front of a sell-out crowd in Long Beach State's tiny cracker box gym, Jerry began his Division-1 college coaching career with a 25-point win over the University of San Diego. The 49ers won 17 of their next 18 games.

Long Beach was beating its league opponents so badly that Cal Poly Pomona Coach Bob Stull, who had coached in the league for 20 years, stated, "This team is the best there has ever been in the California Collegiate Athletic Association."

The 49ers finished the season with a school best 23-3 record, its first league title and six wins outside the state of California. In a telling sign that Long Beach was on its way to becoming a basketball powerhouse, Sam Robinson was named First Team All Coast alongside UCLA's great Lew Alcindor (later Kareem Abdul-Jabbar).

In 1969, Long Beach State joined San Diego State, Fresno State, San Jose State, L.A. State and UC Santa Barbara in forming the Pacific Coast Athletic Association. Over the next 23 years, the PCAA (later known as the Big West) became the second strongest basketball conference in the West, behind only the PAC-10. Jerry coached teams that won every conference title in which they participated, 14 in all.

The top recruit for the following season was the California Junior College Player of the Year, George Trapp. It should have been an easy sell. George and his brother John were star players for Jerry at PCC, and both were close to him. Plus, Mr. and Mrs. Trapp loved Jerry and credited him for their sons' successes. Although, Mrs. Trapp only trusted Jerry so far, and it didn't extend to his driving.

Jerry was a notoriously bad driver. On the only occasion in which she consented to be a passenger in his car, Jerry drove Mrs. Trapp to the airport. The whole way there, she clenched the *Bible* tight to her chest and exclaimed, "O Lord, O Lord, please..." amidst audible bible verses.

In addition to Mr. and Mrs. Trapp, Jerry had the entire Pasadena basketball and football staff and the school's athletic director protecting George's services for Long Beach State. They did everything they could to prevent coaches from other schools from recruiting him.

One weekend, George disappeared and no one knew where he went. PCC's athletic staff panicked. They called Jerry, who drove to Pasadena and joined the search. No one could find him.

Monday morning, George strolled into the Pasadena football offices, whereupon an immediate call was placed to Coach Tarkanian. Jerry asked George where he had been.

"Coach, I went to Tulsa," he said, "and I liked it."

Jerry hung up the phone and drove to Pasadena. When he got there, he asked George, "Where is Tulsa?"

"Utah," George replied.

It turned out George had taken a recruiting visit to Hawaii with his former high school coach, Tony Stinson. Hawaii had promised Stinson a job if he could deliver George.

When Jerry questioned George about the Hawaii trip, George quipped, "Coach, I had a good time. You should have gone with me!"

Later in the year, at the junior college state championship game, a television reporter asked George if there was any truth to the rumor that he was going to follow Coach Tarkanian to Long Beach. "I haven't made up my mind yet," he said. "I want everyone to know I have a B average and I can go anywhere I want."

George's B average was in welding, in the Industrial Arts Program at Pasadena. When he was a boy, he had been involved in a serious accident, which left him with permanent brain damage. It wasn't too severe, but it did create a learning disability for George, making it difficult for him to study most conventional academic subjects. His father was a welder in Detroit, and George wanted to be a welder too.

Even with dozens of people, including George's parents, trying to help Jerry recruit George, the 49ers almost lost him to the University of Detroit.

It was rumored that Detroit was going to be the first Division-1 College to hire a black head coach. Will Robinson, a black candidate for the job, won more games than any other high school coach in Michigan history. In anticipation of his hiring, future Hall of Fame player Spencer Haywood signed with Detroit and it was rumored that other great players, including George Trapp, were to follow.

Detroit narrowed its list to three candidates, with Robinson being one of them. Detroit first offered the job to Don Haskins, from Texas El Paso. Haskins accepted and then backed out. Detroit then offered the job to Tates Locke from Miami of Ohio, but he too declined.

Even though Robinson was the third finalist, Detroit offered the job to the La Salle coach, who was white. Detroit just wasn't going to go against tradition and hire a black head coach.

So far as signing George, Long Beach State wasn't out of the woods yet. Detroit's new head coach had decided to make George their top priority recruit, even enlisting local politicians to help.

When George went home for the summer, the mayor of Detroit had a limousine pick him up at the airport, which was broadcast on all the local TV stations. Mr. Trapp was unimpressed by the media coverage, but his wife was being drawn in toward the siren's song.

When Mr. Trapp called Jerry and told him Detroit was making inroads with his wife, Vicki, Jerry called her and told her that Detroit didn't have welding classes. Vicki was stunned. "Well, George can't go there then."

Two weeks later, Detroit's coach and the dean of the college met with Vicki and told her the school had a new course called "On the Job Training" where the student received course credits *and* a salary by working six to eight weeks as a welder at various automobile companies.

Mr. Trapp called Jerry again and said Vicki was again leaning toward Detroit. Jerry hopped on a plane and stayed at the Trapp's house for ten straight nights, sipping ice tea on the front porch swing with Mr. Trapp. During the day, he took long walks in the all-black neighborhood with Mr. and Mrs. Trapp. In the evenings, he went to St. Cecilia gym and watched George play against the best players in Detroit.

After Jerry's visit, Vicki swung her loyalty back to Long Beach State and George finally signed with the 49ers.

When people question Jerry's success with recruiting inner-city kids, they don't have to look any further than the Trapp story. Remember, this was 1969 and America was still in racial turmoil. Amid all the hatred and chaos drawn along black and white lines, a small white man walked the streets of Detroit in a poor, all-black neighborhood, feeling comfortable and secure. There wasn't another coach in the country willing to do what Jerry did to sign George.

Vicki had only one special request for her son; she wanted him to have his own dorm room, to which Jerry agreed. George arrived on campus on a Sunday and checked in. That night, Jerry received a phone call from the dorm manager.

"What is it with this Trapp fellow?" he asked Jerry. "The first thing he tells me is to take the study desk out of his room because he 'wouldn't need it.'"

George normally made no pretense about his interest in studies outside of welding. Except for one particular occasion.

At the time, the basketball program's budget provided books for only five players, so Jerry didn't include George on the list. On the first day of school, offended that he was not one of the five, George stormed into Jerry's office.

"Coach, where are my books?" George demanded. "I am here for an education. I want a degree!"

"George, you know you are one of my top players," Jerry replied. "Just get me the title and author of each book you need, and I will get you the books."

That was the last Jerry heard from George on the subject. He knew George didn't really want the books but, rather, he just wanted to be viewed as one of the important players.

After college, George became the highest professional draft pick in school history, going 5th overall to the Atlanta Hawks. When he was married the following year, George rented the *Queen Mary* for the reception.

JT with son Danny at a banquet in Long Beach

CHAPTER 11:

LONG BEACH STATE BECOMES A POWERHOUSE

"Some members of the Mormon church told us that they were going to pray that we beat UCLA. I told them I would appreciate it if they would pray a lot."

—Jerry Tarkanian, in a *Press-Telegram* interview

THERE WERE GREAT expectations for the 49ers when the 1969-70 season started; however, the team got off to a poor start, with George playing terribly. After winning two games at home by a single point, Long Beach lost two of its next four before entering the biggest game in school history, at the 5th ranked Houston Cougars.

The 49ers played brilliantly, leading by ten points with 16 minutes to play, before the Cougars staged a frantic rally and won 76-69. Although Jerry was disappointed by the loss, this game was the first indication to everyone that Long Beach could play with the best teams in the country.

After, Long Beach's record stood at 5-3, Jerry's worst since his first year of collegiate coaching. In the locker room, George boldly proclaimed, "We're not gonna lose anymore, Coach, because Big George is going to take over!" And take over he did.

George played great and the 49ers didn't lose a game for the rest of the regular season. Long Beach finished the 1969-70 season with the nation's longest winning streak at 19 games.

In 1970, only 25 teams competed in the NCAA tournament, unlike the 68 teams that qualify today. In just two seasons, Long Beach State was a part of this prestigious group. The entire city was bursting with excitement.

The 49ers opened NCAA tournament play against the Weber State Wildcats. Playing some of their best basketball of the season, the 49ers destroyed a solid Weber State team, 92-73. The victory moved Long Beach State to its first national ranking in school history as they edged into the 15th spot.

In the regional semifinals, Long Beach was matched against the juggernaut UCLA Bruins, who were in the midst of the most dominating dynasty in college sports history. The three-time defending NCAA champions were chasing seven in a row. Their roster was filled with high school All-Americans from across the country and was coached by one of the greatest of all time, John Wooden.

Long Beach State had been a Division-1 member for only two years. There wasn't a single player on the 49ers' roster the Bruins had attempted to recruit. In only his second year of major college coaching, Coach Jerry Tarkanian faced the best of the best, the standard bearer of elite college basketball.

Despite the obvious mismatch, there was great excitement for the game. Dwight Chapin of the *L.A. Times* wrote, "It [UCLA v. LBS] is one of the most interesting Western Regional match-ups in years."

"Some members of the Mormon church told us that they were going to pray that we beat UCLA," Jerry said in a *Press-Telegram* interview. "I told them I would appreciate it if they would pray a lot."

Long Beach State proved to be no match against the powerful Bruins, losing 88-65. In spite of the loss, Jerry had taken his 49ers to new heights.

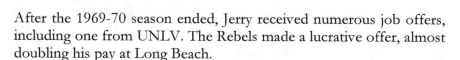

After the 1969-70 season ended, Jerry received numerous job offers, including one from UNLV. The Rebels made a lucrative offer, almost doubling his pay at Long Beach.

"UNLV's affluent businessmen wish to establish a big-time basketball program," wrote Hollingsworth from the *Press-Telegram*, "and their thinking was excellent. In lobbying Tarkanian, they couldn't have made a better move." Rebel boosters considered the offer "impossible to turn down."

"It was a difficult decision," Jerry acknowledged. "Las Vegas has a great, growing program that has unlimited potential and I feel in two to three years it could become another Houston."

In the end, however, Jerry turned down UNLV, and all the other coaching offers as well, to stay at Long Beach State. He knew the 49ers had something special going and he intended to see it come to fruition.

Long Beach's top recruit for the 1970-71 season was L.A. City Player of the Year Bruce Clark, who was being recruited by both USC and UCLA. Jerry knew the inherent difficulties recruiting against these schools. Both programs had great winning traditions and unlimited resources. Long Beach State had neither.

Jerry and his assistant, Ivan Duncan, got in early on Clark, before any other schools knew how good he was. On Sundays in Southern California, there was open gym called fraternity leagues held in gymnasiums located deep inside the projects.

Each week, Jerry and Duncan attended these games looking for talent. No other white coach dared to attend, so they were noticed by the people running the fraternity league. When Jerry entered the gym, the PA announcer customarily broadcast his arrival and he always received a nice round of applause. It was at one of these games that Bruce Clark was first noticed.

Duncan and Jerry recruited Clark for three years and established a great rapport with the young man and his parents. They attended Clark's high school graduation dressed in their best suits and sat in the front seats. They were the only two white guys at the ceremony. Many in attendance gave them strange looks. It was hot and they were sweating profusely.

After each kid was announced, they stood and gave a polite applause. When it was Clark's turn, they hooted and hollered and carried on. Afterward, they were invited to Clark's house for a graduation party, where they were again the only white people there.

After graduation, Clark moved into an apartment near Long Beach's campus and regularly hung out with 49er players. Jerry was confident that he would sign with them.

In the CIF All-Star Game, Clark was outstanding and clearly outshined the other players. Afterward, UCLA Assistant Denny Crum introduced him to Coach Wooden. Jerry drove Clark home from the game and, during the drive, Clark assured him that Long Beach was still even with UCLA.

"How could it be *even?*" Jerry responded angrily. "We have been recruiting you for three years and you just met Wooden!" That was the power Coach Wooden had back in those days.

One Sunday night, Duncan called Jerry and said Mrs. Clark was in great pain and needed to see a dentist. Jerry scrambled to find a local dentist who would treat her on a Sunday, which he did. The dentist told him to have Mrs. Clark come by his office in an hour.

Jerry excitedly called Duncan and told him the good news. When Duncan called Mrs. Clark, she told him not to worry, that USC had already sent a dentist to her home and taken care of the problem.

Clark said he wanted to learn the stock market, so Long Beach found him a job working for a stockbroker. He turned it down when USC got him the same job working only two days a week instead of five. And earning twice the money.

Clark's sister got a job working for a dentist who was a USC alumnus. Clark's father got a job working at a movie studio, which was arranged by legendary actor John Wayne, also a Trojan. Clark's family even moved to Pasadena – just a short drive from the USC campus.

At Dodger Stadium, on a sunny day in Southern California, Bruce Clark announced he was going to play basketball for the University of

Southern California. By 3:00 p.m. that day, he was in the basketball offices at Long Beach State, in tears about his decision.

Jerry was devastated by the news. Late that night, he received a call from Duncan, who told him not to worry, that he was with Clark's father drinking a fifth of scotch and that Mr. Clark had assured him that his son *was* going to Long Beach. After the scotch wore off, Clark signed with the Trojans.

Despondent, Jerry went to visit his brother Myron to lament about the loss of Clark. Myron was the head football coach at PCC and one of his players, Vance Clark, was surreptitiously listening to the conversation. Vance told Jerry to forget Bruce Clark and recruit a kid named Ed Ratleff instead.

Vance enrolled at Pasadena the year Jerry left. He was originally denied admission because he submitted his application after the deadline had passed, but Jerry liked Vance and wanted to help him. So, he went to the university president, who authorized Vance's admission to PCC. In an obvious attempt to return the favor, Vance offered to help recruit Ratleff.

What Vance told Jerry about Ratleff was not news to the coach. He knew all about Ratleff and had even tried to call him, but Ratleff wouldn't return his calls.

Ratleff was a first team All-American from Columbus East High School and on the list of every top university. He was a big-time winner having lost only three games since his 7th grade year.

Vance dialed up Ratleff and put him on the phone with Jerry. By the end of the conversation, Ratleff agreed to visit Long Beach's campus.

As it turned out, the key to signing Ratleff was his desire to play baseball along with basketball. Jerry assured him he could do both at Long Beach State, and he was the only coach who made this promise.

On Ratleff's official visit, Jerry took him by Blair Field, where the 49ers baseball team played some of their home games. Ratleff loved Blair Field and it was the turning point in getting the greatest player in Long Beach history.

After Ratleff returned home from his visit, Jerry received a phone call from his principal, Jack Gibbs. Gibbs was a no-nonsense guy who had played football for Woody Hayes.

"Eddie loves you and he loves the school," Gibbs told Jerry. "But he isn't going anywhere unless his parents, coach and counselor approve."

Gibbs requested information on the school and the basketball program. Jerry sent them and even had Mr. Trapp write a letter of recommendation. After receiving the materials, Gibbs asked Jerry to come to Columbus for a visit.

Jerry spent five days in Columbus meeting Gibbs, the athletic director, Ratleff and his parents. He even went to the Columbus Day fair with Ratleff, strolling around the parade grounds while Ratleff and his girlfriend held hands.

During the visit, Gibbs asked Jerry to take Dwight Bo Lamar along with Ratleff. Jerry didn't know anything about Lamar, his talents largely overshadowed by his two well-known teammates, Ratleff and Illinois recruit Nicky Connors.

Jerry politely told Gibbs that Long Beach State had only eight scholarships and that each out-of-state player cost the program one and two-third scholarships. Therefore, he couldn't take Ratleff *and* Lamar.

Lamar ended up at the University of Southwestern Louisiana (USL) in the Cajun enclave of Lafayette, where he led the nation in scoring and earned All-American honors his senior year. As a senior, he scored 38 points in an upset win over the 6th ranked 49ers. After the game, Lamar met the Long Beach team at the airport.

"Sorry you couldn't use me, Coach," he told Jerry. "I really wanted to come to Long Beach."

After Jerry's visit to Columbus, he and Duncan alternated each day, calling Ratleff, his mother, his father, his girlfriend and Gibbs. One day, when Jerry was at a reunion in Pasadena, Lois called and said Mr. Ratleff needed to speak with him. It was urgent.

Mr. Ratleff told Jerry that Gibbs had changed his mind and was now pushing Eddie to attend USL. Apparently, USL agreed to take the remaining two starters from the high school team with Bo Lamar if Ratleff joined them. Jerry called Eddie and told him not to do anything until he got there.

There was no money in Long Beach State's recruiting budget for another flight to Ohio, so Jerry met with the athletic director and pleaded for the funds. His request was denied. In desperation, Duncan persuaded his father to allow them the use of his credit card to pay for the airfare.

On the way to the airport to catch a red-eye flight to Columbus, Jerry and Duncan stopped at a bar named Hoefly's for a drink. While there, Jerry received a message that Mr. Ratleff wanted to speak with him.

"Don't bother coming," Mr. Ratleff said flatly. Jerry's heart sank, thinking Eddie had decided to go to USL. Then, Mr. Ratleff told *the rest of the story.*

"I chased those USL coaches out of town," Mr. Ratleff said, "and Eddie will be on the morning flight to Long Beach."

After hearing this, Duncan used his father's credit card to buy everyone in the bar drinks as they all toasted "Eddie Ratleff to Long Beach State." The card held out through more rounds than can be recalled, and an elated Coach Tarkanian *crawled* home that night.

Jerry has often said Ratleff was the most important recruit in his entire career. He and Eddie shared an extremely close relationship.

"We're really fortunate," Jerry said, bragging a bit. "A lot of guys will coach a lifetime and never have a person or an athlete like Eddie... There is no finer young man in this country than Ed Ratleff. He is just as beautiful a person as he is a ballplayer... his character and association he has with the other players blends the team together."

"Tarkanian is my kind of coach," Ratleff declared. "He is close to his players... He takes a genuine interest in his players, and that makes a difference in how a man plays... He's been like a father to me and I know that attitude makes me play all the harder. All of Tarkanian's players are like sons to him. The players know it and that's a big factor... Also, his practices are well organized. Everybody is doing something all of the time. Everybody is occupied, every minute of practice."

Ratleff described how other schools had offered him cars, money and phony jobs, but not Long Beach. "You're promised a car and money to buy clothes and that they'll fly your parents to the games … or a little soft job… instead of making $5 you might make $50. Things like that were offered to me. At Long Beach State I only received a $142 per month scholarship check."

Ratleff was also outspoken with his criticism of the NCAA. "Hell, I never accepted any [money] and I know that Tark turned down a lot of players who asked for it…God, the NCAA is screwed up," Ratleff told the *L.A. Times*. "What's wrong with staying at a coach's house, or going to dinner or to a movie with him? They have so many little asinine rules. And to hoot, they pick on who they want…In my opinion, [Long Beach State was] getting too close to [beating] UCLA."

Ratleff had a stellar career. He became a two-time consensus First Team All-American, one of only 12 players to earn that distinction at that time. He was a member of the 1972 U.S. Olympic Basketball Team and was the 6th player taken in the NBA draft by the Houston Rockets.

Joining George and Ratleff on the 1970-71 team was the California Junior College Player of the Year Chuck Terry. Terry also had a successful career. He was the last player cut from the 1972 U.S. Olympic team and a second-round draft pick by the Milwaukee Bucks.

Joining the trio was Eric McWilliams, who was also drafted into the NBA. McWilliams almost didn't start for the 49ers because he played the same position as future Hall of Famer George Gervin, who was on Long Beach State's campus for 19 days taking summer school classes.

Due to the racial violence which was still fairly frequent in the area, Detroit held all high school games in the afternoon. Because of this, the players did not receive much attention from the media or college coaches. One day, Mr. Trapp called Jerry and told him about a great player in Detroit named George Gervin.

At the time, no one knew how good Gervin was, but it didn't take long for Jerry to find out. He quickly offered Gervin a scholarship, which he accepted.

Gervin flew to Long Beach and started attending summer school classes. Long Beach State was not on the Letter of Intent program, so there was nothing to bind him to the school, other than his promise.

Jerry knew that Gervin was homesick and that his girlfriend in Michigan was trying to get him to come back. Gervin was sharing a room with Eric McWilliams at the time, so Jerry told Eric to keep an eye on him and to call him if anything was wrong.

One weekend, Gervin disappeared. Jerry grabbed Eric and asked him what happened. Eric told him that Gervin asked him for a ride to the airport so he could transfer to Eastern Michigan to be closer to home. Eric drove him there.

Jerry learned two important lessons from this experience. First, never allow players competing for the same position to room together. Second, recruit the girlfriend. Jerry learned the hard way that, oftentimes, the girlfriend has more influence over the player than the parents.

Gervin went back to Eastern Michigan and, within a month, broke up with his girlfriend. He was later named one of the top 50 players in NBA history and recognized as one of the league's greatest scorers.

CHAPTER 12:

49ERS PUT A SCARE INTO THE BRUINS

"Long Beach was the finest defensive team the Bruins have played all year… Tarkanian is an absolute master at teaching the zone… (He) is the best teacher of the zone in the country."

—John Wooden, Legendary UCLA Coach

LONG BEACH STATE began the season ranked 15th in the country by UPI (United Press International). *Sports Illustrated* ranked the 49ers in 8th place. Jerry knew he had a problem to fix. Each year, George Trapp played horrible until Christmas. After Christmas, he was sensational.

When he was at Monrovia High School, George had driven his high school coach Tony Stinson nuts with this. He was playing so badly that Stinson disappeared for several days. Some people went so far as to speculate that he might have committed suicide. Yet, after Christmas, George turned it on and led Monrovia to the CIF Championship. Stinson was named Coach of the Year.

George's final season at PCC was no different. George played terribly and caused all kinds of problems in practice.

In the middle of December, PCC Coach Dan Ayala started taking courses to sell mutual funds; he was going to get out of coaching. He even tried to get rid of George over the Christmas holidays. Again, after Christmas, George lifted the Lancers up onto his shoulders and carried them to the state championship.

In his first year at Long Beach State, George drove Jerry nuts as the team started the season 5-3. But, true to form, after Christmas, George led Long Beach State to 19 straight wins and its first NCAA tournament appearance.

Jerry thought he'd be creative for George's senior year and crafted a plan. He had as many Long Beach boosters as possible send George Christmas cards during the Thanksgiving holidays.

Despite the Thanksgiving-timed cards, the season started with disaster. The 49ers opened at the University of Kansas and the team failed to score for the first seven minutes of the game, trailing 32-8 at the half. Long Beach suffered an embarrassing 17-point loss.

A couple weeks later, Long Beach faced a difficult road trip with games at Loyola of Chicago, followed by 2nd ranked Marquette.

The 49ers opened that trip by beating Loyola. The day after the game, Jerry received a phone call from Marquette Coach Al McGuire, who told him that he and his coaches had watched Long Beach beat Loyola and they were impressed. He said that since they were able to scout Long Beach, it was only fair that Jerry be able to scout Marquette's practice the next day.

At the time, there were no film or game tapes. The only way to learn about an opponent was to personally scout them. Jerry was stunned by McGuire's offer. McGuire was a legend in college basketball and Jerry greatly admired him.

Jerry met McGuire at his office. While there, his secretary came in. "Coach, Maurice [Lucas] is outside," she said. "He would like to speak with you." McGuire told his secretary to tell Lucas he was gone. He then escorted Jerry out the back door.

"Why don't you want to speak with Maurice?" Jerry asked. "He's your best player."

"Jerry, if Maurice wants to speak with me, he either has a problem or he wants to get into my wallet," McGuire said. "I don't need either."

As they walked off campus, Maurice spotted McGuire and yelled, "Coach, Coach, I need to speak with you."

McGuire quickly replied, "Maurice, I have been looking for you. I'm glad you caught me. Coach Tarkanian is in town and I was going to take him to lunch, but I left my wallet at home. Can I borrow some money to buy him lunch?"

Maurice was dumbfounded. He apologized and said, "No Coach, I was going to ask *you* for some money."

"That's alright, Maurice. I will get it from someone else," McGuire said, and then walked off.

After lunch, they headed toward the gym, but McGuire maneuvered them to a little detour along the way. "Let's stop off at the bar across from the arena and have a drink," he offered.

As they finished their first drink, Jerry noticed it was almost practice time. He didn't want McGuire to be late, so he suggested they go. "Don't worry about it," McGuire replied. "We have time for one more drink."

By the time they finished their second drink, McGuire was a full 15 minutes late. He strolled into practice unfazed about his tardiness and headed for the bleachers to talk with some friends. His assistant, Hank Raymonds, was running practice.

Players were yelling at each other, getting in one tussle after another. One player yelled at McGuire, who yelled back. After practice, Jerry told his assistants he couldn't believe what he saw. Marquette's practice was so screwed up, he was confident they would upset the 2nd ranked team in the country.

The next night, Marquette played a flawless game and beat the 49ers 83-66. Jerry commented later, "In practice they looked like a disorganized, brawly bunch of kids. But when the game came, they were the most disciplined bunch of kids I think I have ever watched."

Later in December, Long Beach lost to both Tulsa and UNLV in UNLV's tournament. "I thought of jumping off the top of the hotel I was staying in," Jerry said after.

"We were so down after Christmas, we had lost four of eleven games, and I was ready to take up gardening, or anything other than coaching," Jerry commented. After the first of the year, the 49ers turned it around, winning 17 straight games with only one victory within single digits.

As a result of the winning streak, Long Beach earned its second straight NCAA tournament appearance. After beating University of Pacific in the first round, the 49ers earned a rematch with the powerful UCLA Bruins.

No one gave them a chance as UCLA entered the game a huge 13-point favorite. The 49ers rose to the occasion and stunned the nationally televised audience, not to mention the Bruins. Playing great defense and a deliberate offense, Long Beach led by four at the half. Their suffocating zone defense held UCLA starters Henry Bibby, Kenny Booker and Steve Patterson to a combined 0-17 from the field.

Long Beach pulled ahead by 11 points with 14:40 remaining in the game. The Bruins couldn't stop Ratleff, who scored on a variety of shots. They did, however, fight back, scoring nine straight points.

Late in the game, with Long Beach clinging to a small lead, UCLA's powerful athletic director, J.D. Morgan, ran to courtside, pounded his fist on the scorer's table and started screaming at the officials. "Call a foul on 42! Call a foul on 42!"

With 5:23 remaining and Long Beach ahead by two, Ratleff, who wore number 42, was whistled for his fifth foul, disqualifying him from further play. It was the only time in his collegiate career that he fouled out. It was a *horrendous* call.

Forty years later, a film of the game surfaced. On his 80th birthday, Jerry watched the tape with his son Danny. The call was worse than Jerry remembered.

With four fouls, Ratleff was playing tentatively and moved away from the player and out of bounds to avoid contact. The referee under the basket did not make the call, but rather, the referee near mid-court—whose view was blocked by other players—blew his whistle instead.

Ratleff was the leading scorer in the game with 18 points. Long Beach scored only three points the rest of the game.

The score was tied 53-53 with 3:07 to play when Jerry called time-out. He instructed his team to spread the court and shoot only a wide-open shot.

Jerry was going to run the clock down to 10 seconds, call another time-out and diagram a play for George. He was sure George would make the last shot because he had no fear of the Bruins; there was no UCLA mystique for him.

Twice, Long Beach State's Bernard Williams broke free and drove to the basket for layups. First though, Wicks and Larry Farmer came out of nowhere to make blocks.

With 28 seconds left, Ratleff's replacement, Dwight Taylor, caught the ball in the corner. The Bruins refused to guard him. Taylor, a poor shooter, took the wide open 15-foot shot, which missed badly. Wicks rebounded the ball and was fouled.

The crowd roaring and the Bruins' 17 straight NCAA tournament wins at risk, Wicks stepped to the line for a one and one. At the time, a shooter only received a second shot if he made his first.

Wicks' first shot hit the front of the rim with a clank, skidded across the cylinder, hit the back of the rim, then the backboard, before finally ricocheting into the hoop. He made the second shot as well.

UCLA won the game 57-55. It was the closest any team came to beating UCLA in the NCAA tournament during its incredible run of seven straight national championships. It was a heartbreaking loss for Long Beach. For years, Jerry lamented, "It would have been the biggest upset in NCAA history."

After the game, Morgan cynically remarked that they "were *fortunate* to win."

Wooden told the media, "I never expected to be down as far as we were…Long Beach was the finest defensive team the Bruins have played all year… Tarkanian is an absolute master at teaching the zone… (He) is the best teacher of the zone in the country."

"It was the best defense I've ever seen," Bruins guard, Kenny Booker, declared.

Following the game, two hundred and fifty people met the team at the airport at midnight. A sign proclaimed, "Tarkanian for President."

Jerry received hundreds of congratulatory telegrams from fellow coaches, players and even politicians.

The local and national media showered Long Beach State with praise. Mitch Chortkoff of the *Herald-Examiner* wrote, "The *image* of Long Beach State is a wild scattergun array of lads who play the game without discipline. Such was not the case with this edition."

"It was Long Beach State's finest hour… It was the biggest thing ever to happen in this City's sports history," Hank Hollinsworth of the *Press-Telegram* declared.

"Credit Tarkanian with one of the superior coaching efforts of his profession," Loel Schrader wrote.

Another writer proclaimed that "Tarkanian and his team won the hearts of a nation."

As a reward for the great season, Long Beach State paid for Jerry's entire family to vacation in Hawaii. One day, when Jerry was relaxing in the jacuzzi, he got an urgent call from Duncan. Jerry nervously hurried out and went to the telephone.

"You can't win any damn games sitting in the jacuzzi!" Duncan stated emphatically, and then hung up. Jerry and his assistants took great pride in the fact that no one *ever* outworked them, and no one worked harder than Duncan.

During the off-season, Jerry hosted a fundraiser for the 49er basketball program aboard the *Queen Mary*. John Wooden, Al McGuire and Lakers Coach Joe Mullaney attended. Oklahoma City Coach Abe Lemons wrote Jerry, sarcastically declining the invitation:

> *I am sorry I will be unable to attend the Jerry Tarkanian Appreciation Dinner. I think I have to mow the grass or something that day. Second, I might pay $50 for a Rachel Welch appreciation dinner but not for some Armenian coaching basketball…We all thought we would wait until next year when they will have a de-appreciation dinner, then* we *will get fifty bucks for attending.*

Lemons was widely considered the nation's funniest coach. When he coached at Texas Pan American, on the Mexican border, he joked that the school needed to provide more sports for its student body, so they started a swim team. Lemons said their coaches went down to the Rio Grande River and found some great swimmers, but they had one problem – they could only swim north.

When Lemons coached at Texas, he and Arkansas Coach Eddie Sutton did not get along. One year, Sutton had a great player who was ineligible until he passed 14 credits in one summer session. At the league meeting, Lemons told the press, "it was a good thing Sutton's player didn't stay all summer, or he would have gotten his Ph.D."

At the fundraiser, John Wooden joked, "This banquet was misrepresented to me a little. I thought it was a *retirement* dinner for Tarkanian."

Job offers started to again pour in for Jerry. Some were from perennial powers such as Indiana, which inquired after Wooden turned down the job and recommended him instead.

Despite the wonderful offers, Jerry decided to stay at Long Beach. The 49ers were within striking distance of catching the Bruins and Jerry was close to signing his best recruit ever.

To this day, Raymond Lewis is widely considered the greatest high school player in Southern California history. Jerry first saw Lewis play in a pick-up game after his freshman season and fell in love with him. Long Beach State great Chuck Terry tells the story:

> *Ray Gritton, a few of the coaches and I went to some park in Compton to watch some tenth grader play in a full court pick-up game. Tark wanted to see how good this kid was, so he had Ray suit up and guard him. Gritton was a former All-*

PCAA guard at Long Beach. Well, this tenth grader absolutely destroyed Ray. Everyone knew he was the real deal.

Thereafter, on most Sundays, Jerry and Duncan learned where Raymond was playing and they would go and watch. "It was such a joy to watch him play the game," Jerry exclaimed. "I thought he was the finest high school guard I'd ever seen."

"He [Lewis] is the best offensive player for his size [6'2"] that I have seen," UCLA assistant Gary Cunningham remarked.

In his junior year of high school, Raymond put on a dazzling show, dominating a CIF playoff game. After, all the big-time coaches waited for him...John Wooden, Bob Boyd and Denny Crum.

Raymond came out of the locker room and strolled past the other coaches without so much as an acknowledgment. He walked directly up to Jerry and introduced his mother. "Coach, I want you to meet my mother, Ella Mae."

A smiling Ella Mae spoke next. "Coach, I have been gone for a while, but I am back now and I am going to take care of my son."

Raymond loved his mother and she would have the biggest say on where he was going to attend school. So, every week, Duncan and Jerry took Ella Mae to lunch in Compton. On many occasions, her sister joined them.

One day, Don Dyer, a Long Beach booster, called Jerry to say that he heard a rumor that he and Duncan were dating two black ladies. It may not have been a romance, but Jerry's thoughts were so dominated by Raymond's mother that he fell asleep at night mumbling "Ella Mae, Ella Mae."

After his junior year in high school, Raymond played in a three-on-three tournament that included some of the greatest players in Southern California. Paul Westphal and Dana Padgett fielded a USC team, as did some former UCLA players.

Raymond's team consisted of two high school buddies, and they slaughtered *everyone*. The rules were: winner takes out (starts with the ball) and if you made a basket, you kept the ball. It didn't matter how far behind Raymond's team was, once he got the ball, the other team never got it back.

After his senior year in high school, Raymond and his high school buddies played in the inaugural L.A. Summer League. The Los Angeles Laker rookies, USC alumni, LBS alumni and UCLA's alumni all had teams.

In the first game, Raymond scored 52 points as his team beat the Laker rookies. After the next game against the USC alumni, the newspaper ran a big story that Mack Calvin held Lewis to just 32 points.

Raymond's legend was already so big that the local newspaper praised Calvin, an NBA Defensive Player of the Year recipient, for holding a *high school kid* to 32 points. Jerry teased Raymond about the article.

"Coach, Calvin can't guard me," Raymond said. "All he ever did was foul me, but they wouldn't call it because he was a pro and I'm still in high school." Raymond felt he had to explain being held to just 32 points by the best defensive player in the NBA.

During the summer, Raymond moved into Long Beach State's dorm, got a job on campus and enrolled in summer school. Every day, he played pick-up ball in Long Beach's gym.

The 49ers had just inked New York City Player of the Year Ernie Douse and the signing generated great publicity. When Raymond learned of this, he challenged Douse to a one-on-one game. They were on the court playing when someone told Jerry about it.

Jerry immediately jumped out of his chair, rushed to the gym and stopped the game. He was worried Douse would get so discouraged that he would go back home. He was right about one thing; Raymond *was* embarrassing him. The score was 17 to 2.

Nearly 250 colleges from across the country offered Raymond a scholarship, including UCLA, USC and Notre Dame. He was a senior in high school when Long Beach State almost upset UCLA in the Regional Finals.

After the game, Jerry called Raymond and said he wanted to sit down with him and discuss where he wanted to go to college. "Coach, I am coming with you," he said without hesitation, "to Long Beach."

"That's wonderful," Jerry replied. "We will have our Sports Information Director issue a statement."

Long Beach State was not a member of the Letter of Intent program, which bound players to the school they committed to once they signed. Regardless, Jerry was sure Raymond was going to be a 49er.

The day of the CIF All-Star Game, a newscaster grabbed Jerry and asked what he thought of Raymond going to Cal State Los Angeles. Jerry told him he was crazy, that Raymond was going to Long Beach.

Jerry soon learned that Cal State L.A. had given the entire starting line-up on Raymond's high school team full scholarships and bought Raymond a brand-new red Corvette. He was convinced that Raymond thought he could take the Corvette from Cal State L.A. and still attend school at Long Beach State. But such was not the case.

Cal State L.A. had just converted to a quarter system and the school year started earlier than normal. Believing that he was taking summer classes, Lewis attended. He quickly learned that they were fall semester classes so, according to NCAA rules, he was required to play at Cal State L.A.

"I've always loved recruiting," Jerry said, "but I've changed... since the Raymond Lewis thing; a lot of my enthusiasm is gone."

A few weeks later, Randy Elkos, a teammate of Raymond's, told Jerry, "If I received a new Corvette, I would be driving it up and down the coast. Raymond hasn't left Watts with it. He is just cruising Watts." *That* was Raymond!

Before the basketball season started, Santa Barbara's coach, Ralph Barkley, told Jerry not to worry about losing his top recruit. "Raymond was over-rated," Barkley said, "a good scorer but nothing else."

At the time, freshmen could not play on varsity, so they played other freshman teams. Later that year, when the freshmen from L.A. State and Santa Barbara played, Raymond scored 73 points, hitting 30 of 40 shots. After the game, Barkley grabbed Jerry and told him he was wrong about Raymond, that he had just witnessed the greatest performance ever played on a basketball court.

Lewis led all freshmen in scoring, averaging 38.9 points per game while shooting an astonishing 59% from the floor. He also averaged seven assists per game.

Jerry saw Ella Mae at one of the freshman games and asked her what kind of car she had received. When she told him she didn't get one, he responded, "That's not right, you should have gotten a car too."

"Yea, you're right," she replied, "that isn't right."

The next time Jerry saw Ella Mae, she was driving a Buick. He later asked the Cal State L.A. coach, of whom he was very fond, how he could afford all of it. He told Jerry he had to cash in his California State retirement savings. Ella Mae had broken him.

Raymond decided to turn pro after his sophomore season. The Philadelphia 76ers drafted him with the 18th pick. They also had the first pick in the draft, which they used to sign Olympic hero, Doug Collins.

In camp, Raymond destroyed Collins. During one scrimmage, Raymond reportedly scored 60 points in the first half before 76ers coach Gene Shue took Collins out of the game to help him avoid any further embarrassment. The headline in one newspaper read, "Collins Talks a Good Game, but Raymond Lewis Plays it."

As a result, Raymond's agent pulled him out of camp and demanded the same contract Collins had. Philadelphia responded by suspending him. Raymond never made it back into the league. It was a sad ending to an otherwise brilliant career.

For years, Raymond called Jerry and asked for help with jobs or tryouts. Jerry tried to help as much as he could, but Raymond never stuck with anyone.

Raymond never lost his shooting touch. A decade later, he scored 56 points in a summer league game against Michael Cooper, who was later named the NBA's Defensive Player of the Year.

Sadly, Raymond died at 48 from complications following an attempted amputation of an infected leg. After, his father was quoted in an article saying, "Raymond's whole life would have changed dramatically if he had played for Tarkanian—someone who cared about him."

JT with coaching legends, John Wooden and Al Maquire

CHAPTER 13:

REMATCH WITH THE BRUINS

"Coach Tarkanian and his wife have become something of a foster family. I even helped Lois pick pumpkins for deaf children."

—Roscoe Pondexter

THE 1971-72 SEASON looked promising for the 49ers. Long Beach State returned four starters and, although they missed George, he was replaced by the 6'8", 240-pound Leonard Gray.

Jerry described Gray as "a vicious rebounder—the most aggressive player I ever coached—and I love him. I smile every time I see him. [He's] the meanest S.O.B. I've ever seen."

One Long Beach official asserted that "Gray has already knocked out more teeth than the leading orthodontist."

Entering the season, Long Beach State was ranked in the top 10 of every pre-season poll. *Sporting News* even had the 49ers ranked number one.

Traditionally, December had never been kind to Tarkanian teams. In the previous 10 years, his teams won 272 games and lost only 27. Seventeen of those losses came in December, but December 1971 was different.

The 49ers stormed to a 9-1 record with their only loss to future top 10 team, Southwestern Louisiana. Lamar scored 38 points, dished out six assists and was named Tournament MVP.

The 49ers won their next 13 games, playing in front of one record crowd after another. In fact, 9,744 fans squeezed into San Diego State's gym to watch Long Beach State destroy the Aztecs, more than doubling the previous attendance record. The largest crowd in Orange County history watched Long Beach State beat Irvine. San Jose State, Fresno State and Pacific all enjoyed record crowds.

The 49ers had also caught UCLA's attention. John Wooden, who rarely scouted an opponent, was seen scouting the Santa Clara v. Long Beach State game. He also admitted to watching Pacific v. Long Beach State in what proved to be the 49er's toughest regular season game.

The Pacific Tigers had just joined the PCAA after winning the WCAC conference the previous year. They were almost invincible at home, winning 33 straight games. Long Beach State entered the game ranked 3rd in the country; the school's highest ranking to date. The 49ers had never lost a PCAA league game, having won 25 straight. One of those streaks had to end.

The seating capacity for the Civic Memorial Auditorium was 2,800, but more than 3,200 people crammed into its small confines for the game of the year. Frantic fans sat inches from the court. The 49ers' Chuck Terry complained that spectators were pulling the hair on his legs when he took the ball out of bounds.

The scene was complete bedlam and Pacific didn't disappoint their fans, storming to a 20-2 lead. Tigers guard John Errecart hit his first 10 shots of the game and finished with 26 points. Pacific's center John Gianelli scored 17 points and added 27 rebounds. Pacific destroyed Long Beach 104-86.

After the game, Jerry received a call from Wooden, who said, "Goodness gracious, Jerry, I have never seen a team shoot so well."

In their rematch, Long Beach hosted Pacific in the last game of the regular season. The teams were tied in the league standings and only the winner received an NCAA bid.

49er fans were always boisterous and creative, continually finding new ways to become even louder. During Jerry's first year, fans banged wooden blocks together to make a deafening noise. At the end of the season, the newly formed PCAA conference banned these blocks as unsportsmanlike.

The second year, Long Beach fans shook beer cans that were partially filled with rice to create a piercing noise. When that season ended, the PCAA banned this practice as well.

In Jerry's third year, the fans clicked little metal clackers to disrupt the opposing team, a practice that was likewise banned. Finally, the fans turned to old fashioned yelling and screaming to create one of the most intimidating environments in all of college basketball.

The cracker box gym was a frightening sight for opposing teams. It filled to capacity an hour before game time, with fans seated as close as five feet from the court. A large banner hung from the rafters warning, "Welcome to the 'Sweatbox.'"

The acoustics were so bad that it made the noise louder. During introductions, the crowd was so deafening, the announcer had to flash the player's number to the Long Beach assistant coach to identify who was being introduced because it was impossible to understand anything said over the loud speaker.

49er fans were especially animated for the Pacific game, starting their vocalizations a full half hour before tip-off. From the opening of the game to after the final buzzer, the sound in the small gym was ear-splitting, and the temperature inside the gym soared to more than 100 degrees. "Long Beach State's zone was as smoldering as the heat," the *Herald-Examiner* wrote.

The 49ers destroyed Pacific in the rematch, 86-62, and earned a berth in the NCAA tournament. A standing ovation started for the team with three minutes left to play.

Jerry maintained that the Pacific game was "the most rabid crowd we've ever had." Several people told him they would remember the atmosphere in that gym for the rest of their lives.

March Madness, 1972

Long Beach won its first two games and earned a second straight trip to the Regional Finals. For the third consecutive time, they would face the UCLA Bruins. Long Beach entered the game ranked 5th in the country, but UCLA was better than ever. Led by super sophomore Bill Walton, the Bruins won 27 straight games by an average of 32.8 points per game, which is still an NCAA record.

UCLA's team was scheduled to fly on the same plane as Long Beach's for the trip to Salt Lake City. UCLA traveled first class, whereas Long Beach traveled coach so, when Jerry learned of this, he had his team leave on an earlier flight.

After arriving at the Salt Lake airport, Long Beach players were waiting for their things when UCLA's players walked into the baggage claim area. Fifty reporters and 11 cameramen descended upon the Bruins players.

The Bruins were wearing expensive cashmere coats, felt hats and alligator shoes while Long Beach's players wore their traditional letterman jackets, jeans and Converse tennis shoes. One reporter was heard to remark that it seemed only fitting that a team from L.A. comes dressed as if they are going to the Academy Awards presentations in Hollywood.

The contrast between the two teams, the two programs, could not have been more glaring. UCLA was the rich, powerful, glamorous, establishment program. Long Beach State was the poor, blue collar, upstart program.

UCLA players were not the only ones preparing for the big game; their band was as well. While their players stayed in another hotel, their band stayed at the same hotel as the Long Beach team. Obviously in need of additional practice, they held a band rehearsal in the hotel's parking lot at 3:00 a.m. the morning of the game, and again at 9:00 a.m.

Jerry didn't want to do anything to upset the Bruins. He didn't want them more fired up than necessary, so he ordered his team not to say anything bad about their players and to only talk about how fortunate they were to play them.

On the morning of the big game, Jerry sat down for breakfast and to read the newspaper when he came across a quote from his starting center Nate Stephens, who stated in reference to Walton, "The Big Red Head is over-rated."

Jerry almost had a heart attack. The last thing the 49ers could afford was an agitated Bill Walton. But there it was.

The closely contested game Jerry had hoped for never materialized. UCLA played great as Walton humiliated Stephens, scoring 19 points, grabbing 11 rebounds and blocking five shots. UCLA won 73-57.

After the game was over, the media asked Stephens about his quote. "That dude must have some soul in him," Stephens replied.

Despite the loss to UCLA, Long Beach enjoyed a tremendous season. In only its fourth season as a Division-I member, they were ranked as high as 3rd in the country. They reached their second straight regional final, only one win from the coveted Final Four.

The 49ers lost to the most powerful program, and perhaps the best team, in the history of college basketball.

Long Beach State was on the rise, gaining national attention. Traditional Southern California powers USC and UCLA refused to schedule the 49ers for a regular season game. USC's athletic director told Long Beach's athletic director that "USC would never schedule Long Beach State under any circumstances."

At UCLA, John Wooden told the *Press Telegram*, "We don't want to play Long Beach …. The physical match-up of the Long Beach State team may be the best to beat us."

In response to USC's and UCLA's refusal to "come to court," the Long Beach City Council passed a resolution challenging USC and UCLA to play the 49ers. Neither program accepted.

JT with son Danny Tarkanian celebrating first NCAA tournament win at Long Beach State game

The 1972-73 season started with great fanfare. Eddie Ratleff turned down an $800,000 offer from the ABA (American Basketball Association) Indiana Squires to return for his senior season. In spite of receiving lucrative professional offers, Eddie was passionate about seeing his name on a college diploma!

"I turned down a lot of money by not accepting some professional offers," Ratleff said, "but I'm so close to gaining my college degree that I want it, no matter what."

Returning to the 49ers team with Ratleff were future NBA players Leonard Gray (Seattle Super Sonics, Washington Bullets) and Glen McDonald (Boston Celtics, Milwaukee Bucks). Joining them was Roscoe Pondexter (Boston Celtics), the leading scorer in California prep history and winner of the 1971 prestigious California Mr. Basketball award.

Roscoe and his younger brother Clifton were the best high school players to come out of the Central Valley in California. In fact, Clifton was considered by many to be the best high school player in the class of 1973.

The 49ers were able to establish a close relationship with the Pondexter family early on in the recruiting process because of their coaches' close ties to the Central Valley. Not only were Jerry and Lois Fresno State grads, so were Jerry's top assistant and his wife, Lynn and Anne Archibald.

The Pondexter family was destitute. "Their West Fresno neighborhood is too sparse even to qualify for the status of a 'ghetto,'" claimed Rick Roberts of the *Press Telegram*.

Roscoe described the basketball hoop at his home:

> *We had a little goal in the backyard. The backboard was made out of plywood, kind of flimsy, the ball was rough and dirty, and*

the rim was almost falling off. We didn't have a net. The court was dirt.

Fresno State was not about to let a hometown basketball hero slip away. They offered the Pondexter family a "Bonadelle" (a respected homebuilder in Fresno) home for as long as a Pondexter played for Fresno State, which would have been five years if Clifton followed Roscoe to Fresno. They also offered the Pondexters a large sum of cash.

Jerry knew the financial hardships the Pondexter family faced. When Roscoe told him about Fresno State's offer, he told Roscoe that he had to accept it. It was too good to turn down.

When Jerry returned home, he told Lois, Lynn and Anne about his conversation. They were furious with him. "You can't let him go there," they told him. "He doesn't want to play for that coach or that school."

After the browbeating, Jerry called Roscoe and asked him what *he* really wanted to do. "Coach, I don't want to go to Fresno," he said. "I want to play for you." As a result, Roscoe signed with the 49ers.

After the formal commitment, Fresno State's coach Ed Gregory told boosters he lost Roscoe because Long Beach State had *bought him*. It was the pinnacle of hypocrisy.

It was hard for other coaches to understand the close relationship Jerry had with inner-city players. It was far easier to claim he had cheated.

Jerry established close ties with his players by creating a family environment with them. He had done this since his very first days of coaching under Clark Van Galder, and he had seen the effectiveness of this type of player-coach relationship.

"The scene is the most popular hangout of the basketball players at Long Beach State," Jeff Prugh of the *L.A. Times* wrote. "It is the office of head coach Jerry Tarkanian...The players affectionately call him 'JT' or 'The Man.'"

Prugh went on to say, "Tarkanian's players move freely in and out of his office...He talks to them and they listen. They talk to him and he listens... Trapp comes into his office and banters with Tarkanian about the game that night. Ratleff comes in and banters, then other players come in."

Lois agreed. "Our home is open to the boys," she said. "They can use the pool or just visit. It's got to be a family type of feeling. I want them to feel they can come anytime. Most nights there would be one or more players at our home."

"He came to understand them [the players], the way they react, and their feelings," Roscoe Pondexter stated. "He came to understand their situations, knowing that their home life is often difficult, knowing that they have problems as far as not being exposed to reading and not having close-knit families. He came to me as a man of that character.

"Coach Tarkanian and his wife have become something of a foster family," Pondexter went on to say. "I even helped Lois pick pumpkins for deaf children."

Roscoe's close relationship with the Tarkanians remains to this day. In 1995, when Jerry accepted the Fresno State job, he hired Roscoe as the team manager to assist him in getting his college degree. In 2009, when Roscoe's son was drafted in the first round of the NBA draft, Jerry was there to share the excitement with them.

CHAPTER 14:

THE SHARK LEAVES FOR THE DESERT

"You have to take the Vegas job. You won't want to leave, until you go to heaven."

—Mike Toney, UNLV Booster

JT and Mike Toney, one of JT's best and most loyal friends.

JOINING ROSCOE PONDEXTER on the 1972-73 roster was unheralded junior college transfer Rick Aberegg. Undersized and not an especially great athlete, Aberegg was nevertheless the cog that made the 49ers function. His incredible court vision and timing with passes created an up-tempo offense that the 49ers lacked in previous years.

Long Beach started the season ranked in the top ten. They finished the month of December 11-0, winning by an average of more than 30 points per game.

The 49ers participated in the prestigious All-College Tournament, the oldest college basketball tournament in the country. Included in the field were four teams ranked in the top 20.

In the finals, the 49ers battled the 14th ranked BYU Cougars. Everyone expected a close, hard-fought contest. Instead, the sell-out crowd witnessed an astounding first half performance by the 49ers as Long Beach led by 19 points.

Former BYU coach, Stan Watts, told Jerry after the game that it was the greatest half of basketball he had ever seen a team play. "The best half of basketball I think I've ever seen," agreed sportswriter Curry Kirkpatrick.

Oklahoma City coach Abe Lemons was asked at halftime what he would do if he was the BYU coach. "Surrender and ask for amnesty" was his reply.

The accolades poured in for the 49ers. One board member of the All-College Tournament declared, "Long Beach State has to be one of the greatest teams to ever play here."

That included USF's 1954 National Championship Team and Loyola of Chicago's 1962 National Championship Team. Ratleff was named one of the greatest players to ever play in the tournament, a roster that included Bill Russell, Elgin Baylor, Pete Maravich and Calvin Murphy.

In league play, the 49ers still had to face Raymond Lewis and his Cal State L.A. teammates. Despite having lost him as a recruit, Jerry remained Lewis' biggest fan, singing his praises whenever his name was mentioned.

This fact was evidenced by Long Beach's best defender, Glen McDonald, when he mused, "Raymond, Raymond, Raymond. We get tired of coach always talking about how good Raymond is."

The first confrontation was in Long Beach. McDonald was assigned the monstrous task of guarding Raymond one-on-one, and he rose to the occasion. Raymond missed his first 13 shots; McDonald blocked three of them.

Fans taunted Raymond every time he touched the ball yelling, "Shoot Raymond, shoot!" When he finally made a basket, he made such a great move that McDonald pulled a muscle in his leg and had to leave the game.

Raymond finished shooting 8 of 34. Ratleff was phenomenal, finishing with 28 points, 15 rebounds and six assists as the 49ers won by 21 points.

A couple weeks later, 3rd ranked Long Beach State visited Cal State L.A. for a rematch. Five thousand fans witnessed one of the greatest individual performances of all time. Hundreds of 49er fans traveled to the game holding signs, "Raymond Who? We Got Eddie" and "8 for 34."

The 49ers raced to an early 30-15 lead and appeared to be on their way to an easy victory, but Raymond responded by putting on a show for the ages. He just couldn't be stopped.

He finished with 53 points, a conference record. Incredibly, as many as ten of Raymond's shots would have been behind the three-point line, had the rule been in effect. And he did this against a Long Beach State team with four future NBA players. Cal State L.A. prevailed in double overtime, 107-104.

"If anyone had a hotter hand than CSLA's Ray Lewis, against Long Beach the other night, they better put it in ice and send it special delivery to the Hall of Fame," Jim McCormick of the *Press-Telegram* wrote.

Long Beach closed the regular season with the biggest home game in school history, against the Marquette Warriors. Both teams entered the game ranked #4 and #5 in the two wire polls. The game was played in front of a sell-out crowd of 12,987 at the Long Beach Convention Center, which was the first sell-out at this, their overflow venue.

Before the game, McGuire casually strolled to the concession stand for a hot dog and a beer. Once the game started, emotions reached a climax. Seven technical fouls were called, two on McGuire. Long

Beach scored 12 straight points late in the game to pull away 76-66. In a well-deserved, emotional tribute, Eddie Ratleff's number was retired at halftime.

"Clark Kent [Superman] is a fraud," Jerry boasted. "We've got the real Superman here! There is nothing he [Ratleff] can't do with a basketball."

Entering the NCAA tournament, it appeared the 49ers would face the Bruins a fourth consecutive time in the regional finals. In the semifinals, Long Beach State faced the San Francisco Dons, a team they had beaten by 20 points the previous year.

The day before, Ratleff jammed his shooting hand. Playing one of the worst games of his career, he finished 4 for 18 from the field as USF upset the 49ers.

Ratleff made no excuses after the game. "It wasn't the hand," he said. "The ball just wouldn't drop for us." There would be no rematch with the Bruins!

Just before the NCAA tournament, the University of Nevada, Las Vegas offered Jerry the head coaching position for a third time. After several disappointing seasons and an NCAA investigation, UNLV had dismissed its coach.

Although Ratleff was graduating, Long Beach State was now a bona fide powerhouse basketball school. Returning to the team were future professional players Leonard Gray, Glenn McDonald and Roscoe Pondexter, along with the team's great playmaker, Rick Aberegg. Incoming recruits were future NBA star Bobby Gross and the nation's top recruit, Clifton Pondexter.

The 49ers had a chance to be the best team in the country. And Jerry was excited about those prospects.

At practice before the USF game, Las Vegas booster Mike Toney came down onto the court to talk to Jerry. "You have to take the Vegas job," Toney said, adding "you won't want to leave until you go to heaven."

It was an indelible remark that would stay with Jerry the rest of his life. For the first time, he seriously considered the idea of leaving Long Beach.

Jerry faced a difficult decision and changed his mind daily, going back and forth, wrestling with the idea of heading to Vegas. There were pluses and minuses on both sides of the ledger. The night before the deadline, he still had not decided.

Jerry awoke in the morning to a beautiful Southern California day and thought of how happy he and our family were at Long Beach. Once again, he decided to turn down the UNLV offer. The decision made in his mind, he sat down contentedly for breakfast and to read the morning newspaper.

One story jumped out at him. Long Beach State's president, Stephen Horn, was quoted as saying that if Coach Tarkanian was going to remain the 49er's coach, he could hold the press conference (to announce his decision) on Long Beach's campus. But if he were going to accept UNLV's offer, he would have to do it somewhere else.

Horn's comment deeply upset Jerry. He felt that, having done so much to advance the university, the ultimatum issued by Horn was a slap in the face and evidenced a lack of appreciation for all his hard work. At that very moment, he decided to accept the UNLV job.

News of Jerry's departure hit many hard at Long Beach State, particularly his players. Roscoe Pondexter drove the Tarkanians to the airport and begged to go to Vegas with them, expressing a sentiment felt by several other players.

Jerry loved Roscoe and many of the others, but he didn't feel it was fair to the people at Long Beach to leave and take players with him. Despite his personal connection to them all, he refused to take any of his 49ers to UNLV.

Thus, in 1973, a 43-year-old Jerry Tarkanian, the bright young coach with a scintillating winning percentage of .859, the best in college basketball history, decided to leave Long Beach State and head for the Nevada desert.

Coaching college basketball was changing seriously for Jerry because, as he made his move to Las Vegas, the NCAA was moving in on him at Long Beach State.

CHAPTER 15:

THE NATIONAL COLLEGIATE ATHLETIC ASSOCIATION (NCAA)

"Recently, the NCAA got so mad at Kentucky, they put Cleveland State on probation for another two years."

—Jerry Tarkanian

THE NCAA TODAY operates as a self-serving, lucrative bureaucracy with a vindictive, all-powerful enforcement arm. Yet, the university athletic regulatory body's history tells us that, at one time, it was chiefly concerned with player welfare and safety.

More than a century ago, the intense nature of college football—characterized by gang tackling and the infamous flying wedge—led to many serious injuries and even deaths. Eighteen boys were killed during the 1905 season and another 149 were seriously injured.

A hoard of people demanded that football be abolished from intercollegiate athletics unless serious reforms were implemented. To deal with this problem, President Theodore Roosevelt invited college athletic leaders to two White House conferences, hoping to brainstorm a solution.

In 1906, the Intercollegiate Athletic Association of the United States was formed. Four years later, the organization changed its name to the National Collegiate Athletic Association (NCAA). A bronze statue of the flying wedge, an ephemeral reminder of a once-violent facet of the popular American collegiate sport, is featured in the NCAA Hall of Champions in Indianapolis, a tribute to the association's founding.

In 1951, the NCAA hired its first full-time salaried executive director, a 29-year-old, part-time employee named Walter Byers. Byers ruled the NCAA with an autocratic, and often vindictive, grip for more than 36 years. He laughed when he was told by University of Oklahoma President Bill Banowsky that he reminded him of J. Edger Hoover.

"His favorite book .... was *The Godfather*... He read it several times," Byers' second wife Betty stated in Don Yeager's book, *Undue Process*. "I think we had to buy a new copy because he enjoyed it so much...Reading *The Godfather*, I think that had something to do with power. He felt that *he* had that much power."

"Byers clearly wanted to be the Godfather of college sports," Yeager wrote. "In his zeal to make the NCAA the dominant force in amateur athletics, Byers worked ruthlessly to eliminate, or at least weaken, his competition... the Amateur Athletic Union, the United States Olympic Committee, the Association for Intercollegiate Athletics for Women... Generally, he won, and it rarely was pretty."

Under the grim and secretive leadership of Byers, the NCAA became one of the most powerful, and feared, organizations in the country. "Walter built the power of the NCAA on enforcement," former PAC 10 Commissioner Wiles Hallock stated, "...Before the NCAA was involved in an enforcement program, it didn't have any power."

"To complete his mission, Byers surrounded himself with an incredibly loyal staff," Yeager said on the topic, "so loyal some wondered if they were clones of the master. In return, Byers defended his staff unconditionally."

Byers claimed that when he took office, the NCAA had a dual mission: keep intercollegiate sports clean and, simultaneously, generate millions of dollars of income for the member colleges.

"We proved barely adequate in the first instance," Byers wrote in his memoir, *More than a Game*, "but enormously successful in our second mission."

Admittedly, Byers' *real* mission was to generate as much money as possible, not only for member colleges, but also for the use of the NCAA and its top brass, including himself.

The association earned nearly $1.1 billion in 2017 and, thanks to its status as an educational, nonprofit organization, it pays no state or federal taxes on its income. It gets to keep every penny it receives.

In the past 25 years, its total revenues have increased more than 8,000 percent. Its $10.8 billion television contract for basketball is bigger than any single professional sports league deal with any network. So substantial is their contract, that it is nearly *twice* what the Department of Defense pays colleges for research.

The NCAA has its own private jet, its own real estate subsidiary and its own marketing division. *Money* is the reason top NCAA officials enjoy benefits that stretch the limits of tax laws, and ethical rules.

The association spends more than $50 million per year on salaries and expenses for approximately 400 full-time employees. In 2009, during the height of the Great Recession, it spent nearly $6 million to compensate 14 of its highest-ranking executives.

Top NCAA employees travel first class in the organization's private jet and stay at the most luxurious hotels in each city. Out of tax-exempt proceeds generated by the hard work of student-athletes, certain select NCAA staff members have received unheard of six-figure *interest-free* loans.

In November 1985, the *Washington Post* reported that "in the seven previous years, the NCAA arranged more than $600,000 in no-interest mortgage loans for its staff, the largest being the $118,000 provided to Byers."

In an even more questionable ethical arrangement, *The Post* reported that Byers received $455,000 in low-interest loans from the only bank authorized to receive unlimited deposits from the NCAA. Banking officials throughout Missouri point out that the low interest loans represented "preferential treatment."

A few years ago, Harvard economists named the NCAA America's best monopoly. It is a monopoly that provides generously for its owners while overlooking the needs, and often the interests, of the people it was chartered to protect – the student-athletes.

Under NCAA rules, member institutions are permitted to provide student-athletes a full-ride scholarship which includes the cost of a dorm room, food and books.

At one time, "books" included all course-related supplies. Now NCAA regulations limit books to the actual course assigned textbooks and exclude note pads, study guides and even pens, pencils and markers. The student-athlete is expected to pay for all other course-related supplies.

At one time, NCAA rules also allowed student-athletes to receive a stipend for laundry. The association has since eliminated the laundry allowance, while at the same time shamefully increasing monetary benefits for its own officials.

When the NCAA first published its rules on recruitment, athletes at these institutions were mostly white, upper-middle class kids from affluent families. These were families that were able to financially assist their children while in school. While the rules may have worked for them, they don't work for the student-athletes who dominate major college sports today.

During the past 50 years, the majority of revenue generated for the NCAA comes from student-athletes in basketball and football, which consists primarily of poor, black, inner-city kids with little or no financial support from their homes.

The NCAA generates more than a *billion dollars* each year in revenue from these student-athletes, which it spends lavishly on its top brass. At the same time, many of these student-athletes live at or near poverty level, far below fellow classmates.

Instead of allowing the "revenue-producers" to live a normal college life, the NCAA has made rules that strip them of their dignity. Rules that create an atmosphere that *necessitates* rule breaking.

Financially needy students can apply for and receive Federal Pell Grants. Even then, the NCAA does not allow scholarship athletes to keep all of the money.

Originally, the NCAA required student-athletes to offset all of the Pell Grant money from their scholarship money. As an example, if the student-athlete received $2,000 in scholarship money but received a $1,500 Pell Grant, the scholarship money was *reduced* to $500.

Over the years, the NCAA has allowed student-athletes to keep at least part of their Pell Grant money. In 1982, the NCAA allowed student-athletes to keep $900, or half of the $1,800 Pell Grant. By the 1990s, it was allowing student-athletes to keep $1,700 of the $2,300 provided by the Pell.

Neither the NCAA nor its member institutions have provided justification for why it takes federal money from needy student-athletes. "The Pell Grant was designed to help the individual person in need," stated Bob Timmons, who retired with four NCAA championships in track and field. "It is not to finance athletic departments."

And it's not just Pell Grants. The array of NCAA rules prohibits student-athletes from supplementing their scholarship check in any way possible. For instance, they are prohibited from working during the school year or from keeping any money generated from their name or likeness.

At the same time, member institutions and the NCAA use the student-athlete's name and likeness for their own commercial purposes. And they keep all the money.

In addition to meeting their own needs, many student-athletes must care for their parents and/or siblings. At Fresno State, one of Jerry's players, Noel Felix, was always short on funds. He couldn't pay his rent and often had no money for food.

Danny Tarkanian, an assistant coach at the time, asked Noel what he did with his Pell Grant and scholarship money. He told Danny that he had to send it back home or his mother would be evicted from her house and his brother would have nothing to eat. This is not unusual for many student-athletes.

In an article written by David Zirin titled "Stop the Insanity of March Madness: Pay the Damn Players," Zirin boldly asserted that the NCAA propagates the "biggest labor swindle since Reconstruction."

The gulf between the practical needs of student-athletes and the arcane and Draconian rules imposed by the NCAA has led to a system that forces athletes and coaches to make impossible choices. Many student-athletes are forced to live in poverty and well below the standard of living enjoyed by their fellow students, or NCAA rules must be broken.

The following is an illustration of what many student-athletes face when they are offered a scholarship to a university, far away from home.

The student-athlete needs transportation to the university. Often this constitutes hundreds of miles of travel from their home. The student-athlete's family cannot afford an airline ticket, or even a bus ticket. What often happens is the coaching staff finds someone close to the family to pay for the ticket, then they reimburse that person. Of course, this is a clear NCAA violation.

To hide the violation, all parties claim that no one connected with the university had anything to do with the ticket. Most of the time the NCAA accepts these statements and concludes that there was no violation. It does, however, have discretion in these matters and the enforcement staff uses this discretion to *target* certain schools and coaches.

In Jerry's final year at Fresno State, he signed a junior college kid from New York City named Chris Sandy. Just days after his best game as a Fresno Bulldog, in an upset win over nationally ranked Oklahoma State, the NCAA declared Sandy ineligible for the rest of the regular season because his godfather's best friend, who was from New York and had no ties to Fresno State, had paid for his airline ticket to Fresno.

The NCAA *used its discretion* to conclude that Sandy was provided the ticket because of his athletic ability. No evidence was ever provided, nor apparently required, to reach that decision.

For many years, NCAA rules prevented athletic department personnel from meeting the student-athletes at the airport or bus terminal to provide them a ride to their housing. Student-athletes were supposed to procure their own ride, despite the fact that, on most occasions, the only people in town that were known to them were from the athletic department.

As a result, one of the coaches would arrange for a current player to pick up the new player. It is a violation if the coach *arranges* the pick-up, but acceptable if an individual other than the coach made the arrangements. So typically, if questioned, all parties claimed that no coaches were involved.

If a student-athlete rents an apartment instead of staying in the dormitories, he or she is usually required to pay a deposit and first month's rent. Student-athletes don't receive their first scholarship checks until after school starts and many of their parents can't pay their *own* rent, let alone rent for their child at college. But someone must pay for it.

In addition to housing costs, utility companies often require deposits for first-time users. Most student-athletes are first-time users who don't have money for the deposit. Someone must pay it or the student-athlete does not have electricity, heat and water, which are basic life necessities.

Once school begins, the situation improves, but only marginally. While student-athletes receive their first scholarship check, they still cannot live like their fellow classmates. They do not have money to pay for course-related materials, wash their clothes, buy new clothes, go to the movies, go out to dinner, go on a date or attend many other social functions.

These student-athletes—who earn more than a *billion* dollars a year for the NCAA so its brass can stay at five-star hotels, fly in their private plane, and enjoy substantial salaries and benefits—are forced to live in poverty conditions.

As a result of this glaring inequity between students' economic classes, NCAA rules are broken by every major college athletic program in the country by student-athletes in need. The number of violations and their severity often depend upon the number of student-athletes from economically deprived families and the degree of economic deprivation.

Every coach, player and most administrators and media personnel with insight into college athletics are aware of what is happening.

In an article on the problem of big business in college athletics, former LSU Basketball Coach Dale Brown quoted Duke Coach Mike Krzyzewski: "No college program, including my own, could withstand a thorough NCAA investigation without taking some kind of a fall."

In the late 1970s, legendary Penn State Football Coach Joe Paterno stated, "There are forty some cases of illegal recruitment in the Ivy League, that I know about right now."[2]

"The crime in the NCAA is not in breaking the rules," respected American University Coach Ed Tapscott declared, "it's in getting caught."

Tapscott noted that coaches have a veil of silence. "We have our own MAD – Mutually Assured Destruction. There's a threshold of dirty linen we can all build up, and know that all of us agree tacitly, not to disclose it. Because, none of us could succeed without breaking the rules."

"I've never met a coach, with a modicum of intellect, who had any real regard for the NCAA and its laws," award winning Kansas City Star columnist, Jason Whitlock, wrote. "You do what you think is fair, and what you think <u>won't</u> get you caught."

Whitlock noted that he covered college basketball his entire life, and has spent time on nearly every big-time college basketball campus in the country, and he has seen the exact same thing at every stop. "Coaches are stretchers of NCAA rules they don't believe in."

Columnist Adrian Wojnarowski wrote, "The nature of the job calls for cover-ups." He quoted one Division-I coach who said, "I wonder how guys in our business can sleep at night, with the fear that it all could come crashing down any minute on them." Wojnarowski noted that, "it isn't so much an issue of cheating, in college basketball—just *degrees* of cheating."

Wojnarowski is correct, on both counts! Breaking NCAA rules is the norm. The difference is in the *degrees of cheating.*

Most programs provide only minimal extra benefits to student-athletes so that they have an opportunity to attend school and live comparably to other college students. There are also a number of programs that actually buy players.

---

[2] In 2014, the National Labor Relations Board ruled that Northwestern student-athletes could organize as a union. In response to the ruling, the NCAA agreed to allow member institutions the discretion to raise the amount of scholarship money provided to its student-athletes, to cover the full cost of attending college.

While the NCAA claims that number is 10-20%, a 1989 survey by Allen L. Stack, a sociology professor at the University of New Haven, put the number at 30-50%.

For decades, certain coaches, boosters and other representatives of athletic programs paid top-tier student-athletes and/or their families large sums of money, cars and other luxury items to entice the student-athlete to participate in their program.

During the past three decades, it has changed. Now, for the most talented student-athletes, AAU coaches, street-agents, shoe companies and the like provide these "extra benefits" to star players and their families in the hopes of cashing in when the player turns pro.

Instead of actively participating as they did in the past, coaches now cultivate relationships with these groups who deliver the players to the coaches' respective programs and the coaches feign ignorance. Whether the money is coming from college boosters or street agents, it is still *buying athletes* for their ability.

When Walter Byers took over leadership of the NCAA, he said his dual mission was "keeping intercollegiate sports clean, while generating millions of dollars each year as income for the colleges." Yet, in the infancy of big-time college athletics, there was an inherent conflict between the two missions.

It may be hard to imagine today but, in the early stages, the NCAA basketball tournament was not especially popular. It had to scratch and claw just to get a television contract and the arenas were sparsely filled.

The association relied upon big-name programs with big boosters to generate interest and excitement, and thus, *money*. Turns out, it was often the big-name programs that proved to be the worst <u>cheaters</u>.

If the NCAA actually cleaned up intercollegiate sports, it would not be able to generate the money Byers desired. So, it typically looked the other way on violations committed by perennial cash cows.

Cash cows such as the UCLA Bruins.

CHAPTER 16:

THE NCAA AND THE UCLA DYNASTY

"If the UCLA basketball teams of the late 1960's and early 1970's were subjected to the kind of scrutiny Jerry Tarkanian and his players have been, UCLA would probably have to forfeit about eight NCAA Championships, and be on probation for the next one hundred years."

—Jack Scott, author of *Bill Walton,*

On the Road with the Portland Trailblazers

THE MOST SUCCESSFUL basketball program in the history of the NCAA is the UCLA Bruins, who have won more national championships than any other school. In 1948, John Wooden took over the UCLA program and coached the Bruins for 27 seasons.

Under Wooden's tutelage, UCLA created a dynasty that will never again be matched in college sports. In 1964, his 16th year at UCLA, Wooden won his first national championship. He went on to win 10 of 12, including seven in a row (1966-1973). During this span, the Bruins had four undefeated seasons and, at one point, won 88 consecutive games.

Throughout Wooden's coaching career, it was never publicly mentioned that the Bruins program violated any NCAA rules. In fact, Wooden and the Bruins were viewed as the *model program* of the NCAA, the one others should emulate.

From the early 1960s through the 1970s, during the span of UCLA's championship run, coaches and other insiders privately discussed the widespread cheating which was occurring at UCLA. It was common knowledge.

It wasn't until 1978, three years after Wooden retired, that anyone disclosed it. The true picture of UCLA's dynasty was first revealed by an unabashed admirer of Coach Wooden and UCLA loyalist, former Bruins great, Bill Walton.

In the book titled *"Bill Walton on the road with the Portland Trailblazers"* by Jack Scott, it was disclosed that Sam Gilbert and several other wealthy alumni of UCLA, provided star basketball players at UCLA with whatever "help" they might need. The book summarized that "UCLA players were so well taken care of—far beyond the rules of the NCAA—that even players from poor backgrounds never left UCLA prematurely to turn pro during John Wooden's championship years."

"If the UCLA basketball teams of the late 1960's and early 1970's were subjected to the kind of scrutiny Jerry Tarkanian and his players have been, UCLA would probably have to forfeit about eight NCAA Championships, and be on probation for the next one hundred years," Scott adds.

Scott also reports that Walton stated: "It's hard for me to have a proper perspective on financial matters, since I've always had whatever I wanted, since I enrolled at UCLA... I hate to say anything that may hurt UCLA, but I can't be quiet when I see what the NCAA is doing to Jerry Tarkanian, only because he has a reputation for giving a second chance to many black athletes other coaches have branded as troublemakers. The NCAA is working day and night trying to get Jerry, but no one from the NCAA ever questioned me during my four years at UCLA."

UCLA booster Sam Gilbert was even quoted in the book in saying, "Tarkanian's violations were nickel-and-dime stuff compared to what goes on at UCLA and USC."

Gilbert could be a scary man. He saw Lois at a NCAA playoff game shortly after she was quoted in *Sports Illustrated* discussing the expensive clothing UCLA team members were wearing. Gilbert told Lois she should keep her mouth shut. Then he told her in a truly frightening manner that Jack Scott might be found at the bottom of a lake someday. Lois was shocked at his bluntness.

Jack Scott made it clear in a 1978 *L.A. Times* article that he and Walton's intent was not to hurt UCLA, but "to point to the hypocrisy of the double standards that exist." Scott explained, "We spent three weeks, I think, writing that part of the book. We tried to write it with enough discretion so that it hopefully wouldn't hurt UCLA but would bring about much needed changes."

Scott had a copy of a letter that was sent by a UCLA basketball star, presumably Bill Walton, to Gilbert stating that the athlete was paying back more than $4,500 Gilbert had paid to him while he played basketball for UCLA.

"Are you going to use that letter?" Gilbert asked, when confronted with it. "UCLA would have to return four NCAA championships. What I did is a total violation of NCAA rules."

When Gilbert denied the allegation to the *L.A. Times*, Scott played for the publication's staff members a tape recording corroborating the above conversation.

UCLA's response to the well-documented infractions was predictable. Its powerful athletic director, J.D. Morgan, called Gilbert "a humanitarian."

"I'm sincere in my feelings that no illegal payments were made," Coach Wooden responded. "When you are successful, the NCAA likes to investigate you, and they investigated us while I was at UCLA...And I know that Sam was investigated by the NCAA and nothing came of it."

The NCAA's response was predictable as well. Nothing was done and the story died after the book was published. UCLA's dynasty under Wooden maintained its false image of honesty and integrity.

In 1980, the *L.A. Times* published an article detailing four sporty automobiles that were purchased for four star recruits of the Bruins. The article disclosed that Rod Foster, Cliff Pruitt, Michael Holton and Darren Daye—all high school All-Americans who helped lead UCLA to the championship game as freshmen—had each acquired a new sports car within a short time of each other.

All of the cars were purchased outright, with no financing. They were bought from two separate dealers, both of whom were boosters of the Bruins.

UCLA Athletic Director Robert Fischer investigated the matter and determined no violations had been committed. His investigation concluded that each of the parents turned in an old automobile and bought a newer one.

Both the car dealers and two of the parents contradicted this conclusion. Cliff Pruitt, Sr. told the *L.A. Times* he still owned his former car and Holton's father didn't own his own car; he was leasing one.

The story revealed additional contradictions between the car dealers, players and parents concerning who *actually* paid for the cars. It certainly was *not* the players or their parents.

As a result of the negative publicity and the contradictions from the *L.A. Times* article, the NCAA was *forced* to investigate UCLA's basketball program. A little over a year later, it concluded that nine violations had occurred, most of them minor. One of the boosters named in the three most serious violations was Sam Gilbert.

Once again, UCLA rallied its support for Gilbert. "Mr. Gilbert and his wife have served as surrogate parents, counselors and advisers [to the UCLA players]," stated UCLA Chancellor Charles Young. "They have also been helpful to them in achieving academically. In my opinion, the actions of Mr. Gilbert have grown out of those concerns."

UCLA coach and former player Larry Farmer added, "For over a decade, I've seen him [Gilbert] do so many good things for student-athletes. I believe to single him out is unfair."

UCLA and the NCAA hoped the conclusion of the investigation and the finding of nine violations would end all discussions concerning Gilbert and the UCLA basketball program. "If there could have been a more intensive investigation by the NCAA or us, I'd like to know about it," Chancellor Young challenged.

Much to the Chancellor's chagrin, on January 31, 1982, the *L.A. Times* responded. In an article titled "NCAA Missed the Iceberg in Westwood," two *Times* reporters, Mike Littwin and Alan Greenberg, exposed the true underbelly of the UCLA program.

Together, Littwin and Greenberg interviewed more than 45 people connected with UCLA basketball, many of them former Bruins players and coaches who allowed their names to be made public. During these interviews, the former players and coaches disclosed a continual and flagrant pattern of serious NCAA rule violations committed by UCLA boosters, starting as early as the school's first championship season.

NCAA investigators often claim that they are severely handicapped in gathering information because they lack subpoena power. The *L.A. Times* staff managed, in just a short time with a limited story budget and no subpoena power, to document more than 15 years of serious NCAA violations by the its *marquee program*, the UCLA Bruins.

The article described how UCLA players and their families were lavished with gifts, money, clothes and cars. It even detailed how boosters paid for abortions for some of the athletes' girlfriends.

Jack Hirsch, the starting forward on UCLA's 1964 National Championship Team, admitted UCLA alumni paid players $5 for each rebound, up to ten per game, and $10 for each rebound beyond that. "It was a helluva great feeling to pick up $100 for a night's work..." Hirsch told the *L.A. Times*. "Believe me; we really went all out for the rebounds."

Keith Erickson, a teammate of Hirsh's, confirmed the story. Despite having the shortest average-height players in what was then the Athletic Association of Western Universities, UCLA led the league in rebounding. Cash incentives will do that.

The cheating intensified in subsequent years, when UCLA alumnus Sam Gilbert became more involved. For more than 15 years, Gilbert, a multimillionaire who is rumored to have made his fortune in racketeering and money laundering for the mob, befriended UCLA players and, according to the school's chancellor, served as a surrogate father, counselor and adviser to these players.

Gilbert had limited involvement in the UCLA program until 1967, when Lew Alcindor and Lucius Allen, the linchpins of the program, felt alienated and considered transferring. In a desperate effort to stop this from happening, an athletic department administrator enlisted Gilbert's help. Gilbert persuaded both to stay at UCLA.

Years later, Allen admitted that if it wasn't for Gilbert, he would have left. "There were two people I listened to," Allen stated, "Coach Wooden, as long as we were between the lines, and outside the court, Sam Gilbert."

Gilbert's involvement in the UCLA program led to some of the most blatant cheating that ever occurred in college sports. The *L.A. Times* reported that "players who led UCLA to seven of its NCAA-record 10 national championships, said Gilbert helped them obtain cars, stereos, clothes, airline tickets and scalpers' prices for their basketball season tickets. Thanks to his largesse, Gilbert became known as 'Papa Sam' to many of the Bruin players."

Lucius Allen also told the *L.A. Times* that when he or other players got a girl pregnant, they went to see Gilbert and he would arrange and pay for the abortion. Allen boasted that players often got women pregnant at UCLA in those days.

Gilbert even arranged for one of UCLA's greatest players, Lew Alcindor (Kareem Abdul-Jabbar), to live in his Encino guesthouse at little or no cost. A few years later, another Bruins great, Larry Farmer, also lived there. Farmer later became UCLA's head basketball coach.

Gilbert's comfortable Pacific Palisades residence was a second home to many of the Bruins players. Hardly a weekend or holiday passed that some of them didn't flock there. The house contained a wall that would pass as a Bruins Hall of Fame, replete with autographed pictures of nine Bruins All-Americans, including Bill Walton, Jamaal Wilkes, Sidney Wicks, Curtis Rowe, Lucius Allen, Henry Bibby, David Greenwood, Richard Washington and numerous lesser stars.

"The older guys would bring the younger guys by Gilbert's home," Marques Johnson explained. "That's how you got indoctrinated."

"Interviews with UCLA players, coaches, and administrators led to one inescapable conclusion—that Gilbert has been the enduring presence during UCLA's extraordinary success," the *L.A. Times* article summarized.

"UCLA wouldn't have won *any* championships without athletes," Lucius Allen concluded. "And without Sam Gilbert, they wouldn't have had the athletes."

"The Bruins eviscerated the rule book like no program before or after," reporter Dan Wetzel wrote. "But [UCLA] went largely unpunished by an NCAA that wanted no part of taking down its marquee team. During the 1960's and '70's, the organization [NCAA], run by old white men, was too busy going after small, upstart programs that dared to play too many African-Americans, launching inquiries into Texas Western/UTEP, Western Kentucky, Centenary and Long Beach State."

After the blockbuster *L.A. Times* story was published, Wooden claimed he had a distant but cordial relationship with Gilbert. He contended he was never concerned about Gilbert and had no reason to believe he was breaking any rules. "Maybe I had tunnel vision," Wooden acknowledged. "I still don't think he's had any great impact on the basketball program."

Former UCLA great Greg Lee stated, "On the one hand he [Wooden] was glad about his [Gilbert's] presence, but whatever was happening was going to be out of sight, out of mind."

"I think he [Wooden] knew that things were going on, and he just didn't *want* to know," Keith Erickson said. "It was like the rebound money."

David Greenwood, a star player for the Bruins, stated, "Everybody knew what was going on. Nobody was so naïve. It was common knowledge in the whole town."

Athletic Director J. D. Morgan was an outspoken supporter of Gilbert but, in 1978, he told the *L.A. Times*, "I can't sit here and tell you, Sam Gilbert has never done anything wrong, any more than I can tell you that I've never broken a traffic law."

"I knew he [Gilbert] and J.D. Morgan had kind of an arm's length truce," UCLA's Chancellor Young conceded. "I don't think J.D. wanted to stir up the pot too much."

Gene Bartow replaced Wooden as UCLA's coach in 1975. David Greenwood told the *L.A. Times* that there was always a power struggle between Bartow and Gilbert. The story goes that soon after Bartow arrived at UCLA, he had breakfast with Gilbert, who explained his considerable role in UCLA basketball affairs. Bartow quit two years later.

Gary Cunningham replaced Bartow as UCLA's coach in 1977. Cunningham had a close relationship with Gilbert, dating back to his days as an assistant under Wooden. Once Cunningham was named head coach, Gilbert became more involved in the Bruins program, even helping in the recruitment of players. Until Cunningham's reign, there is no evidence Gilbert was actively involved in this activity.

Cunningham's assistant, Larry Farmer, told the *L.A. Times* that Gilbert became involved in recruiting "because we were struggling so much. They [Gilbert and Cunningham] cared about each other a great deal."

During this time period, several Bruins recruits who signed with other schools told NCAA investigators that Gilbert offered them cars. Greg Goorjian who attended Arizona State, Michael Johnson who attended UNLV and Darryl Mitchell who attended Minnesota all admitted that Gilbert offered them cars as an inducement to attend UCLA.

So, why wasn't the cheating that was occurring at UCLA made public? Why wasn't there an official NCAA investigation? There were many reasons.

J.D. Morgan was the most powerful athletic director in the NCAA. He was a close personal friend of the executive director of the NCAA, Walter Byers.

Further, John Wooden was, without question, a man of integrity. No one in the NCAA wanted to question his ethics or hurt his reputation. UCLA is also one of the top academic institutions in the country and held in high esteem.

Lastly, but most importantly, UCLA was the NCAA's biggest draw! They were *the* money maker for the association.

Former NCAA investigator Brent Clark provided insight into how the NCAA operated when he testified under oath before Congress in 1978. Clark testified that, as an NCAA field investigator, he recommended a full-scale investigation of UCLA after he interviewed Gilbert and that "Gilbert was well known by the NCAA for years and years." Clark further testified that Bill Hunt, his superior in the enforcement department, pulled him aside and told him, "We're just not going after the institution [UCLA], right now."

"If I had spent a month in Los Angeles, I could have put them [UCLA] on indefinite suspension," Clark told the *L.A. Times*. "But as long as Wooden was there, the NCAA would never take any action."

Clark asserted that this was an example of a school that was too big, too powerful and too well respected by the public, and that the *timing* was not right to proceed against them. Clark believed that the decision was made "not to pursue the individual since it would involve one of the NCAA's leading moneymakers, a major basketball power."

Two days after the scathing *L.A. Times* article, David Berst, head of the NCAA's enforcement division, declared, "As of now the NCAA has no intention of reopening its investigation of UCLA." He cited the enforcement code's four-year statute of limitations, unless there is information "to indicate a pattern of willful violations on the part of the institution or individual involved."

The *L.A. Times* interviewed dozens of former Bruins players and coaches who stated their names for the record and verified *habitual violations* spanning 15 years. The report included gifts of cars, stereos, clothes, airline tickets, scalpers' prices for basketball season tickets and even abortions for player's girlfriends.

Despite all of this, the NCAA was unable to find a "pattern of willful violations."

CHAPTER 17:

THE NCAA AND THE REST OF THE "MONEY MAKERS"

"They were paying players cash, $12,000, 15,000 to sign. 25 to 30 boosters would meet in Birmingham, and 15 to 20 would meet in Georgia. They would give $5,000 each."

—Terry Bowden, Auburn Football Coach

THE UNIVERSITY OF Kentucky basketball program has won more games than any other program in college basketball history. They have the best all-time winning percentage, the most NCAA tournament wins and the second most national championships with eight.

Adolph Rupp started Kentucky's basketball dynasty in 1930. He coached the Wildcats for 42 years, until 1972, and retired with the most wins in college basketball history. His Wildcat teams won four NCAA championships, went to six Final Fours and won 27 Southeastern Conference titles. However, Rupp's program was embroiled in one of the worst scandals in college basketball history, which included point shaving, paying of players and knowingly playing ineligible players.

Three members of Rupp's 1951 team admitted to taking a bribe to fix an NIT (National Invitation Tournament) game and they pled guilty to point shaving. During the point shaving investigation, it was disclosed that several players were receiving cash payments from Rupp and other boosters of Kentucky.

The judge concluded that Kentucky covertly subsidized its players, illegally recruited athletes, tolerated cribbing in examinations and admitted star athletes into the university when they were not qualified for admittance.

Rupp retired in 1972, but the proud basketball program at the University of Kentucky continued to be exposed for its widespread recruiting violations. In 1976, the NCAA cited its basketball and football programs for 50 violations, which included offering high school prospects cash, clothing, free transportation, use of automobiles, lodging, theater tickets and, in one instance, a race horse.

In 1985, the *Lexington Herald-Leader* published a series of articles in which 26 former basketball players *admitted* that they had accepted "$100 handshakes," other cash payments, clothing and extravagant gifts during their school years at Kentucky.

The NCAA investigated the allegations and concluded that *no violations occurred.*

Five weeks after the investigation ended, the Kentucky basketball program was rocked when an overnight package sent from the basketball office to the father of high school sensation, Chris Mills, popped open and approximately $1,000 was discovered inside.

Even the NCAA couldn't ignore another newspaper story with such obvious implications. After a short investigation, the organization determined an assistant coach at Kentucky sent the money to Mill's father and Kentucky was placed on probation.

At a coaching clinic, Darryl Dawkins, one of the first high school players to skip college and go directly into the pros, recounted his recruiting trip to Kentucky.

While at dinner, Kentucky's head coach, Joe B. Hall, excused himself to go to the restroom. While Hall was gone, the assistant coach handed Dawkins an envelope filled with cash. He told Dawkins not to mention this to Hall because he would get in trouble.

When Dawkins returned home, he showed his mother the envelope. Dawkins' mother responded, "Darryl, you should take more recruiting trips." Jerry learned, in time, that it was pointless to recruit against Kentucky.

In 1979, UNLV recruited Sam Bowie, a high school All-American from Lebanon, Pennsylvania. On three or four occasions, Jerry flew to Lebanon to watch Bowie play. When he arrived, he checked into the only hotel in town, the Roadway Inn. Each time he did, he learned that Kentucky's assistant coach was *also* registered there.

Years later, Jerry asked the assistant about this. The assistant admitted that the assistant coach wasn't there most of the time, but that Kentucky kept the room year-round for Bowie to use as he wanted. There are similar stories involving major college programs across the country.

Wilt Chamberlain is one of the greatest basketball players of all time. In 1955, he joined the University of Kansas basketball team. By May of 1956, Chamberlain was driving a 1953 Oldsmobile which came from a dealership owned by a major booster of Kansas. By 1957, he had a 1956 Oldsmobile convertible obtained from *another* booster.

In the late 1970s, Eric Dickerson was one of the most sought-after high school football players in the country. After signing with Southern Methodist University (SMU), he was seen driving around campus in a new, $15,000 Trans-Am. At the time, he claimed his grandmother from Houston bought it. After graduating, he admitted it was purchased by a Texas A&M booster who was recruiting him for the Aggies.

In 1986, David Stanley, a key football player for SMU, admitted that he was paid $25,000 to sign with the Mustangs. He also received continuing cash payments of $750 per month. Stanley asserted other players were receiving payments as well.

A further investigation of the program confirmed widespread cash payments to numerous SMU football players and that involvement in the scandal went as high up as the State of Texas's governor's office.

In 1991, five of the top high school basketball players in the country signed with the University of Michigan. They were dubbed the "Fab Five" and led Michigan to two straight NCAA championship games in their two seasons together.

During a federal gambling and money laundering probe, it was discovered that Ed Martin, a prominent Michigan booster, provided four of the players with hundreds of thousands of dollars from as early as their freshman year of high school throughout their playing tenure at Michigan.

According to the indictment, Chris Webber received $280,000, Robert "Tractor" Traylor received $160,000, Maurice Taylor received $105,000 and Louis Bullock received $71,000. Fellow Fab Five player Jalen Rose admitted he received money from Martin while attending Michigan, but in smaller amounts, what he deemed "pocket money."

Former Auburn football coach Terry Bowden disclosed that boosters were funneling tens of thousands of dollars to football players when he became head coach in 1993. "They were paying players' cash, $12,000, 15,000 to sign," Bowden stated. "25 to 30 boosters would meet in Birmingham, and 15 to 20 would meet in Georgia. They would give $5,000 each."

In 2002, a local newspaper reported that South Carolina's star football recruit, Derek Watson, who was named "Mr. Football" and "Mr. Basketball" for the State of South Carolina in his senior year of high school, was driving a $60,000 *Cadillac Escalade*. The car belonged to a Gamecock booster, but Watson was driving it regularly within months after signing to play. The vehicle was stolen while under Watson's care and Watson reported the theft to the police.

In 2006, the University of Kansas was placed on probation because a booster provided cash, transportation, clothing and other benefits totaling more than $5,000 to two basketball players.

In 2010, both USC's football and basketball programs were put on probation. With respect to the football program, two wannabe sports agents provided approximately $300,000 in cash, clothing, housing and other benefits to Heisman Trophy winner Reggie Bush and his family. The Trojans' basketball coach allegedly provided $1,000 in cash to future NBA star O.J. Mayo.

Instances of large cash payments, free automobiles and the lavishing of other expensive gifts by major college programs are endless. Early on, the NCAA was reluctant to go after these traditional cash cow programs and only did so after a well-publicized newspaper story or court case disclosed the violations, making ignoring it an impossibility.

Instead, the association typically went after the smaller, more vulnerable upstart programs who challenged the old bulls. One such rising program that felt the full wrath of the NCAA's enforcement arm was Jerry's at Long Beach State. And it was the beginning of a long, bitter fight.

JT celebrating championship win at 1986-87 pre-season NIT

CHAPTER 18:

THE NCAA STARTS AFTER TARK

"I wonder whether [Tarkanian] considers California State University at Long Beach, in the 'big money maker' category. Keep smiling."

—Warren Brown, Director of Enforcement,

in a written threat about Coach Tarkanian

JERRY UNDERSTOOD the challenges he faced at Long Beach, both on the court and off, by taking on two prestigious and established institutions in the West: UCLA and USC. These institutions had all the resources necessary for successful athletic programs.

NCAA regulations allow student-athletes to work over the summer. These summer jobs are crucial for the financial support of most athletes. While UCLA and USC players received the best jobs with the highest pay, Long Beach State was happy when their players landed any job.

When questioned by the NCAA, New York City Player of the Year Ernie Douse told the investigator that his summer job while playing at Long Beach State was washing trucks for the City of Long Beach.

While Bruins and Trojans players stayed in nice apartments or the guesthouse of millionaire booster Sam Gilbert, most of the Long Beach players lived in modest campus dorms available to the regular student body, usually two men to a room.

Dave McLucas, who was 6'7", stated his "biggest problem was getting sleep" since none of the beds in the campus dorms was long enough to contain his elongated frame. For the few who lived off campus, they had trouble getting to and from school because they didn't have a car.

In another interview, an NCAA investigator asked Glen McDonald, the star forward for the 49ers and future NBA player, what kind of car he owned. McDonald said he didn't own a car and had to ride the public bus to his apartment every night after practice. McDonald was one of few, if any, future NBA players taking the bus home every night.

While 49er players watched their rivals parade around in expensive, stylish clothes, the Long Beach players wore letterman jackets, jeans and tennis shoes.

Despite limited department resources and the players' sparse existence, the NCAA investigated Long Beach State for rule violations. It did *not* investigate UCLA, USC or other big money-making schools. Or, if they did conduct any limited investigations, the resulting punishment was a mere slap on the wrist.

Jerry had tremendous success at Long Beach State because he was able to build a close personal relationship with the class of athletes who were beginning to dominate college basketball – poor, inner-city black kids. He bonded with these athletes and their families based upon trust, understanding and loyalty. To coach them and establish that kind of relationship, archaic NCAA rules had to be broken.

Jerry's programs admittedly broke NCAA rules, but none of the major violations that were occurring regularly at UCLA, USC, Kentucky and other top programs around the country.

Jerry coached major college basketball for 31 years. Half that time, or approximately 15 years, the NCAA conducted official investigations of his programs. Even when there wasn't an official investigation, court documents show that the association continued to scrutinize Jerry's program, looking for violations everywhere possible.

More money, more time, more effort and more questionable actions were undertaken by the NCAA in an attempt to find violations by Jerry's programs than any other school or coach in the history of the organization. Despite this, it never found one violation of offering money to a player or recruit (except one dubious claim of $65), providing a player or recruit a car or providing anything of substantial value to a player or recruit by Jerry, his coaches or boosters of his programs. Given the level of scrutiny, if these violations were occurring, the NCAA would have found at least one. They never did.

In March of 1971, starting four inner-city black players and a local junior college transfer, Long Beach State came within an eyelash of upsetting the powerful UCLA Bruins. Shockwaves spread throughout Westwood.

Within months after the Bruins close win, J. D. Morgan turned Long Beach State in for violating a minor, obscure NCAA rule and demanded an investigation into its basketball program. Morgan was the most powerful athletic director in the country and close personal friends with NCAA boss Walter Byers. When Morgan called, Byers was always quick to respond.

What transgression did Morgan claim Long Beach had made? Long Beach brought two players who were redshirting (sitting out the season) to the NCAA tournament and allowed them to practice with the team. Jerry didn't even know it was a violation. He allowed those ineligible players to participate in a practice which was open to the public and attended by NCAA brass.

For years, Morgan's involvement was unknown. Only after Jerry sued the NCAA and the court ordered the NCAA to turn over relevant documents did this fact come to light.

One of the documents disclosed was a February 10, 1972 letter from Warren Brown, the executive director of enforcement, to Morgan. Brown wrote:

> *Thank you for the information which you forwarded to Tom Hansen (Pac-8 Commissioner) concerning Leonard Gray (Long Beach State player who was ineligible). Please rest assured that the source of this information will remain personal and confidential, as you have requested.*

In March 1972, Jerry wrote the first of two newspaper articles critical of the NCAA enforcement staff's selective enforcement of rules. In this article, he detailed the obvious pattern of going after the small, upstart schools while ignoring the bigger, money-making schools. The article was titled "NCAA 'Witch Hunt' is Embarrassing" and here is an excerpt:

> *The University of Kentucky basketball program breaks more rules in a day than Western Kentucky does in a year... The NCAA just doesn't want to take on the big boys.*

Seven months later, the NCAA notified Long Beach State that they were conducting a preliminary investigation into its athletic program.

In January of 1973, Jerry wrote another article critical of the enforcement staff titled "Investigate the Big Guys, 'NCAA must go further.'" He wrote:

> *The NCAA investigates and then places on probation the New Mexico States, Western Kentuckys, Centenarys, and Florida States while the big money-makers go free. It is a crime that Western Kentucky is placed on probation, but the famous University of Kentucky isn't even investigated...*
>
> *...Southwestern Louisiana has one-tenth of the income and one-tenth of the support of LSU, but who does the NCAA persecute, USL...It seems totally unfair that the NCAA doesn't look at the schools that are making money for the NCAA through television appearances.*

In retrospect, you have to wonder why Jerry, a new coach with little power or influence, would write such a thing? Why take on the most powerful organization in sports?

While his actions were motivated by principle, Jerry has admitted that writing those articles was the biggest mistake of his life and that they fostered an antagonistic relationship with the NCAA which forced an early end to his career.

On January 26, 1973, in response to Jerry's second article, NCAA Enforcement Chief Warren Brown wrote the commissioner of the PCAA, Jesse Hill:

> *Enclosed for your leisure reading is a copy of a newspaper article which I presume was written by Jerry Tarkanian. It always amazes me when successful coaches become instant authorities. As in the case of this article, such instant authorities reflect an obvious unfamiliarity with the facts. Tarkanian is no exception in this regard.*
>
> *I wonder whether he considers California State University at Long Beach, in the 'big money maker' category.*
>
> *Keep smiling.*

The most chilling aspect of Brown's letter is the cavalier bluntness of his threat. Did he believe the NCAA was untouchable?

True to Brown's word, on April 5, 1973—approximately two months after his letter to Hill—the NCAA launched an official inquiry into Long Beach State's basketball program. The timing was obvious, as the following appeared in the *L.A. Times*:

> *The NCAA began its Long Beach investigation in 1971, (the same year Long Beach almost upset UCLA and Morgan turned the school in for violations). It intensified in 1972, when Tarkanian wrote the first article critical of NCAA, and continued it in 1973 after another.*

On December 17, 1973, Long Beach State's president, athletic director and other representatives appeared before the NCAA Committee on Infractions to present the school's response to the allegations. Jerry, who was coaching UNLV at the time, was not invited.

The next day, the lead investigator and chief prosecutor of the case, David Berst, wrote the opinion for the infractions committee in Confidential Report Number 78.

After two years of a full-scale investigation riddled with threats, bribes and racial connotations, the Committee on Infractions found no violations of cars, clothes or cash payments by anyone connected to the Long Beach State basketball program. The one exception was a dubious claim by a former player who flunked out of school and said he was given $65.

The committee ruled that Jerry gave Ernie Douse $35 and that booster Vic Weiss gave him $30 more at a high school basketball tournament. In his first two interviews with the NCAA, Douse maintained he was never given anything. He even signed an affidavit stating the same.

In a third interview, Berst threatened Douse's eligibility and bribed him with immunity. It was in this interview, for the first time, that Douse claimed Jerry and Weiss provided him small amounts of money.

Douse also claimed that Jerry placed him in classes at Pomona Junior College where he received credits when he did not attend. Douse's Pomona transcript proved he was lying, so no charge was made.

Despite the fact that Douse initially denied the allegation that his eligibility was threatened by an NCAA investigator, that he was offered immunity as an enticement to make the claim, that another claim of his was proven to be false and that Jerry and Weiss vehemently denied the charge, the infractions committee nevertheless determined that a violation existed.

One of the worst charges that can be levied against a coach is academic fraud.

In the Long Beach State investigation, Berst alleged four players had their ACT tests taken for them to ensure their eligibility. Ernie Douse was named in this charge as well, but denied that anyone took the ACT test for him in his first two interviews. He even told Berst he took the test, paid the fee and that many other students were present.

After Berst threatened his eligibility, Douse changed his story. "This other guy took the test…" he stated, under threat. "It was this white guy, and I couldn't remember his name."

In a 1974 interview with the Long Beach *Press-Telegram,* Douse changed his mind on three different occasions about the name of the person who was supposed to have arranged for someone to take the test for him.

At one point, he offered the name of an assistant coach who was not even employed by Long Beach State at the time. When this was noted, Douse said, "I really can't remember for sure who it was." Later Douse retracted the entire story.

A second player named in the charge was George Gervin. Berst, in his own memorandum, disclosed the flimsy evidence he used to make this charge: "It is the writer's opinion that Gervin was assisted on the test, based on the young man's inability to recall [in which] building the test was administered."

Gervin had taken the test more than two years before his interview with Berst and was only on Long Beach State's campus for a few weeks.

Roscoe Pondexter was the third player charged with academic fraud. In his first interview, Berst wrote, "Pondexter appeared to be willing to provide complete information to the best of his recollection… Pondexter reported that he took an ACT examination on the college's campus during July 1971."

In his *second* interview, Berst stated, "the writer is definitely of the opinion that Pondexter did not take the ACT exam." When the truth was not good enough for Berst, he threatened Pondexter.

"The only way you would have a chance to *participate* this year… would be to cooperate with the NCAA," Berst told him.

"I will not lie…or make up any fairy tales," Pondexter replied.

When Pondexter wouldn't change his story, the NCAA suspended him. It was no coincidence that every single athlete that the NCAA charged with academic fraud in this investigation was *black*.

The NCAA didn't hide the fact that it was targeting black athletes in its investigation of Long Beach State. In a January 1974 article, the

L.A. Times quoted an ex-Long Beach State coach who said: "I think every player they talked to on the basketball team was black...They slap down *every school* that is challenging the big powers...All the *new* powers were using black players."

"No white guy, past or present, was ever called in and questioned by the NCAA, for anything," added John Cashmere, a white player on the 49er team.

Berst's internal memos and personal comments candidly showed his racial prejudice. "Pondexter may not have the *tools* to finesse his way through the situation, very well," Berst wrote in a November 1973 interview. Was he claiming that Pondexter was not *bright enough*?

"It's easier not to ask a white kid the same questions you might ask a black guy," Berst stated, in a recorded interview on October 26, 1976, "because you know the black, or you think, in your mind, you know the black kid doesn't have a damn thing..."

During the 1978 Congressional investigations, Berst even admitted he used a racial slur against Jerry calling him a "rug merchant," a derogatory statement against Armenians.

The Committee on Infractions believed everything its investigators presented, as well as the conclusions they reached. Despite an overwhelming lack of *evidence* to support the allegation, it concluded the players had committed academic fraud and ordered Long Beach State to declare Pondexter and Glenn McDonald ineligible.

Long Beach State's administration did not agree with the decision. "It was our strong belief that this had not taken place," a school spokesman was quoted. "It seems to me that this is the basis of our judicial system in this country—that a person is innocent until proven guilty." Pondexter and McDonald were forced to go to court to regain their eligibility.

On January 23, 1974, Berst told former Long Beach State player Amen Rahh that "he's [Pondexter] challenged us to prove that he didn't take the ACT, and I think we can do it... no sweat. Our lawyers are in a position they want to go in there, and prove it, and that's the end of it. They [Pondexter and McDonald] are not playing again."

Despite Berst's bravado to Rahh, a United States district court hearing officer ruled there was *not enough evidence* to support the suspension of either player. The court re-instated both. It was the first in a series of embarrassing courtroom defeats for the NCAA in its battles against Jerry Tarkanian.

Excluding Douse's flimsy claim of nominal cash payments and the disproved charge of academic fraud, the NCAA was left with only minor violations that occur on every campus that recruits inner-city kids or students who need financial help to cover expenses not paid for by their scholarships.

The rest of the charges against Long Beach's basketball program were: free airline flights to and from school, free lodging for short periods of time, an assistant coach bought an athlete lunch and had him over for dinner, an assistant coach drove an athlete to different places because the athlete did not have a car and an assistant coach watched a summer pick-up game involving Long Beach State and UCLA players. And yes, according to the NCAA, all of these minor things are violations of its rules.

The most serious of these charges was providing players airline tickets to school and back home. Neither Jerry nor his assistant Ivan Duncan disputed the charges. Berst, in summarizing his interview with Duncan, wrote, "Duncan made no apologies for the account with the travel agent, and it was his opinion that most universities do something similar for black athletes or student-athletes' who are a long distance from home."

"If you take any school in America, that has black kids or that comes from far away, now you know as well as I, that their parents aren't taking their money out of welfare, or wherever it is, to buy an airline ticket," Jerry told Berst.

The NCAA did everything it could to make the violations by the basketball program look as serious and as *disgraceful* as possible. To increase the number of violations to a shocking amount, it listed the *same charge* as numerous violations under several different sections of the NCAA code.

To make the violations look more severe, the NCAA grouped the nationally renowned basketball program's violations with the far more serious violations committed by their relatively unknown football program. The infractions committee concluded that the Long Beach football program provided regular cash payments and additional car payments for numerous players and recruits.

By failing to distinguish *which* violations were committed by the basketball program and which were by the football program, the media and general public assumed it was the more successful *basketball program* that committed these serious violations.

In part, the NCAA's press release stated: "In the judgment of the Council, the violations involved in this case were among the most serious which it has ever considered."

In a January 1974 interview with Berst, Jerry complained. "The NCAA Press Release comes out with some of the most serious violations ever and practically all of the real serious ones dealt with football, and yet I take the brunt of the entire thing..." he said. "All over the country I am accused of tampering with grades and giving money to players and buying cars for players...I had dinner last night with Ara Parseghian... he took me aside and said I had to be careful. I said I didn't do those things. I defended myself to the guy...I got punished probably worse than any coach has ever gotten punished. My name is dirt all over the country and for what? For airline tickets...The Wizard of Westwood [was giving] $10 a rebound."

"That was back in 1964..." Berst defended. "That's so far back, and evidently they [John Wooden of UCLA and the Bruins] quit doing that."

CHAPTER 19:

THE BIRTH OF RUNNIN' REBELS BASKETBALL

"You guys are all a bunch of bandits. The university pays for your schooling, gives you a scholarship check and you won't play hard; you won't give a maximum effort. The next time you pick up your scholarship check, wear a mask and gun because you are stealing from the university."

—Jerry Tarkanian, using sarcasm and wit

to cajole his players to play hard

TO SAY THAT the UNLV athletic program was in disarray when Jerry was hired is an understatement at best. The school's first football coach, Bill Ireland, resigned after a 1-10 season. The basketball program had just finished 13-15 and their last game was halted because of near-riot conditions at the Las Vegas Convention Center.

The team's starting center was declared ineligible because he wasn't registered in *any* classes and, unbeknownst to Jerry, the NCAA had commenced a preliminary investigation into the 15-year-old basketball program.

"People fed up with a loser in both major sports were threatening to cancel their scholarships," wrote columnist Royce Feour. "And, there was a general air of gloom about the prospects of soliciting funds...Boom! Presto! Jerry Tarkanian arrives like a knight on a white horse and it's a whole new ballgame. Tarkanian's coming to UNLV to coach basketball has given the school perhaps more publicity, and coverage, on a nationwide basis, than the University had ever received before."

Scholarship donations jumped 50% Jerry's first year.

"We have been happy in Long Beach," Jerry said. "But we feel the potential of the program in Las Vegas is unlimited ...The people there go basketball crazy ...I have never been in a community with such interest in basketball. Every place you go there are people talking about it."

Two weeks into the job, Jerry and his assistants inked one of the best recruiting classes in the country. UNLV signed high school standouts Jeep Kelly, Lewis Brown, Eddie Owens, Jackie Robinson and Glen Gondrezick, as well as junior college players Ricky Sobers and Lawrence Williams. On paper, it looked very promising.

As a sophomore at Schenley High School in Pittsburgh, Jeep Kelly was considered one of the country's best players. When he played, fans screamed "Beep, Beep! Here comes the Jeep!" Although he failed to improve as he got older, Jeep was still recruited by many of the top universities.

Jerry's assistant at Long Beach, Tony Morocco, was from Pittsburgh. He knew about Jeep early on and established a close relationship with him and his aunt. When Jerry took the UNLV job, Morocco followed and, with Morocco, came Jeep.

Jeep played little at UNLV, became disillusioned and flunked out of school after his first year. Later, he, his aunt and Tony Morocco would become key participants in the NCAA efforts to eradicate Jerry from college basketball.

Jerry considered Lawrence Williams one of the best shooters he had ever seen, but he wasn't much of a student. During his first semester, one of his professors called to complain that the player wasn't attending class. Jerry confronted and ripped into him.

"Coach, the professor don't know how much I already know," Williams replied calmly, and with a straight face. Apparently, Williams didn't know as much as he thought. He flunked out of school after his first year.

Lewis Brown was a two-time CIF AAAA Player of the Year, a feat never accomplished before. His high school teams won 88 games and lost only four, winning three straight Southern Sectional Championships. Brown was not a typical inner-city basketball player. He came from a close, attentive family.

"I've been fortunate that I had two very strong parents and a great high school coach," Brown said. "They taught me things about life and dealing with people."

When Brown signed with UNLV, he told reporter David Israel, "I'm the type of player that, I try to be very honest with coaches. In turn, when they were recruiting me, I wanted them to be honest with me. Tark was one of the two or three who was completely honest with me. He didn't try to pull any gimmicks."

When asked later why he trusted Jerry, a white man, Brown responded, "Tark isn't white. He's Armenian."

Brown adored Lois. She spent hours helping him in his studies and talking about his various interests. In return, Brown helped her any way he could, including spending part of his first summer in the Las Vegas heat planting huge almond trees in the front yard of the Tarkanian's home.

"I know for a fact that she's a big part of Tark's success," Brown said about Lois. "With the exception of my mother, she's the strongest woman I've seen. She's sensitive and intelligent. She's always there to help and give advice. But she will never try to jive you in any way. She won't lie to you, just to make you feel good. In many ways, I think she is the backbone of the team."

In spite of this, Jerry still had trouble motivating Brown and getting him to play up to his enormous potential. In frustration, after his sophomore season, Jerry suggested Brown transfer to another school. Jerry felt he wasn't getting through to him.

"No, Coach, I really like you. If I didn't, I wouldn't have planted those almond trees for you," Brown responded.

"Lew, I'll plant the damn trees if you just play hard for me," Jerry replied.

Eddie Owens was the Texas High School Player of the Year. Jerry recruited Owens personally, battling the Reverend Oral Roberts himself.

Roberts twice called Owens' home while Jerry was there trying to convince him to attend Oral Roberts. Owens turned down the noted television evangelist and became a Runnin' Rebel. He would finish his career as the leading scorer in UNLV history.

The easiest catch of the six recruits was Jackie Robinson. The younger brother of Sam Robinson, Jackie was Jerry's star player at Pasadena City College and Long Beach State. When Jerry accepted the UNLV job, Jackie was the first recruit he called.

Without question, the most important recruit was Ricky Sobers, who grew up in the Andrew Jackson housing projects in the Bronx, New York. Remarkably, Sobers never played basketball in high school, but earned first team All-American honors in junior college. Initially, Sobers and Jerry had a rocky relationship.

"Like most black players from ghetto backgrounds, Ricky never had any reason to trust a white man," wrote Peter Bodo of the *National Star*, "and in the end, no matter how you sliced it, Tark was a white man."

Sobers almost transferred after his first season but decided to stay. He became UNLV's first All-American basketball player and the first to be drafted in the first round of the NBA draft.

If Sobers was the most important recruit, Glen Gondrezick, or Gondo as he was known, was the most surprising.

Gondo was not highly recruited out of high school. Oregon was the only college to offer him a scholarship, but they kept putting him off hoping to sign future NBA great, Adrian Dantley. If Oregon signed Dantley, they would not have a scholarship for Gondo. After continual delays, Gondo finally decided to sign with the Rebels.

Gondo was the toughest kid on the team. He came from a family of 15 that took turns beating up one another. A common sight was Gondo flying through the air into the stands or diving hard onto the court to chase a loose ball.

The sight most often seen was Gondo standing in front of an opposing player who was barreling full speed ahead, not flinching, standing upright and taking a charge for his team. He took more charges than any player in the country. He took so many his junior year that he had to have a cyst removed from his chest.

Because of his hard work, determination and toughness, Gondo is one of the all-time favorite Rebels. His number is retired, alongside that of Sobers in the Thomas & Mack Center. He died of heart failure at the age of 53.

Although the Rebels signed some great recruits in Jerry's first year, they lost possibly the best high school player to ever come out of Nevada.

In 1972, Lionel Hollins was named Nevada State Player of the Year, leading his Rancho Rams to the Southern Zone title. He wanted to attend UNLV, but its basketball coach at the time, John Bayer, didn't think he could play for the Rebels. "I wasn't recruited by Bayer," Hollins remarked. "Bayer said I couldn't play college basketball."

Instead, Hollins attended Dixie Junior College, an hour and half drive from Las Vegas, earning All-American honors in his sophomore season. Jerry was named UNLV's coach the same year Hollins graduated from Dixie. He asked Bayer if Hollins was any good. Bayer responded, "Coach, I could beat him in a one-on-one game."

Hollins signed with Arizona State and enjoyed a brilliant career leading the Sun Devils to its best season ever. His second half effort in the Western Regional Semifinals resulted in a come-from-behind victory for Arizona State over UNLV. After the game, Jerry sarcastically asked his assistant if Bayer had any eligibility left.

Hollins was the sixth overall pick in the NBA draft by the Portland Trailblazers and enjoyed a long and successful professional career.

Even without Hollins, UNLV fans were expecting big things from their Rebels. After all, Jerry won 86 percent of his games at Long Beach State, never losing a home game. The program had one of the top recruiting classes in the country and had two talented players returning from the previous year, Bobby Florence and Jimmy Baker. The pre-season polls ranked UNLV 19th in the country and picked the Rebels a close second to win the conference behind the University of San Francisco.

On December 1, 1973, the Tarkanian era at UNLV began at home against the defending Southwest Conference Champions, the Texas Tech Red Raiders. Anticipation for the game built for weeks. It was a sell-out and fans were rocking the Convention Center by opening tip.

UNLV led by 13 points with 15 minutes to play, but then the players started to play selfishly. They took bad shots and turned the ball over. Texas Tech came back and won the game 82-76. It was Jerry's first home loss in *eleven* years.

Before the season, Jerry was hired to do his first radio show, something he never had at Long Beach. He was so excited. After the loss, the station's owner grabbed him on the way out of the arena and told him, "Shove that radio show up your ass!" It was the shortest running broadcast of all time.

Las Vegas' political consultant Sig Rogich, a key player in recruiting Jerry to UNLV, went home and vomited. The next day, the *Las Vegas Sun* headlines screamed, "Rebs flop in debut" and "Young Rebels Choke."

"We [the coaches] were wrong for letting this happen and for being too lax the past three weeks," Tarkanian explained to the media. "This loss hurts, really hurts...this is unbelievable...I'm in a state of shock.... We played as badly as we could play."

Jerry noted that one of his successes as a coach had "always been to get kids to play together." However, he failed this time. "We played as individuals," he said, "and you just can't play that way. We must get the kids to play together, to discover unity."

To have the team best prepared for its opening game, Jerry put the Rebels through grueling three-hour practices for 35 days, rarely having a day off. He felt this may have backfired and that the players were "mentally and physically exhausted."

After the stunning defeat, Jerry gave the team the next day off, their first in over a month. It responded by winning nine straight games to tie a school record.

The week before league season, the NCAA placed Long Beach State on probation, calling the violations some of the *most serious* in the organization's history. Jerry and Lois were devastated. "I hope the problems I had [at Long Beach State] don't affect [my UNLV] team," Jerry said. "I hope we don't lose any concentration."

Unfortunately, the team *did*. UNLV lost its first two league games, to St. Mary's and to Seattle. The Rebels came back strong, winning three straight games, including a 14-point upset over league favorite USF. The Rebels had a chance to win the league championship if they swept Santa Clara and USF on the road. More than 3,000 fans traveled with the team for this crucial road trip.

"Since I have been coaching college basketball, I've never seen that kind of a crowd on a road trip...," Jerry said. "If the players aren't determined to win, then I don't know what it would take to motivate them."

Neither Coach Tarkanian nor the crowd could motivate this Rebel team, as they played uninspired ball and lost both games.

As the season continued, Jerry became more and more frustrated with his players. They didn't get along with each other, *on or off the court*. They rarely talked or socialized with each other and there were even instances of players refusing to ride in elevators because of the presence of one or two others.

On one occasion, Bobby Florence was walking to school in the rain when a car pulled up alongside him. Bobby noticed it was his teammate, Jeep Kelly. Instead of stopping the car and giving him a ride, Jeep drove off, leaving his teammate in the rain. Jerry asked Jeep about the incident. "Coach, would you give him a ride?" Jeep replied sarcastically.

In a late season trip to Reno, the team stopped at a sparsely filled café for dinner. Two players went to one table, two others went across the room to another table, and three others went to a third table, until the team was spread out all over the restaurant. The assistant coaches didn't like the players, so they went across the street to eat. Jerry figured that since it was his team, he better eat with the players.

When he walked into the restaurant, the waitress asked if he could bring his team closer together. Using his trademark humor, Jerry replied, "Ma'am, I've been trying to do that all year but I haven't had any luck."

Going into the last game of the regular season, the Rebels held out hope for a bid to the NIT. At halftime, Jerry gave an emotional and passionate speech in an effort to motivate the players.

Upon leaving the locker-room, assistant coach Dan Ayala grabbed him and said, "Do you know what an NIT bid means? We will have to spend another week with these SOB's!"

The Rebels won the game, but did not receive an NIT invitation. They finished the season 20-6, which was the school's first 20-win season.

"We've got to spend the off-season straightening out the thinking of some of the players," Jerry explained to the press. "We have to get them to understand the concept of team orientation—get a feeling of deep commitment to UNLV, the community and teammates…the need to build pride was obvious, all season…Our biggest goal is just to encourage everyone that's unhappy *not* to come back."

He started with the team's best player, Ricky Sobers. Jerry called him into his office and told him he had a bad attitude and was hurting the team. He suggested Sobers transfer to the school where his junior college coach was recently hired.

"Coach, you are half the problem because you worked us too long and hard," Sobers responded. "My legs were shot and I hated to come to practice."

One of Jerry's best traits is his willingness to listen to others. He decided to address Sobers' concerns. The next year, the Rebels practiced four days and took the fifth day off. Jerry had never given a team that much time off before. He followed this routine the rest of his career.

Sobers, meanwhile, worked his tail off and became the ultimate team leader as the Rebels became a cohesive and selfless unit. Jerry's philosophy of teamwork, pride and hard work finally took hold.

A key addition to the team was 5'10" sophomore point guard Robert Smith. Robert was a teammate of UCLA's star player, Marques Johnson, at Crenshaw High School. Two years later, after a brilliant game in the Western Regional Semifinals, John Wooden asked Jerry where he found such a great player.

Wooden, who recruited Johnson for UCLA, had never noticed Robert on the Crenshaw team. And he wasn't the only one. Smith didn't receive any scholarship offers out of high school, so he decided to attend Arizona Western Junior College.

During the previous frustrating year, Jerry decided to get away from his players for a few days, so he and a couple of boosters took a trip to watch Arizona Western play. When Robert noticed Jerry walk into the gym, he broke into this big, beautiful smile and waved to him. Jerry said Robert's smile made him feel so good he decided to offer him a scholarship on the spot. As a result, UNLV signed the best point guard in school history.

Smith had an incredible career at UNLV. By the time he finished, he held all of the school's assist and free throw percentage records. But, even as good as Robert played basketball, he was a better person. His hard work and engaging personality made everyone on the team like and respect him.

The most important addition for the Rebels was David Vaughn, a 7'0" center. Vaughn was a highly recruited transfer from Oral Roberts University. While on his recruiting visit to UNLV, Vaughn and his wife stayed at Caesar's Palace where they met several movie stars. His wife said meeting the stars was a contributing factor in David choosing UNLV.

Jerry was oblivious to anything not involving basketball or his family, and that included movie stars. On one occasion, he was in the casino boss' office at Caesar's Palace. While there, a black man who was modestly dressed wearing jeans, with a towel hanging from his shoulders, walked in.

The boss, Ash Resnick, introduced him as Harry. He was so embarrassed when Resnick informed him that the man was actually Harry Belafonte. Jerry mistook him for a custodian.

A few years later, Jerry attended a large pre-game dinner with Jerry Buss, the Lakers owner, and several other guests. When he got home, he told his daughter that he sat next to this "fruitcake wearing a sports coat over a tee shirt." She later learned it was Don Johnson.

On another occasion, Jerry came into his office and heard his assistant say, "Bo Derek is a 10!" Jerry interjected and said, "If Derek is a 10, we need to start recruiting him right away!"

Jerry was ecstatic about the prospect of Vaughn joining his Rebel team. "He's as good as anybody besides Walton," Jerry told the press, "We thought with Vaughn we could challenge for the national title."

Just before school started, Vaughn moved out of his apartment without telling anyone. Four days later, Jerry learned he had signed a $1.4 million dollar contract with the Virginia Squires of the ABA basketball league. Vaughn's departure left UNLV with only one big man, the talented Lewis Brown. Jerry knew that if Brown felt the team was relying upon him, he would be impossible to coach.

Jerry's teams had always played a great zone defense and were patient and deliberate on offense. Yet, without Vaughn, the Rebels were too small for this kind of strategy.

Instead, Jerry decided to implement a "run and gun" style of play. He figured that they would play pressure man-to-man defense all over the court and, on offense, they would race the ball up court looking for quick, easy transition baskets. This style of play is less reliant upon a big man and played into the Rebel's natural strengths – their speed and agility.

Jerry and his assistants traveled to Albuquerque, New Mexico, to visit with the Lobos coaching staff and learn how its pressure defense was taught by their coach, Norm Ellenberger. Ellenberger's teams played great man defense, so he was the ideal coach to learn from.

Jerry always felt he could learn a little more from each coach he spoke with. While other coaches were golfing or playing tennis at the Nike coaching clinic, Jerry held court in the jacuzzi listening to other coaches' secrets of success. His willingness to listen and his ability to learn were among his greatest traits.

Jerry took Ellenberger's techniques, blended them with his own and *completely altered* his coaching style. No coach in college basketball history had ever been successful playing two dramatically different styles.

As a result of Vaughn's decision to turn pro and Jerry's willingness to change his style of play, the most entertaining brand of college basketball materialized. The *Runnin' Rebels* were born.

Over the next several years, UNLV's basketball teams shattered virtually every scoring record in NCAA play. Amazingly, these records, many of which remained for decades, were obtained with no three-point line or shot clock.

Certain members of the media and many casual fans believed the Rebels simply ran up and down the court, took quick shots and played no defense. In reality, these teams played the best pressure man defense in college basketball.

It all began in practice. Jerry put his teams through grueling three-hour practices, two hours of which were reserved for defensive drills, maximizing effort and perfecting technique.

Jerry assigned an assistant coach to each position, one player on offense and one on defense. The assistant only watched his two players, exhorting their effort and correcting their mistakes.

Technique and maximum effort were demanded of the players in every drill. The assistant's primary responsibility was to make the players compete as hard as they could.

Practices were quite the sight. Five different coaches barking incessantly at players—encouraging, correcting and, oftentimes, baiting them—to play harder. It reached the point at UNLV that the players wouldn't accept less than full effort and maximum competitiveness from their teammates.

This was "Rebel Pride." It wasn't something you talked about. It was something you did.

After watching one such practice, Basketball Hall of Fame Coach Red Auerbach commented that he had never seen a college team practice that hard.

Many coaches tried to emulate the effort and intensity of the Rebels by yelling or threatening their players. Jerry, on the other hand, had the ability to get a maximum effort from his players without chastising or demeaning them. He did it with sarcasm and wit. On occasions, when his players did not play hard, he called them together:

"You guys are all a bunch of bandits," he'd say. "The university pays for your schooling, gives you a scholarship check and you won't play hard; you won't give a maximum effort. The next time you pick up your scholarship check, wear a mask and gun because you are *stealing* from the university. That's what you are, you're stealing from the university."

On another occasion, he told his players he didn't want them playing like a bunch of cool guys trying to show off for their girlfriends and family in the stands. Then he took a basketball and imitated a cool guy, dribbling to the basket and shooting a layup, which he missed badly.

In a game when UNLV was out-rebounded and losing at halftime to a team with no starter taller than 6'6", Jerry quickly ushered his players into the locker room, and said: "Please, please, sit down. You all must be tired after how hard you played. You red-blooded Americans, you hardnosed athletes. How else could you get out-rebounded and outplayed by a team that small?"

Once, during the halftime of a game in which the Rebels were not playing well, Jerry ripped into the team for five minutes. The players were totally embarrassed. Then he browsed through the stat sheet and addressed his center, who was the tallest person out there. "Wow-wee, you have two more rebounds than my wife!" The whole locker room burst into laughter!

"At halftime, Tark would take the chalk he used to diagram plays and slam it against the black board," UNLV player James Jones said. "He would do this over and over again. By the end of the halftime, he would try to diagram a play and there wouldn't be any chalk left, and he would get so upset."

Eldridge Hudson, who played for the Rebels from 1983-1987, said: "Tark once got so upset at halftime that he threw an eraser at the chalk board so hard it ricocheted back and hit him. The players tried to hold their laughter but it was tough."

Tapp Nixon, who played for Jerry at Pasadena City College and Long Beach State, added: "At halftime of a PCC game, Tark started pacing back and forth, biting his nails, then he put his fist through the black board. We didn't know if we should laugh or be scared. At Long Beach State, he tried to kick the basketball and instead hit the ball rack and broke his toe. All the players laughed."

Because Jerry had the ability to get a maximum effort from his players without chastising and demeaning them, it helped create the close bond he had with his players.

CHAPTER 20:

REBELMANIA

"How could UNLV be so good, when it started four Blacks, a Pole, and was coached by an Armenian?"

—from *The Philadelphia Inquirer*

JT with former Rebel player, Lewis Brown at the 25-year anniversary of Tarkanian's coaching career (1986)

U NLV OPENED THE 1974-75 season with consecutive road losses to 15th ranked Arizona and 18th ranked Oregon. Despite the losses, Jerry never wavered from the new style of play. By league season, it all came together and the wins started rolling in. When UNLV thrashed UNR 126-87, they tied the school record with nine straight wins.

UNLV won the school's first and only WCAC title in any sport, by an incredible four-game advantage. Upon clinching the championship, Rebel players dragged a kicking and screaming but smiling Coach Tarkanian into the showers fully clothed.

"I am as proud of this ball club as *any* I've coached," Jerry stated after he dried off. "This team comes as close to realizing its potential as any I've coached."

UNLV finished the regular season ranked 14th in the country and earned the school's first NCAA tournament appearance. And 2,600 Rebel fans followed their team to Tempe, Arizona for UNLV's first-round game against San Diego State. The Rebels did not disappoint, prevailing 90-80 and advancing to the Sweet 16.

In the Western Regional Semifinals, the Rebels faced 7th ranked Arizona State and its All-American guard Lionel Hollins. ASU was called the quickest team to come out of the WCAC in years. To counter ASU's vaunted full-court press, Robert Smith started at the point guard spot and Ricky Sobers moved to shooting guard.

In his only start as a sophomore, Smith destroyed ASU's press, but it wasn't enough. With 5:53 to play and UNLV leading by eight, Hollins led a frantic comeback as ASU prevailed 84-81. The Rebels finished the season 24-5.

Left: JT with UNLV player, Jackie Robinson, UNLV assistant George McQuarn, and Sammy Davis Jr

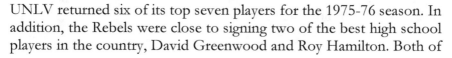

UNLV returned six of its top seven players for the 1975-76 season. In addition, the Rebels were close to signing two of the best high school players in the country, David Greenwood and Roy Hamilton. Both of

157

these young men played at Verbum Dei High School under Coach George McQuarn. McQuarn was one of Jerry's closest friends and would soon become one of his assistant coaches.

Although Greenwood and Hamilton were recruited by UCLA, Jerry felt certain they would sign with the Runnin' Rebels. He and his staff spent an enormous amount of time establishing a close personal relationship with the players and their families. With McQuarn's support, Jerry truly believed he would finally beat the Bruins for a recruit.

All that changed just two days before the signing date, when Jerry called Greenwood's home and a family member answered. The person on the other end of the phone mistook Jerry's voice and yelled, "David, Sam is on the phone."

"Sam" was, of course, Sam Gilbert, UCLA's notorious booster. Sam never lost a recruit and wouldn't this time either. Both players signed with the Bruins. Years later, in 1977, both Greenwood and Hamilton proclaimed the biggest mistake they ever made was not attending UNLV.

"We have concentrated almost all of our efforts on two of the best preps in the nation and came in runner-up...," Jerry lamented. "It is probably better to have not tried at all, than to come in second."

For many years thereafter, Jerry refused to recruit any kid that UCLA was also recruiting. As fortune would have it, after losing its two top recruits, UNLV ended up signing one of its best players ever, Reggie Theus.

"He's just a great talent; I think he'll be one of the best players anywhere," Jerry said of Theus. "There isn't anything he can't do and do it great... He's not only talented, but he is a tough kid. He takes charges, falls on the floor, dives for the ball, runs through screens. He's just a tough player." Theus later became the 9th player selected in the NBA draft and he enjoyed a 13-year pro career.

UNLV signed one other player in 1974, "Sudden Sam" Smith. Sam played high school ball in Vegas but wasn't highly recruited. He decided to attend Seminole Community College in Oklahoma, where he averaged 30 points per game.

During the previous summer, Jerry was in the campus gym when he noticed this kid knocking down the longest jump shots he had ever seen. After learning the kid was from Vegas, he decided to recruit him. Initially, Sam wanted to join his brother Willie at Missouri, but when the Tigers didn't offer him a scholarship, he decided to return home to UNLV.

Sam is arguably the greatest shooter to ever don a Rebel jersey. He had no limit in his range, casting jumpers from 30 feet and beyond with uncanny accuracy. "A chorus of 'oohs, and ahhs' is not uncommon whenever Sam releases one of his projectiles toward the rim, from a distance which defies reality, if not imagination," explained an article in the local newspaper.

Sam also had a sense of humor. He told the media that shooting came naturally to him at Seminole Community College. "There'd be 200 people in the stands; Indians on one side and Cowboys on the other," he said.

He earned his nickname Sudden Sam in a game with UNR, when he came off the bench with less than five minutes to play. The Rebels were trailing 93-91 when Sam scored *seven straight points* ***in 15-seconds*** to propel UNLV to the win.

With Theus and Sam Smith, Jerry had his eight-man rotation for the upcoming season. The "Hardway Eight" as they were called tied or eclipsed 29 school records and seven NCAA records—a feat never accomplished before by any team in NCAA history.

The Runnin' Rebels shattered the NCAA season scoring record averaging 110.5 points per game, more than five points higher than the previous mark. They shattered the NCAA single game scoring record with a 164-111 shellacking of Hawaii-Hilo. They also scored 100 or more points in 80% of their games. All of this was done without a three-point line or shot clock.

Many teams tried to stall the entire game, but couldn't maintain possession of the ball because of UNLV's relentless pressure defense. UNLV started the season by upsetting 9th ranked Arizona, 20th ranked Centenary, PAC-8 power Oregon State and WAC power University of Utah. The highlight of the regular season was a 108-94 triumph over NCAA runner-up Michigan.

The Rebels pressure defense was the key to victory in each game. To put it in perspective, if a team had 10 or more turnovers, for the *entire game,* it was considered a lot. Houston, with All-American guard Otis Birdsong, had 24 turnovers in the *first half.* Centenary had 19 turnovers in the *first half.* Michigan turned the ball over on 25% of its possessions.

Runnin' Rebel basketball took the country by storm. With its exciting style of play, high-octane offense, pressure defense and the creativity of the Hardway Eight, fans across the nation jumped on the Rebel bandwagon. One reporter termed it "Rebelmania."

After beating Syracuse by 22 points, a reporter for the *Philadelphia Inquirer* wondered, "How UNLV could be so good, when it started four Blacks, a Pole, and was coached by an Armenian?"

UNLV had been unranked when the season began but, after winning 23 straight games, the Rebels climbed to number 2 in the nation. Game 24 was against the Pepperdine Waves, led by future Hall of Famer Dennis Johnson.

The Rebels beat Pepperdine by 17 points one week earlier. In the rematch, 4,500 fans crammed into Pepperdine's 3,500-seat gymnasium to witness an epic battle.

UNLV was up two-points with 2:36 to go when Sam Smith flew through the air for an offensive tip-in. He went up so high with such power and force that he ended up slamming the ball through the rim. The only problem was that dunking was illegal in 1976. Sam's determined play resulted in "no basket" and a technical foul against the Rebels.

With 13 seconds to play and the score tied, Pepperdine fouled UNLV's all-time leading scorer Eddie Owens, but he missed the first shot of the one-and-one. Pepperdine's Ollie Matson grabbed the rebound, raced up court and sank a 14-foot running jumper with five seconds remaining. The Rebels lost 93-91. It was UNLV's *only loss* of the regular season.

March Madness, 1976

The 3rd ranked Rebels opened the NCAA Tournament with a 25-point thrashing of Boise State. In the Western Regional Semifinals, UNLV faced 12th ranked Arizona, a team they had defeated earlier in the year. The winner faced the suddenly vulnerable UCLA Bruins. Wooden had retired the previous year and the Bruins subsequently struggled through PAC-8 play.

The Rebels played well and led Arizona for most of the game. When Eddie Owens fouled out with a little over 11 minutes left to play, the momentum changed.

UNLV still had a chance to win in regulation, but *twice* missed the front-end shot of one-and-one free throws, both in the last minute. Arizona won in overtime, 114-109. For the third time in four years, Jerry came up short in his bid for a rematch with the Bruins.

Despite the heartbreaking loss, Rebelmania was sweeping through Nevada like a wildfire! Bell captains wore portable radios tuned to the games and cab drivers boasted about "their team" to passengers.

From *The New York Times*: "A recent visitor to Las Vegas asked a cab driver, what was the best show in town? The cab driver responded, 'The Runnin' Rebels and a guy they call Steady Eddie [Owens].'"

Before it became popular for celebrities to attend Los Angeles Lakers games, they were attending Runnin' Rebel games. On any given night, fans might hear Lou Rawls or Wayne Newton sing the National Anthem. Or they might catch a glimpse of stars such as Diana Ross, Don Rickles, Totie Fields, Lola Falana or Sugar Ray Leonard lead cheers from their courtside seats, which were aptly named "Gucci Row."

Indeed, it was not unusual for any of these or other stars to walk into the campus gym unannounced and plop down on the wooden bleachers just to watch the team *practice*. Hollywood celebrities were so enthralled with Rebel basketball that some even acted as scouts and recruiters. "When they [celebrities] entertain in various parts of the country, they send me newspaper clippings about our future opponents or future prospects," Jerry remarked.

Frank Sinatra once tried to use his Italian heritage to recruit a player for the Rebels. Jim Graziano was a high school All-American from New York. Sinatra knew someone in his family and tried to persuade him to attend UNLV. Graziano chose South Carolina instead, coached by Frank McGuire.

Years later, Sinatra was at a New York restaurant that had a picture of McGuire hanging on the wall. On his way out, Sinatra grabbed the picture and said, "He stole Jim Graziano from me. So, I am going to steal his picture."

In the entertainment capital of the world, UNLV basketball was Las Vegas' most popular attraction. "Tickets to Rebel games are harder to get than the big shows on the strip," read a story in the local newspaper.

Every game in the Las Vegas Convention Center was a sell-out. The demand was so great, there just weren't enough tickets. So, the university created a pass list where certain special invitees gained admittance through the back door. They didn't have seats, but they were in the arena. Many ended up sitting in the aisles. Others simply stood.

Sinatra was close with his bodyguard, Gilly Rizzo. He was so close, the story goes, that when Sinatra was born and started crying, the doctor slapped Rizzo. At Sinatra's personal request, Rizzo's son was added to the pass list.

In the early 1980s, UNLV hired a new athletic director who canceled the pass list, claiming there were too many complaints from people who didn't make the cut. Before the season started, Rizzo called to confirm his son's name was on the list.

Jerry explained what had happened and that the list had been canceled. He said he would talk to the new athletic director and hoped that once he knew it was for Frank Sinatra, he would have a change of heart. The athletic director, however, told him there were no exceptions. Embarrassed, Jerry called Rizzo and told him there was nothing he could do.

A short time later, Frank Sinatra called the Tarkanian's home. Lois, who idolized Sinatra, answered the phone and asked who it was. "Frank Sinatra" was the response.

"Yea, right, who is this?" Lois responded, growing a little irritated.

Needless to say, she was rather embarrassed when she learned it actually *was* Frank Sinatra. A few seconds later, Jerry got on the phone.

"Jerry, this is Frank. I just want to thank you for getting Rizzo's son into the games. I know it is difficult, but I know you will get it done." He then hung up. That was Sinatra – he expected results. Jerry understood that you simply didn't tell Sinatra no, so he met with the school president, who was also new.

Jerry explained how much Sinatra had helped the university. For years, Sinatra hosted the annual fundraising drive for the basketball program. He arranged for entertainers like Dean Martin, Jerry Lewis, Bob Hope, Norm Crosby, Joey Bishop, Jackie Gayle, Don Rickles, Shecky Greene, Helen Reddy and Phyllis McGuire to appear.

Each year, attendees boasted, "UNLV will never top this one." But every year, they did.

The basketball program raised hundreds of thousands of dollars from these events. The president agreed with Jerry, and they made a special exception, just for Sinatra.

In a town where collecting and cashing-in favors is routine, casino owners, managers and hosts often deluged Jerry with last minute calls asking for game tickets. Many of these requests were for high rollers who wanted to see the game, which is always a top priority for casinos.

Jerry always saved some of his personal tickets for these special requests. In return, he could go to almost any restaurant or show in town at no cost. In his 19 years at UNLV, Jerry rarely ate at home, and he *never* paid for a meal.

No basketball program, no university, not even an NBA franchise ever held a pre-game show as exciting as the one for a UNLV home game. The UNLV cheerleaders would enter the arena and roll out a large red carpet for the players to enter the court for warm-ups while the band blasted the school fight song.

When the buzzer sounded for team introductions, the lights in the arena dimmed and the fans quieted, awaiting the announcement of the opposing team's starting lineup. One spotlight followed each opposing player from their bench to mid-court. After each name was announced, the crowd exploded into a thunderous, "Booooooooooo!"

After the last opposing player was introduced, the announcer, with the flair of a title fight ring announcer and a low voice that rose in decibels, screamed: "...and now, Yourrr Runninnn' Rebels!"

The arena pulsated. Fans sprang from their seats and clapped and cheered while the UNLV fight song again blasted. The noise was so intense, it felt like your ears would burst. Blue, green, red and orange spotlights danced around the arena. In later years, theatrical light explosions worked the crowd to a frenzy, bringing this breathtaking moment to a conclusion.

When the light show finished, the announcer began his dramatic individual introductions, "From Bouuulder, Colorado, Glen 'Gondo' Gondrezick," giving each player star-like treatment. The crowd erupted as each player took center stage. After the starting five were introduced, the announcer roared, "...and your head coach, Jerrrrry Tarkanian!"

After the introductions, the UNLV band would play the ominous theme song from the motion picture *Jaws*. Standing fans, clapping their hands up and down, would emulate a shark's bite. All the while, a giant shark produced by laser traveled through the rafters, passing a huge sign that warned: "Welcome to Tark's Shark Tank."

The shark would run around the arena and look to devour anyone in its path. A few years later, UNLV retired the Rebel mascot in favor of a Shark mascot.

The scene was so intimidating to opposing teams that many coaches took their players back to their locker room until the fireworks and light show were over. Oklahoma coach Billy Tubbs had another approach. He and his team stayed on the court waving lit sparklers up and down as a sarcastic gesture to the UNLV fireworks show.

But the cheerleaders seemed to be the fan favorite. The *Rocky Mountain News* had this to say about them: "They are the Los Angeles Laker Girls of college basketball...more accurately...the Laker girls might be the NBA's answer to the UNLV cheerleaders. Flower shops love them. They get letters from admirers in Europe. Notes carrying telephone numbers from love-struck fans were passed to the squad members...they were besieged with requests for personal appearances...at the all-star game the other night we heard that more people were trying to get the cheerleaders autographs than the players."

Just as Rebelmania was erupting and Jerry's adaptive style of coaching was showing its unlimited potential, the NCAA publicly announced that it was investigating UNLV. The NCAA's own rules prohibited such comments, but the NCAA was desperate to stop UNLV and Rebelmania in its tracks.

Jerry had the opportunity to get away from the NCAA harassment when the Los Angeles Lakers offered him a five-year $350,000 contract. He loved coaching at the collegiate level and didn't want to leave but, under the circumstances, he had to consider the offer. "If it weren't for the NCAA thing, I wouldn't even consider it," he commented.

In the end, despite his apprehensions, Jerry decided to return to UNLV for his fourth and most promising season.

JT with TV personality, Dick Vitale

CHAPTER 21:

THE FINAL FOUR

"There is little question the NCAA would have preferred almost any team, other than Las Vegas, to reach the Final Four...Mention his [Tarkanian's] name and people think of his NCAA problems. But link his coaching record with any other name, and that person would be acclaimed a genius."

—*The Washington Post*

These five players took UNLV to the 1977 Final Four—Robert Smith, Sam Smith, Lewis Brown, Glen Gondrezick, and Eddie Owens

U NLV ENTERED THE 1976-77 basketball season with its top eight players returning, six of them were seniors. The Rebels signed only one player, Larry Moffitt, as a backup center to Lewis Brown.

Moffitt ended up being more than a backup. By year's end, he was starting and was one of the team's winning components. He played so well that he was drafted in the 2nd round of the NBA draft after only one season of college ball.

When the season began, *Sports Illustrated* ranked UNLV 5th in the nation and wrote that the Rebels may be ranked number one "if you are not behind bars," a reference to the NCAA investigation which was deceitfully made public by the NCAA. UNLV began the season with a 174-90 thumping of the Chinese National Team.

Late in the season, UNLV played the most thrilling game ever played in the Las Vegas Convention Center. It was against the 3rd ranked Louisville Cardinals, nick-named "Doctors of the Dunk," and their starring freshman sensation Darryl Griffin. The Cardinals came into the game with a school record 15-game win streak. Their coach, Denny Crum, was so sure of his team's success, he got married while in Vegas.

The Convention Center was not only sold out for this game, but three large television screens were placed in the rotunda for those who couldn't be crammed into the playing floor area. It was the largest crowd to witness a basketball game in Southern Nevada history.

UNLV fell behind by 17 points, but fought back in dramatic fashion, its pressure defense inspired by the deafening crowd. "We've never been higher," Jerry declared. "The crowd has never been higher." UNLV prevailed 99-96 and Jerry credited the Louisville win as the catalyst that solidified the school's reputation as a national powerhouse.

During the regular season, the Runnin' Rebels averaged an amazing 108.6 points per game, falling just short of the NCAA record it set the previous year. They broke the NCAA record with 12 consecutive 100-point games. UNLV's style of play produced an astonishing *2 ½ shots per minute.*

It was the Rebels' defense that provided the opportunity for its run and gun offense by forcing opposing teams into averaging 16 turnovers per game.

March Madness, 1977

UNLV opened NCAA tournament play against the 2nd ranked San Francisco Dons, led by a trio of superlative sophomores: Winfred Boynes, Bill Cartwright and James Hardy.

USF Coach Bob Gaillard, who had just been named National Coach of the Year over Jerry, boasted that his players did not have curfew. So, the night before the game, some of UNLV's cheerleaders, several of whom were girlfriends of Rebel players, went to USF's hotel and partied and danced with USF's star players until the early morning hours.

More than 4,000 fanatical Rebel fans made the trip to Tucson, Arizona. When the Rebels ran onto the court, they witnessed a magnificent display of red and silver pom-poms. The fans were expecting "Rebel Magic," and the team didn't disappoint, putting on one of the greatest displays of basketball artistry the game had ever seen.

UNLV scored 12 points in the first 90 seconds of the game. The Dons looked fatigued as the early afternoon game was essentially over by halftime with UNLV ahead 63-44. The Rebels led by more than 30 points numerous times before settling for a 121-95 win.

The Runnin' Rebels tied the NCAA record for most points scored in a tournament game. Their defense created 32 turnovers, leading to countless easy-baskets. "It was almost as perfect a basketball game a college team could play," USF Coach Gaillard remarked.

Jerry claimed the game was won "Tuesday, Wednesday and Thursday," with grueling two hour practices each day. The UNLV cheerleaders believed the game was won *the night before*.

It was a momentous victory for Jerry and his rebels, but there was no time to celebrate. He and his attorneys caught an early morning flight to Kansas City for a third NCAA infractions committee hearing.

While all the other tournament teams were preparing for their next opponent, Jerry was fighting to keep his job.

UNLV was in the Western Regional Semifinals for the third year in a row and, for the third straight year, the Rebels were matched against the WAC champion, this time the Utah Utes.

For the second consecutive weekend, more than 4,000 fans traveled with the Rebels, this time to Provo, Utah. The northwest end of the arena was a mass of scarlet and white, with customary red and silver pom-poms.

In an effort to get rid of his semifinal jinx, Jerry discarded several superstitions. He let someone sit in the chair next to him on the bench—a spot normally off limits to everyone—and, for the first time in history, he allowed his former manager Gil Castillo to drive him to the game. The towel chewing remained.

For a while, it appeared the jinx would continue as Utah led for most of the second half. However, UNLV fought back to take a one-point lead late in the game.

Three straight times, Utah scored to go up one. Each time, Eddie Owens answered with a basket of his own. With 4:00 to play, Utah point guard Jeff Jonas, the fourth best free throw shooter in the country, missed the front end of a one-and-one. His teammate Buster Matheny soared high for the rebound, but as he went to lay the ball in the basket, UNLV's Tony Smith came from nowhere and stole it.

Jerry ordered his team into a delay game. The play of the game came when Reggie Theus drove to the basket and Buster Matheny stepped in his path to take a charge. Instead of calling a charge, the referee called a blocking foul. Theus hit both free throws and the Rebels prevailed 88-83. UNLV's defense shined once again, forcing Utah, a great ball handling team, to give up 24 turnovers.

Jerry was back to the regional finals for the first time since his Long Beach State team fought a losing battle against Bill Walton and the UCLA Bruins. After the Utah game, UNLV's coaches and players sat in the stands at the Marriott Center, scouting UCLA for a much-anticipated match-up.

UNLV fans started chanting, "We want the Bruins! We want the Bruins!" until the refrain rang through the rafters of the Marriot

Center. Just then, UCLA's team took the floor against unheralded Idaho State with the Bruins band chanting, "U rah rah rah, C rah rah rah, L rah rah rah, A rah rah rah, UCLA fight fight fight!" This was the chant that made teams shiver in their sneakers. On this occasion, it had no effect on Idaho State.

The Bengals stunned the college basketball world by upsetting the Bruins. For the first time in 11 years, someone *other than* UCLA would represent the West in the Final Four.

The Western Regional Finals was billed "Killer vs. Shark." Idaho State coach Jim "the Killer" Killingsworth and "Tark the Shark" had been close friends since their junior college days.

"We used to spend nights drinking coffee at the Red Bell and drawing X's and O's on the tablecloth," Killingsworth told the press.

Before the game, he told Jerry he was happy one of them was going to make it to the Final Four. Jerry responded in kind.

UNLV started the game flat and Idaho State led 52-51 at the half-time break. In the locker room, Jerry lit into his players, acknowledging afterward that it was "as hard as I had ever been with my team."

He closed his tirade by telling them, "Next week, I am going to Atlanta [the site of the Final Four and Coaches Clinic] with or without you. I hope to Hell you will be joining me."

In the second half, the Rebels played with passion and urgency, blowing Idaho State off the floor. Coach Killingsworth sat back, smiled and relaxed, realizing there was nothing he could do. UNLV won with a final score of 107-90.

In Vegas, Wayne Newton interrupted his show for five minutes to boast about the Rebels' win. The Tropicana Hotel stopped gaming activities while they were playing. It was the first time gambling had ceased in that hotel since the assassination of President John F. Kennedy.

During the week of the Final Four, the *Washington Post* reported, "NCAA sources at the annual national basketball playoffs say that the University of Nevada at Las Vegas... will be placed on probation soon after the conclusion of the tournament."

At a time when Jerry should have been celebrating a major milestone in his coaching career, he and his players, all of whom had sacrificed to reach the pinnacle of college basketball, were viciously dogged by the NCAA.

From story in the *Washington Post*: "There is little question the NCAA would have preferred almost any team, other than Las Vegas, to reach the Final Four...Mention his name [Tarkanian's] and people think of his NCAA problems. But link his coaching record with any other name and that person would be acclaimed a genius."

Tarkanian's coaching record after the 1976-77 season, his last year before NCAA probation, was an astounding 224-36 for a winning percentage of .860%, far surpassing Claire Bee, who held the next highest winning percentage at .826.

The *Washington Post* story continued: "What makes this more impressive is that Tarkanian has won with two completely opposite styles. In junior college and at Long Beach, he was a ball control coach, emphasizing defense and high percentage inside shots... at Vegas, without physical big men, he switched to run and gun, non-stop basketball."

In just its 7th year at the Division-I level, UNLV's basketball program was participating in the Final Four against one of the premier programs, the North Carolina Tar Heels. The Tar Heels were led by one of the greatest coaches of all-time, Dean Smith, and had played in four of the previous 11 Final Fours. Four of its players were members of the 1976 Gold Medal Olympic Team, which was coached by Dean Smith.

The Rebels entered the game sky high and played with tremendous emotion. Their pressure defense was suffocating, forcing 16 first half turnovers against a team led by three-time All American point guard, Phil Ford.

UNLV extended its six-point halftime lead to ten (55-45) early in the second half. And just when it appeared that the Rebels might run the Tar Heels right off the court, one play changed the game.

Glen Gondrezick went high in the air for a rebound. After snatching the ball at its peak, his elbow came down on Larry Moffitt's nose, causing a cessation of play as Moffitt's gushing bloody nose was treated. Moffitt, who had been playing great for the Rebels, had to leave the game.

UNC proceeded to score 14 unanswered points and took a four-point lead. With fifteen minutes left, Smith directed the Tar Heels into his famed four-corner offense which consisted of Phil Ford controlling the ball in the middle of the court near the half-court line and the other four Tar Heels standing in the four corners. The purpose of the offense was to spread the defense as far as possible and either run time off the clock or shoot an uncontested layup.

There was no shot clock in college basketball at the time, so a team could hold the ball on offense as long as they wanted. Many basketball enthusiasts criticized this tactic.

Jerry countered Smith's four-corner offense by placing 6'7" Reggie Theus on Ford. Theus was one of the few people quick enough to stay in front of Ford and tall enough to deny him the ball once he passed it. For over fifteen minutes, the Rebels pressured the Tar Heels all over the floor causing numerous turnovers, but also allowing numerous back-door layups.

UNC led by six points with 2:23 to play. During a time-out, television cameras zoomed into the UNC huddle where Dean Smith smiled and joked with his players. After, UNLV staged a tremendous comeback.

Seldom used sophomore Tony Smith scored on two consecutive long jump shots causing Coach Smith to call a time-out. "I guarantee you Smith won't be smiling during this time-out!" CBS color analyst Billy Packer remarked.

Once the game resumed, Tony hit another 25-foot jumper to cut UNC's lead to two with 23 seconds left to play. On the inbound pass, Tony leapt high in the air and knocked the ball away from a UNC player and into the waiting hands of Reggie Theus.

Reggie drove to the free throw line, jumped, and threw a pass to Eddie Owens for a shot that would have tied the score. Instead, John Kuester of North Carolina stepped in front of Theus and drew a charge. Kuester sank both free throws to preserve the Tar Heels' win, 84-83.

UNLV's team trudged dejectedly off the court. Jerry was the last to leave, slowly walking with his head down, in obvious pain. Jackie Robinson, who was injured before the season started, put his arm around him to console him.

Post-game, a reporter asked Ford if he thought UNLV could play in the tough ACC. Ford responded, "Las Vegas could play in the NBA."

After the disappointing loss, the Rebels faced North Carolina at Charlotte in the consolation game. Jerry told the team during its pre-game meal that if "they went out and played a real good game today, it would be a reflection on their pride and character."

The players heeded his advice, forcing UNCC into 28 turnovers en route to a 106-94 victory and allowing them to finish the season third in the country. After the game, senior Robert Smith wept in the locker room. His UNLV career was over.

As was customary post-game at the time, an NCAA representative entered the locker room, congratulated the coaches and players and handed each a ceremonial watch. Jerry receive his first. He opened it, but nothing was in it.

"It's empty. Coach!" one of the players yelled. "The NCAA stole your watch too!" The room erupted in laughter.

Upon their arrival home, a motorcade met the team at the airport and ferried them to the Charleston Plaza Mall, where 2,500 fans waited for a welcome home ceremony to honor them. The Clark County Commissioners proclaimed it "Runnin' Rebel Week," a fitting honor for a special team.

The 1976-77 Runnin' Rebels set 14 NCAA single season, single game and tournament scoring records and equaled another six. UNLV finished in the top four for the second consecutive year. All six Rebel seniors were selected in the first four rounds of the NBA draft, the most ever by a team.

To many fans in Las Vegas, this was the greatest Rebel team of all-time. If not the greatest, it certainly was the most entertaining.

JT and LT celebrating big win at Long Beach State

CHAPTER 22:
THE NCAA SHUTS DOWN RUNNIN' REBEL BASKETBALL

"The NCAA is not only going to get Tarkanian, it is going to run him out of coaching."

—John Hunt, NCAA investigator

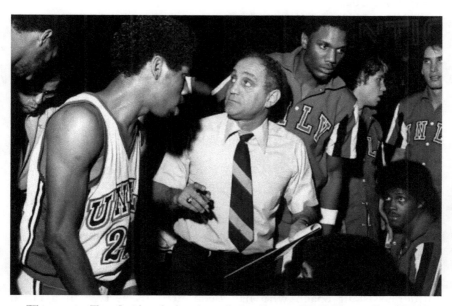

JT instructing Tony Smith and other players during timeout of UNLV game (late 1970's)

ON MARCH 29, 1973, ten days after Jerry Tarkanian accepted the head coaching job at UNLV, the NCAA opened an old, dormant investigation into the UNLV basketball program. One of the documents found in its file on Long Beach State was an article of Jerry accepting the UNLV job. David Berst, the lead investigator at Long Beach, was immediately assigned as lead investigator in UNLV's case.

When UNLV's president Donald Baepler learned of the investigation, he asked Jerry if there was anything to be worried about. "Remember after our win over Oregon State the previous year, our first against a PAC-8 school, you bought three players breakfast?" Jerry asked. "That's a violation," he explained. Baepler couldn't believe it. But it wouldn't be the last time the NCAA shocked him.

Over the course of the next four years, the NCAA maliciously investigated Jerry's program. Many absurd allegations were reported. Among the more ridiculous was one made by Jim Poore, a sportswriter from Boise, Idaho.

Poore reported there was a "rumor that basketball players from UNLV kept a key in their possession to enable them to open a slot machine in one of the local casinos. At designated times; the young men open a machine for the purpose of obtaining cash payments."

Anyone familiar with the professionalism of the Nevada gaming community and the function and accountability of the Nevada Gaming Commission knows this was laughable, and still is. And yet, it was investigated by the NCAA.

In this environment, Berst commenced his investigation of UNLV, searching for bitter former coaches and players with the biggest axes to grind. All it took was a half-willing participant and Berst would provide the emotional fuel to work the alleged witness into becoming the linchpin of his investigation.

The individual Berst chose for this purpose was Tony Morocco, a former assistant coach who had been fired by Jerry. In a taped interview, Morocco described how he became the centerpiece in what the NCAA itself labeled the longest, most expensive and most adversarial investigation in NCAA history.

Berst flew to Pittsburgh and introduced himself to Morocco. He told Morocco people in Las Vegas said he was "a really bad person— a less desirable character" and that Jerry had fired him.

Years later, Morocco confessed that he was hurt by what Berst told him. That he was in "extreme anger" and "exaggerated things" concerning possible NCAA violations.

Still, after his interview, Morocco told Berst to speak with Jeep Kelley because Kelley was also upset at UNLV since he had flunked out of school. Morocco set up a meeting between Berst and Kelley. After that meeting, Morocco gave Berst the phone number of Kelley's aunt, Frances Parker, and told him to call her.

"She [Parker] was very, very bitter about what happened to Jeep," Morocco stated, "how he was mistreated … She's bitter… against Nevada, [and] Jerry, particularly."

Berst maintained close contact with Morocco throughout the investigation and used him as his main source. To retain Morocco's trust, Berst funneled confidential information to him concerning the investigation—in flagrant violation of the NCAA's own rules which require confidentiality. One of these confidentiality violations was when Berst discussed with Morocco the infractions committee hearing, which Jerry attended.

Berst told him: "Jerry was being extremely nervous, and always looking at him [Berst]," and "when he opened his file and went through it, Jerry would wipe his brow and become more nervous."

"He [Berst] was a bit amused with that," Morocco remarked.

"In extreme anger and vindictiveness to get back at Tark" for firing him, Morocco told Berst that Jerry and his assistant coaches discussed ways to set up Berst with drugs and a prostitute, and that they intended to use that compromising information to encourage him to drop the case against UNLV. Morocco later admitted the story was not true.

In response, Berst wrote a memo to the Director of Enforcement Warren Brown stating, UNLV assistant "[Dan] Ayala recommended that someone be hired to scare the investigators, by working them over… there was serious consideration given to setting the investigator up on a false narcotics charge, or arranging for him to be photographed in the company of a prostitute… Arrangements were also discussed to place cocaine in the writer's [Berst's] motel room, or his automobile during his next visit."

Brown discussed the matter with NCAA Executive Director Walter Byers, who suggested, "...we should be on record with someone, that we have heard the rumor, in case the incident ever took place." Understandably, this story infuriated the enforcement staff. It fueled their malice and steeled their resolve to nail Jerry, even though there was no truth to the story.

Former North Carolina State coach Norm Sloan informed Jerry of a discussion he had with NCAA Investigator Bill Hunt. Hunt told Sloan that the NCAA was not only going to *get Tarkanian*, it was going to run him out of coaching altogether because they believed that he had tried to discredit several of the NCAA investigators by having them arrested in a Las Vegas hotel room with prostitutes and drugs.

Sloan told Jerry he did not want to get involved because "the NCAA can get any school at any time" and he didn't want them coming after *him*.

UNLV brought Sloan's statement to the attention of the infractions committee. In response, Warren Brown angrily called Sloan and confronted him. "If I did [make the statement], I sure don't remember when it was," Sloan responded. "Bill [Hunt] wouldn't tell me something like that in the first place."

"Right...that's what we think," Brown replied.

Brown used Sloan's feeble denial to obliterate Jerry's credibility in the eyes of the Committee on Infractions. Brown's memo to them stated that the "telephone transcript... supports... the apparent and obvious attempt by Jerry Tarkanian to mislead, fabricate, and submit... erroneous statements... for the purposes of misdirecting attention from his activities, to the alleged improper activities of the NCAA enforcement staff."

U*nder oath* during the 1978 Congressional hearings, Sloan admitted Hunt made the statement. He further testified that he had denied the statement to Brown because "the NCAA can get anybody it wants at any time, and I believe that with every bone in my body. The NCAA is powerful and has a great deal of influence over coaches."

Enraged that Jerry escaped punishment at Long Beach State and now running under the erroneous assumption that he was conspiring to set them up on fake criminal charges, the investigators intensified their actions. Over the next four years, they contacted every significant recruit and player of the UNLV Rebels, interviewing many of them three or more times. They also interviewed boosters, administrators, high school coaches, street agents, friends and girlfriends—anybody they could find.

As with the Long Beach State investigation, many of these individuals complained that *the investigators* threatened, intimidated and lied about Jerry and UNLV in an effort to find NCAA violations.

Rodney Parker, a street agent from New York City whom Berst cited as a credible source in his investigation, swore in an affidavit that Berst told him, "He had nothing against the University, but it was their head coach he wanted. He said their coach did a lot of illegal recruiting at another school and left just before the school got punished. He said he [Tarkanian] was bad for college athletics and that the NCAA was going to bury him, with or without my help."

Jerry Baskerville, who transferred from UNLV after Tarkanian arrived, asserted in his sworn affidavit:

> *NCAA investigators asked me numerous questions and wouldn't accept my answers as true, and, for all practical purposes, said I was a liar. They also said they were going to get Tarkanian. They said they had been after him for a long time and were going to get him because he recruited illegally.*

When the investigators weren't coercing and intimidating student-athletes for damning information, they relied upon bitter coaching adversaries.

Jim Harrick, who was later fired from UCLA, Rhode Island and Georgia for committing major NCAA rule violations, including academic fraud involving his son, called the NCAA to complain about Jerry's recruitment of one of his high school players, Jackie Robinson.

"I certainly wouldn't want this to get out that I called," Harrick began. "I have no ax to grind...I just feel bitter that the kids are used in an unnecessary manner," Harrick told Berst. "You can't tell me he [Sam Robinson, Jackie's brother, who played at Long Beach State] didn't get money. Don't write that down, that's just an opinion."

Harrick asked Berst to send an NCAA investigator to interview Jackie. "I will set you up in a room, anything you want," Harrick said, closing with: "This is between you and me and your office."

Three days later, an NCAA investigator named Lester Burke showed up at Jackie's high school to interview him. Burke started the interview by asking Jackie what schools had recruited him and if he was *offered* anything.

"USC said I would graduate, no matter what," Jackie told Burke. "And they offered transportation and extra cash. When I mentioned Fresno State, he [Burke] said, 'I heard they offered you the same thing they offered Roscoe Pondexter,' and I said 'yes.' They had offered my family a home to live in and me a car and extra cash. They also offered to pay some of my mom's telephone bills, but when I brought them the bills, they said they couldn't do it until after I signed a letter of intent."

Despite these *major recruiting violations* by USC and Fresno State, the NCAA never investigated. Jackie said when he mentioned UNLV, Burke "stopped and put down his pencil for a while."

"To tell you the truth, if I were a kid coming out of high school, I wouldn't go there [UNLV]," Burke told him. "You were recruited by UCLA, weren't you? They told me they wanted you. Why did you choose Las Vegas over UCLA? ... If you break your leg and can't play, and you go to a man and ask for a job, what do you think will mean more, if you can tell him your degree is from UCLA or from University of Nevada?"

Burke asked if any of the coaches said anything about Jerry. Jackie told him the coaches from USC and Fresno State had mentioned him. "What did they have to say?" Burke asked.

"They said he [Tarkanian] was cheating...," Jackie responded. "I said the only thing I know ... he didn't cheat to get me."

Burke told Jackie that Long Beach State was going on probation. This was *eight months before* the school appeared before the infractions committee and the final decision was announced.

Jackie said that Burke stated that "the NCAA was investigating Las Vegas...," adding, "He said he didn't know for sure, but he felt there was a good chance Las Vegas would go on probation. I asked for how long, and he said two or three years."

"Tarkanian, he's just one step ahead of us," Burke declared. "But we are *out to get him,* and we will."

That night, Burke visited Mrs. Robinson, who was dying of cancer. He told her "he didn't think Las Vegas was a good place for a person to go, coming out of high school. He said there was too much to distract and too much gambling...he said Jackie would not get a good education there." Burke also told her "they were out to get Tarkanian, and would, no matter where he went."

Harrick met with Jackie after his interview with Burke and told him Burke had confirmed that "Las Vegas would probably go on probation."

"You can still come to Utah State," Harrick told him, which is where he was just hired as an assistant. "Just tell that man who visited today from the NCAA that Tarkanian gave you some little thing...just tell him he loaned you $5 or something."

In their response to the official inquiry, UNLV's legal counsel compiled these statements and others into what they called the "pink file." Over twenty different sources claimed misconduct by NCAA investigators, many of whom had no allegiance to UNLV or Jerry.

Some transferred when Jerry got the job; others flunked out of school while he was coach. Most of the claims were made under oath in an affidavit or in a deposition. Instead of causing concern within the NCAA that there may have been misconduct by its investigators, the top brass circled the wagons to protect them.

"I do want to assure you that I have not taken lightly criticisms of our staff and charges that they behaved improperly," Walter Byers wrote to the Chairman of the Committee on Infractions. "But I have been surprised, to put it mildly, at the lack of substance to the allegations and criticisms."

Really? The NCAA investigators told "witnesses" explicitly *to lie* in their statements… with other witnesses present. And the top man at the NCAA says there is a *lack of substance to the allegations?*

When NCAA Council Member Franklin Lindeburg advised Byers that he had received numerous complaints concerning the investigators' methods and that he had "come to the conclusion that there is probably some substance to the claims," Byers answered with a terse letter.

"Jerry Tarkanian, of course, has been broadcasting and promoting the type of allegation you quote…" Byers said in it. "I am somewhat disappointed you would embrace them."

When the *entire NCAA Council* reported criticism of enforcement techniques, Byers again became defensive. "The criticism raised in the instant case, are for the most part if not exclusively, the result of one coach's attempt to discredit the NCAA," he said.

Byers assured the Council that he "had given the criticisms serious attention and pursued every available avenue in checking the allegations." A paid employee of the NCAA, he was misleading the council, of course. Neither Byers nor anyone else in the organization made any attempt to contact *ANY* of the sources of the allegations to determine the truth.

The entire internal investigation of investigator misconduct consisted of Byers asking the investigators if the allegations were, in fact, true. *Amazingly*, the investigators denied the allegations.

To everyone's surprise, investigator misconduct was not the biggest obstacle UNLV faced. It was the lack of any procedural guidelines and no standard of proof.

Because of the magnitude of the task and the NCAA's posture, UNLV enlisted the Nevada State Attorney General's office to assist in the investigation. On March 24, 1976, David Berst scheduled an interview with a student-athlete on UNLV's campus. At the direction of the attorney general, Assistant Attorney General Lyle Rivera was to monitor the hearing.

Five minutes before the hearing started, Berst advised Rivera that "he [the assistant attorney general] could not be present during the interview and the university might be charged with being uncooperative if he remained."

Rivera told Berst that "if he [Berst] would point out the rule in the manual prohibiting his presence, he [the assistant attorney general] would leave immediately." Berst could cite no such rule.

As a result of this first encounter, Rivera thought it was important to identify the *procedures* used in an NCAA investigation. He wrote a series of letters to the enforcement staff simply requesting copies of the organization's procedures in a rule infractions case. Despite numerous requests, the information was *never* provided to the university.

In its appeal to the NCAA Council, the university wrote: "It is inconceivable that a member institution, of a voluntary organization, would be asked to conduct an investigation under a set of rules, procedures and policies, which it is never allowed to see….Certainly, true justice is obtained more through education than surprise."

Without specific guidelines to follow, the university made a series of basic requests to the NCAA. First, they requested to see the information collected by NCAA investigators in advance of the hearing. This *full disclosure* of evidence is the bedrock in our judicial system, but the NCAA denied UNLV's request.

The university followed with a request to be provided the names of the sources of the allegations so that the sources could be contacted. This too was denied. The university was expected to investigate charges of NCAA violations, without knowing *who* made the charges or *what* was said.

While the enforcement staff refused to reveal their sources and evidence to UNLV, the university *was required* to submit their response weeks in advance of the hearing, listing all the people interviewed and what was said. The enforcement staff used this information to try and refute the university's evidence.

Fair play? Cooperative Investigation? Hardly!

As bad as the procedures were before the hearing, they were worse *at* the hearing. The University had no right to confront its accuser, cross-examine a witness or even call its own witnesses. The only people allowed to attend the hearing were *current* university personnel.

The NCAA claimed witnesses were not allowed because it did not have subpoena power and the costs would be prohibitive. The association—which makes more than a billion dollars a year and spends lavishly on its staff, whose personnel fly to the hearings in the association's private planes, and who conducts hearings in luxurious hotels across the country—did not have the financial resources to pay the cost of a willing witness to give personal testimony to resolve important conflicts between NCAA investigators and the university. The *university* even offered to pay the expenses, but the NCAA denied the request.

This decision became important when NCAA investigators presented their case. Their sole evidence was a memorandum prepared by an investigator, written as late as several weeks <u>after</u> the interview, of *his impressions* of what was said.

The investigators claim they took notes of the interviews and used these notes to prepare the memorandums. But when the university asked to see the notes, the investigators claimed they had destroyed them.

Enforcement Director Warren Brown acknowledged witnesses were not afforded the opportunity to read the memorandums and/or confirm their accuracy. In fact, the witnesses never saw the memorandums of their own testimony.

In 1984, Berst admitted *under oath*, "the NCAA had no sworn statements, no depositions, no transcripts, no affidavits, no physical evidence or other documentation" to support the charges against Jerry's program.

The university, on the other hand, through the State Attorney General's Office, provided sworn affidavits, depositions and other documentation refuting the memorandums prepared by the investigators *regarding every allegation* against Jerry and his program.

During the course of its investigation, the Attorney General's Office discovered numerous statements made by NCAA investigators that were erroneous and exhibited sloppiness, incompetence and/or outright misrepresentation.

For example, Allegation #22 said that Eddie Owens, Glen Gondrezick and Dan Cunningham resided in the Flamingo East

Apartments free of charge. In investigating this, the *Nevada State Attorney General's Office* learned that *none of the players* ever resided there.

One of the most absurd "findings" by the infractions committee was that Jerry arranged for Jeep Kelly to take a junket (a casino-chartered flight for customers) home to Pittsburgh at the end of November. There was only one problem: There were *no junket flights* at that time.

In a case teetering entirely on credibility, the university caught a break when one of the NCAA's key witnesses, Rodney Parker, secretly recorded a conversation he had with Berst. The taped transcript showed that Berst totally misrepresented the conversation he had with Parker to the infractions committee.

When the university tried to play the tape before the committee, its chairman Arthur Reynolds incredulously refused to permit the playing of the tape. "UNLV is on trial here, not the investigators!" he remarked.

If the tape wasn't enough to discredit Berst, additional witnesses identified by Berst denied the statements attributed to them and, in some instances, claimed they never even spoke with him.

Despite the numerous inaccurate statements, contradictions and misrepresentations from its investigators, the Committee on Infractions and NCAA Council completely supported them. When UNLV first raised the specter of investigator misconduct at the infractions committee hearing, Chairman Reynolds objected, saying, "You should be careful making charges about the investigative staff not doing the appropriate thing."

When an attorney questioned the integrity of an investigator at the council hearing, Chairman J. Neils Thompson snapped, "I think that is enough of that point. Because, this group [Council and NCAA investigators] has, for years, worked in solid fashion."

In Jerry's ensuing lawsuit against the NCAA, committee member Henry Cross testified, "the infractions committee never wavered from its faith in the objectivity of the NCAA investigators" and that "he never had heard of NCAA investigators not using objectivity."

"The NCAA had to back its own personnel first," Cross added.

The NCAA Manual says all investigations and hearings are to be cooperative. Nevertheless, Cross declared the UNLV hearings "the most adversarial in NCAA history."

The reason the investigation and hearings were adversarial was simple. The university learned during the course of its investigation that NCAA investigators threatened, coerced and misrepresented statements from key witnesses. The university had to decide whether to challenge the investigators' motives and credibility or to *ignore the evidence* and work amicably with the investigators in hopes of leniency. As crazy as it sounds, most schools and coaches choose the latter; the alternative is simply too dangerous.

Lou Henson, who was coaching at New Mexico State at the time, and Hugh Durham, who was coaching at Florida State, warned Jerry that it was a mistake to fight the NCAA. Henson told him he should take the punishment, thank them and "hope they leave you alone."

Durham told him to make friends with the investigators and to call them constantly for rule interpretations. It was the only way to survive.

Despite the fear encountered in challenging the NCAA, UNLV President Donald Baepler and Athletic Director Bill Ireland showed unwavering support for Jerry. At both the infraction committee hearing and on appeal, Baepler and Ireland maintained that during Coach Tarkanian's tenure at the university, he followed all NCAA rules and performed his work in an ethical manner.

And during the course of the university's investigation, the school spoke with numerous recruits, coaches and athletic administrators who praised Coach Tarkanian's professionalism and ethical manner in which he conducted his basketball program. With the hearings complete, there was nothing left to do but wait for the NCAA's decision.

JT with Don Rickles

CHAPTER 23:

THE NCAA ORDERS TARKANIAN SUSPENDED

"The subcommittee is astounded that the [NCAA] Infractions Committee could have resolved this particular issue against the accused, in favor of its <u>own investigators,</u> and with a straight face, professed to adherence to any sort of evidentiary standard or sense of burden of proof."

—Chairman of the U.S. Congressional Subcommittee, investigating the NCAA

I N THE SPRING of 1977, the NCAA issued its findings against UNLV's basketball program in what was termed the "Confidential Report." The infractions committee concluded that the former head coach, John Bayer, and his program committed 16 violations including providing cash payments, cars and free apartments to players and cheated-on ACT tests in an effort to obtain eligibility for their players. "Information related to Bayer's program was not very difficult to obtain," Berst remarked.

After four years of the most intense, expensive and adversarial investigation in NCAA history, the infractions committee did not find *one* violation of cash payments, free cars, free use of apartments or anything else of substantial value against Jerry, his assistant coaches, boosters or anyone else connected with the basketball program under his leadership.

Nevertheless, the NCAA maintained an intense suspicion and, indeed, a vendetta against Jerry. They wanted to make an example of him. They ordered him suspended from coaching NCAA teams for a period of two years—the first time in NCAA history this penalty was imposed upon a coach. To rationalize its decision, the NCAA fabricated the worst charge that can be made against a coach: academic fraud.

The NCAA claimed that during the 1973-74 academic year, Jerry arranged with Harvey Munford, a part-time instructor at UNLV, to provide David Vaughn a B grade "with the understanding Vaughn would not attend any classes or do any course work."

The NCAA further alleged "arrangements were made by Tarkanian, so that the course could be transferred to Clark County Community College...to assist Vaughn in earning sufficient credit, to receive an associate degree in art."

The only evidence presented by the NCAA of this most serious violation was an unsigned memorandum by its investigator, Hale McMenamin, of his recollection of conversations he allegedly had with Munford. He claimed he discarded his notes from the interviews.

There were many problems with this allegation, not the least of which was that the class Vaughn took from Munford could not and did not transfer to Clark County Community College. Therefore, it could not and did not help him attain his associate's degree, meaning that there was no *motivation* to commit the alleged academic fraud.

UNLV provided a plethora of *evidence* to disprove this allegation. There were sworn affidavits from everyone involved that Jerry did not even meet Munford until two months *after* the start of his Black Studies class. There was also a sworn statement from Munford that he worked with Vaughn *on his own* after class, to help him, and that Vaughn turned in his term paper and received a below average grade in the class.

There was a sworn affidavit from Vaughn that Jerry did not arrange the class and that Vaughn regularly attended the class, did the required course work himself and worked with Munford after class to improve his grade.

Also submitted as evidence were signed statements from six additional students who remembered seeing Vaughn in class, stating

189

that he participated in class and gave an oral presentation on his term paper. There was a sworn statement from a person who said she typed Vaughn's term paper for the class.

And finally, there were the results of a polygraph test and voice analyzer test proving that Munford gave truthful answers when he stated that neither Jerry nor any member of his staff had anything to do with Vaughn's class attendance or grade.

Despite overwhelming evidence to the contrary, the infractions committee *nevertheless* determined that a violation had occurred. If they could find a violation in this situation, then they can find one in *any* situation.

In testimony to a Congressional subcommittee investigating NCAA misconduct, one Committee on Infractions member, Charles Alan Wright, a law professor at the University of Texas for 45 years, avowed he voted against the finding. The rest of the committee members who appeared before the subcommittee *could not remember* how they voted.

"In the most celebrated of all infraction cases in the history of the NCAA ... [the Infractions Committee members] could not *remember*...how they voted?" the subcommittee Chairman remarked. "The subcommittee is astounded that the Infractions Committee could have resolved this particular issue against the accused, in favor of its own investigators, and with a straight face, professed to adherence to any sort of evidentiary standard or sense of burden of proof."

UNLV admitted to most of the violations against Bayer's program, including the cash payments and car offers. Conversely, it appealed the decision of the infractions committee with respect to *all* violations against Jerry's program. The appeal was heard by the NCAA Council.

The university argued that "the great weight of evidence before the Committee on Infractions clearly showed no involvement by Tarkanian" of any NCAA violations and that, after four years of intensive investigation, "the enforcement staff was not able to present one single piece of documented evidence to support their allegations."

David Berst, the lead investigator in the case, wrote the report which was submitted to the NCAA's Council on behalf of the infractions committee *defending the NCAA investigators.* "It is the

[Infractions] Committee's opinion that the NCAA enforcement staff has investigated this case in accordance with the high standards of personal integrity required in the processing of all infractions cases ..." he wrote.

NCAA Executive Director Walter Byers added: "It seems to me a great deal of the commentary...has been to attack the integrity of the investigators involved... you obviously have it fixed in your mind that these people essentially are dishonorable individuals... My inquiry is based on motivation... there is obviously a great amount of conflicting evidence...look at the motivation behind this...what motivates them [the investigators] to distort evidence or manufacture evidence, and to lie before this Committee...Do they get a distinction, do they get increased salaries, are they only motivated against Las Vegas?"

Byers answered this question himself following the UNLV case when he *promoted* David Berst to the head of the enforcement department and provided him with a *substantial pay raise*. The investigator who distorted and *manufactured* the most evidence, and who lied multiple times to the infractions committee, was now the head of the NCAA enforcement division under Byers' guidance and protection. Byers demonstrated to all that unwavering loyalty to the cause, regardless of truth or ethics, would always be rewarded in *his* NCAA.

The NCAA Council rubber stamped the committee decision and upheld Jerry's suspension as it had done *in every past case.* investigators had made a promise, years before, that they were going to run Jerry out of coaching and the Committee on Infractions and NCAA Council were not about to stop them.

It looked like they were going to keep that promise, except for one thing: The United States Constitution. Since Jerry was a state employee, he could only be suspended from his job after a hearing in front of the school's disciplinary board. His due process rights were guaranteed by the 14th Amendment.

The university's hearing officer reviewed the evidence and concluded that the NCAA did not have sufficient evidence to suspend Jerry. In fact, in several instances, there was "complete and convincing evidence that Tarkanian had not done the things that he has been alleged to have done."

Nevertheless, the hearing officer advised President Baepler to follow the NCAA directive, noting the substantial risk to the university in not doing so: heavier sanctions by the NCAA against the entire athletic department.

On September 7, 1977, less than five months after leading his team to the NCAA Final Four, President Baepler delivered a letter to Jerry which stated:

The Committee on Infractions rejected any and all alternatives. As a result, I feel it would be impossible for the University to show-cause why additional penalties should not be imposed if the University fails to take the action directed by the Committee, and the University is simply left without alternative... It is therefore, my unpleasant task to inform you that...you shall be completely severed of any and all relations...with the University's intercollegiate athletic program during the period of the University's NCAA probation (two years).

Despite a lack of evidence against Jerry, and with considerable evidence exonerating him from the NCAA charges, even UNLV, the institution that benefited from his leadership and clearly understood that the charges brought against him were fabrications, had to surrender. The power of the NCAA to *punish* the institution was simply too great.

Jerry was quickly running out of options to save his job. There was only one arena left for him to bring the battle for his career: the American Judicial System. It was his last hope!

Right: JT with Frank Sinatra

CHAPTER 24:

CONGRESS AND THE COURTS

"There is no legal, credible evidence to support the findings and the action of the NCAA... The Committee on Infractions, and its staff, conducted a star chamber proceeding, and a trial by ambush against the plaintiff... When one sifts through the evidence presented to this Court, the action demanded by the NCAA against the plaintiff can be reduced to one word: 'Incredible.'"

—James Brennan, District Court Judge

(Top) Freddy Glusman, one of JT's best and most loyal friends, owner of Piero's Restaurant, with Tark. JT ate at this restaurant more than 200 times a year.

J ERRY FILED a lawsuit in the Clark County District Court alleging that his 14th Amendment due process rights were violated. There are two parts of due process: substantive and procedural. The latter, procedural due process, requires certain procedural safeguards be followed based upon the intrusiveness of the action.

On the least intrusive side of the spectrum, a child being suspended from school for instance, all that is required is notice of the charge and an opportunity to be heard before an impartial board.

On the other end of the spectrum, such as with a criminal trial, a long list of protective procedures are mandated. Among them are the right to face your accuser, the right to call witnesses and cross-examine them, the right to examine all evidence (both exculpatory and incriminating) and hearsay—the report of another person's words—is prohibited.

The NCAA argued that their sanctions were akin to suspending a child from school, wherein only the minimal safeguards and procedures were required. But removing a man from his primary source of income and denying him the opportunity to earn a living in his chosen field of expertise is a far cry from a child missing a few days of school.

The question to ask oneself is what safeguards and guidelines would *you* desire and expect before you were removed from your job, deprived of making a living and publicly branded a crook, liar and cheat throughout your community and across the nation?

The second part of due process is substantive due process, which requires decisions to be based upon *credible evidence* and are not to be arbitrary and capricious. Jerry claimed both his procedural and substantive due process rights were violated when UNLV, under the direction of the NCAA, suspended him as its basketball coach.

Jerry was forced to file his lawsuit against UNLV because it was his *employer* who wrongfully terminated him, even if at the direction of the NCAA. The NCAA was given an opportunity to be a part of the case as an indispensable party, but they declined to do so.

On September 20, 1977, the district court handed down a blistering review of the NCAA investigation/decision and UNLV's subsequent action. The court concluded:

"There is no legal, credible evidence to support the findings and the action of the NCAA... The Committee on Infractions, and its staff, conducted a star chamber proceeding and a trial by ambush against the plaintiff... When one sifts through the evidence presented to this Court, the action demanded by the NCAA against the plaintiff can be reduced to one word: 'Incredible!'"

The Court ruled that UNLV, at the direction of the NCAA, deprived Jerry of his procedural and substantive due process rights and blocked his suspension.

At the NCAA's urging, UNLV appealed the case to the Nevada Supreme Court where the NCAA, for the first time, requested to be made a party to the suit. The Nevada Supreme Court agreed, remanding the case to the district court for retrial.

Finally, in 1984, Jerry had his day in court with the NCAA. Both parties had a full and complete opportunity for discovery with all witnesses testifying under oath, swearing to tell the truth. After hearing testimony from both sides, the district court concluded that the NCAA violated Jerry's due process rights as guaranteed by the 14th Amendment.

"The NCAA did not, and has not, 'heeded the bounds of reason, common sense and fairness, and the decision by the NCAA was arbitrary and capricious," the court ruled. "This case presents a classic example of how misperception becomes suspicion, which in turn becomes hostility, which leads, inevitably, to a deprivation of one's rights... what started out as an association whose members met, and exceeded, certain lofty goals, ended up as the NCAA-bureaucracy, which looks upon its friends with feigned pleasure, and its enemies with barely-concealed malevolence... The NCAA is an association which exists for the purpose of seeing that there is fair play; it also has the obligation to play fairly."

The NCAA appealed the decision to the Nevada Supreme Court. After briefs were filed and a hearing was held, the Supreme Court affirmed the district court's decision. Jerry was able to continue to coach at UNLV.

Because of Jerry's willingness to stand up and fight the NCAA, and the success he achieved, a movement started around the country to reform the abusive enforcement procedures of the NCAA.

The Big Eight and the Missouri Valley Conferences submitted a resolution to the NCAA Council requesting the appointment of a special committee to thoroughly investigate the practices and procedures used in enforcement matters. This caused a flurry of activity by the infractions committee and NCAA staff.

Both the committee chairman and the president of the NCAA wrote letters questioning the resolution's motives. The "iron-fist" of the NCAA worked by frightening those submitting the resolution and it was tabled. The NCAA was still able to intimidate its member colleges into submission.

In 1978, the United States Congress decided to weigh in on the matter and convened a special subcommittee to investigate the fairness of NCAA investigations. This subcommittee held ten days of hearings over a ten-month period. It considered 41 witnesses, examined thousands of documents, interviewed hundreds of individuals and deliberated dozens of potential findings and recommendations.

When it was done, the Congressional subcommittee concluded that the NCAA enforcement procedures were unfair and one-sided. It stated that, while all institutional representatives are required to cooperate with the NCAA, representatives of the NCAA are not required to do the same with the institutions. And while full and complete disclosure is required by all institutional representatives, it is *not required* by representatives of the NCAA.

When questioned why an NCAA investigator did not disclose evidence which exonerated a school, the Chairman of the Infractions Committee Dean Reynolds incredulously testified the NCAA policy is "that the staff would develop exculpatory information, *not that they would reveal it.*" The arrogance and duplicity of the NCAA in these instances were as unforgivable as they were un-American.

The subcommittee was also stunned to learn that the *source* of an allegation is omitted in the official inquiry and that the accused institution, which must respond to the allegation, may not even know the source exists.

Additionally, the subcommittee found that hearsay, even double and triple hearsay, was embraced by the infractions committee. And when a conflict in evidence exists, the institution is prevented from calling witnesses to resolve it.

The subcommittee also concluded that the NCAA policy of not providing member institutions a copy of the transcript of the infractions committee hearing "is fatally defective to the fundamental fairness of the appeals system."

In addition to the procedural defects, the subcommittee found that the infractions hearing process lacked all evidentiary standards or burden of proof and that "such standards are essential to fundamental fairness in the system."

Further, there was an unseemly alliance between NCAA investigators and infractions committee members. It was disclosed that on weekends in which there were infractions hearings, investigators and committee members routinely had dinner together or went golfing.

The NCAA tried to downplay the close relationship between the two groups, but was embarrassed when it was disclosed that one of its investigators, Dave Didion, married an infractions committee member, Marilyn Yarborough, shortly after he presented part of the NCAA case to the committee on which she sat.

NCAA Members testified that current NCAA rules were "vague, impractical and confusing." Former NCAA President (1975-76) John A. Fuzak noted, "an investigation of almost any institution in the country could reveal a number of minor or technical violations..."

The Congressional subcommittee heard testimony of the vindictiveness of the NCAA when an institution challenged its decision. For instance, the NCAA had directed Minnesota to declare three of its players ineligible. Minnesota refused to do so after a due process hearing exonerated the players. The NCAA responded by placing Minnesota's entire athletic program on probation.

When Minnesota still refused to suspend the players, NCAA brass met privately with Minnesota's president and advised him of the "allied conference rule" whereby, if Minnesota did not declare its athletes ineligible, the Big Ten conference could also receive NCAA sanctions if it continued to compete in sports with Minnesota.

After ten months of hearings, the subcommittee made 46 recommendations to improve the policy and procedures of the NCAA enforcement process. The following year, the NCAA reported that it had implemented 25 of those recommendations, in whole or in part. Nineteen others were being considered by the NCAA, and two others were under review toward possible action.

The one recommendation the NCAA has refused to consider is the public release of the transcripts of infractions committee hearings. To do so would bring public awareness of the flawed and corrupt nature of its hearings.

One of the legacies of which Jerry was most proud, is being part of the movement that forced the NCAA to change its archaic rules and enforcement methods.

JT with Mike Tyson and Don King

CHAPTER 25:

RESTORING REBEL GLORY

"The Rebels are going to win with character, not characters."

—Jerry Tarkanian

Left: JT coaching son, Danny, at UNLV in 1984

GROWING UP, Jerry's son Danny followed his father everywhere. When Jerry went to his office, Danny accompanied him and shot baskets in the gym nearby, and when he visited one of the many inner-city gyms to evaluate players, Danny sat with him in the bleachers.

When Jerry coached games, Danny was the ball boy sitting at the end of the bench. When his team went on a road trip, Danny was with him on the bus or plane. Danny loved every minute of it.

However, Danny never thought about *playing* for him. Truthfully, Danny never thought he was good enough to play for the great Runnin' Rebel teams he idolized as a youngster.

When Danny graduated high school, he was named Player of the Year in football and All-State in basketball. Lois wanted him to go to Stanford or Penn. Academics were her top concern.

Jerry, on the other hand, wanted his son to attend a small school where he could play both football and basketball. He discouraged Danny from participating in major college sports, sharing the story of Billy Cunningham.

Billy had signed with Indiana out of high school but became disillusioned with Bobby Knight's coaching philosophy and transferred to UNLV. Though he was projected to start, Larry Anderson beat him out for the spot.

In the last game of the year, UNLV had a chance to make the NCAA tournament if it beat Wyoming. The Rebels led by 15 points in the second half, but Wyoming cut the lead to one with seconds to play.

Jerry called a time-out and inserted Billy in the game to take the ball out of bounds because he was a high school quarterback and could throw the long pass.

Jerry diagramed a play. Three players were supposed to break toward the basketball and the fourth, Michael Burns, was to break long. If Burns was open, Billy was to throw him the ball.

The play worked perfectly. Burns was wide open, but Billy threw the ball to Sidney Green instead. Green threw it back to Billy, who was fouled.

Billy missed the free throw and Wyoming threw a half court desperation shot at the buzzer which somehow went in. The team was devastated. Players sprawled on the floor and cried.

When Jerry came into the locker room, Burns had Billy up against the wall by his throat. On the plane ride home, none of the players would talk to him. Jerry tried to console him.

Billy told Jerry that big-time athletics "had been nothing but one heartache after another" for him. Jerry didn't want his son in that environment, but Billy's story didn't deter him.

Danny wanted to play major college sports, but he also wanted a chance to *play*. One day, Stanford's assistant football coach came by his high school and told Danny that Stanford had a quarterback they really liked who was a sophomore. The assistant coach also said they were looking for someone to back the sophomore quarterback up for a year, then sit out (redshirt) a year, then back him up for another year. As a junior, Danny could compete for the job.

Danny asked if he would be given a chance to beat out the sophomore. The coach told him no, that they really liked the kid. Much to Lois's chagrin, Danny declined the offer. Stanford knew what they were doing. The sophomore they liked was future Hall of Famer John Elway.

Danny took a recruiting visit to the University of Nevada for football. On Sunday morning, all the recruits had breakfast at the head coach's house. During the meal, UNLV's basketball team was playing Kentucky on national TV. Needless to say, Danny was glued to the screen.

The Rebels kept the game close, but the 5th ranked Wildcats pulled away late in the second half. Suddenly, a Nevada assistant blurted out, "Turn off the TV. The game is over." Danny decided then and there that he wouldn't play football at Nevada. Basketball was going to be Danny's choice.

It was clear from the beginning that Danny would not attend UNLV because its starting point guard, Michael Lloyd, was a freshman. In addition, the leading scorer in California high school history, Greg Goorjian, had just transferred to UNLV.

Goorjian originally signed with Arizona State, coached by the enigmatic Ned Wulk who, at the time, appeared in television commercials preaching the virtues of college athletics and asking anyone who knew of cheating to "please notify the NCAA."

Goorjian had a disappointing freshman year and decided to transfer to UNLV. When he arrived in Vegas, he drove a white Fiat convertible. He told Jerry Arizona State had bought him the car and also paid for its insurance. He went on to ask Jerry if UNLV would take over the insurance payments.

Jerry told him no, but jokingly offered to call Wulk to see if Arizona State would continue to do so. This led to one of Jerry's favorite lines: "I love four-year transfers because they all have their own car."

Although UNLV was not among them, Danny was recruited by several schools to play basketball. His preference was USC. Several of his close friends attended school there. It had great academics, was a member of the prestigious Pac-8 Conference, and its basketball coach, Stan Morrison, really liked him.

Jerry wanted Danny to attend the University of Nevada and play basketball. He felt it was important for his son to go to an in-state school because Danny planned to make Nevada his home. Jerry warned that USC's starting point guard was only a freshman and that it would be difficult to beat him out.

Danny experienced firsthand his father's persuasive recruiting skills as Jerry convinced him that Nevada was the better choice for him than USC. Over the summer, Danny committed to play basketball for them.

The day Danny was to leave for college, he learned that Nevada's new head basketball coach, Sonny Allen, was bringing his son Billy to Nevada with him to play point guard. Jerry, who was in Hawaii at the time, called and told Danny not to do anything until he got home.

When Jerry returned, he used those same persuasive recruiting skills to convince Danny Nevada *was not* right for him. By then, it was mid-August.

There was little chance of Danny finding a Division-I school to attend, so he decided to go to Dixie Junior College in St. George, Utah. Before he left, Stan Morrison called and, again, offered him a scholarship to USC. Danny was so excited, he was ready to accept on the spot.

To this day, Danny doesn't know how his father did it, but he again convinced Danny that Dixie Junior College was better for him than USC. One of the most embarrassing calls Danny ever had to make was to Coach Morrison telling him he was turning down USC for Dixie.

He could hardly imagine what his Mom thought. Danny turned down Princeton, Pennsylvania, Stanford and USC to go to Dixie Junior College. His dad was just too persuasive.

The NCAA mandated probationary period from 1977-79 knocked UNLV from atop the basketball world. The program was limited to three scholarships per year and banned from television and post-season play.

Such sanctions normally devastate a program, but Jerry kept UNLV competitive, winning more than 20 games per year despite the difficulties. The biggest impact was in recruiting. None of the top recruits would consider the Rebels until the sanctions ended.

In 1980, UNLV signed two great recruits: Larry Anderson and Sidney Green. Green's signing was important for UNLV because he was one of the country's top ten high school players.

Jerry got involved with Sid through a New York contact, Winston Karim, and spent several weeks in the state recruiting him. During the day, Jerry joined the legion of coaches waiting at Thomas Jefferson High School to say hello to Sid when he finished classes. The coaches lined up in the front of the school, jockeying for the best position. There were so many coaches there, it was like a coaching convention.

Afterward, Jerry and Winston followed Sid to one of the playgrounds in the projects and watched him play. Usually the only coach there, when Jerry entered the park, he was treated like a celebrity. Dice games stopped and people came over to say hello and shake his hand.

After several weeks of constant recruiting, Sid committed to the Rebels. But he didn't want to sign the Letter of Intent until the anniversary of his brother's death. Jerry didn't want to leave New York until Sid signed, but had to go back to Vegas. Before he left, he pleaded with Sid to sign the Letter of Intent. Instead, Sid gave Jerry a handwritten note. It read: "I'm coming. – Sid."

Once Jerry left, Sid took a recruiting trip to UCLA. When he returned, he told Winston he was going to UCLA because "they had more beautiful women than even Las Vegas."

Jerry jumped on the next plane to New York and spent five days wooing Sid back to UNLV until he finally agreed to sign with the Rebels. When Jerry went to Sid's apartment to get him to sign the Letter of Intent, Sid kept delaying him. He was waiting for UCLA's coach, Larry Brown, to call.

Winston, who was with Jerry, went into the kitchen and took the phone off the hook. When it made that beeping noise, he put it back on, only to take it off again. Despite his efforts, one call made it through. Winston answered the phone. It was Larry Brown.

Winston yelled to Sid, "The Oregon coach is on the line, do you want to speak with him?"

"No, tell him I'm not here," Sid replied.

That was the last chance for Brown and the Bruins. After an hour and a half of Jerry sweating profusely from the unrelenting New York heat, Sid's mother, feeling sorry for Tark, told her son to sign with the Rebels. Jerry was relieved, but did not find out until much later how close he came to losing Sid.

After signing with UNLV, Sid confided that he had signed a Letter of Intent with another school, but that his mother wouldn't sign it.

According to Sid, a head coach from a perennial top 10 program came to his house with a briefcase filled with $10,000 cash. He took Sid to the bedroom, showed him the money and told him it was *his* if he signed a letter.

Sid signed on the spot, but when he went to his mother for her signature, she demanded the coach leave the house. "You don't need to sell yourself by taking that money!" she admonished. "There will be a pot of gold waiting for you, when you finish college." Sid's mother later confirmed this story.

UNLV players with showgirls, this was the cover of the UNLV media guide for the 1984 season

With the signing of Sid and Larry Anderson, the 1980-81 season looked promising. That aside, it turned out to be Jerry's worst.

Over the summer, Michael Lloyd was involved in a car accident and broke his neck. Greg Goorjian moved from shooting guard to point guard, but the move backfired. Goorjian was a great scorer, but the team had scorers. They needed a point guard who was a passer first.

There was also a lot jealousy on the team. If Sid scored a basket, Larry Anderson complained that he didn't get the pass. If Larry scored, Sid claimed Goorjian was freezing him out.

During one game, Goorjian raced the ball up court on a 3-on-1 fast break with Larry on one side and Sid on the other. Instead of passing, Goorjian pulled up from 15 feet and shot it. Jerry immediately called time-out.

As the players approached the bench, Sid was muttering under his breath, "That MF won't pass me the ball! That MF won't pass me the ball!" Jerry went over to Larry, who was muttering something similar.

Jerry pulled Goorjian aside and asked him why he shot the ball. "Coach, if I pass to Larry, Sid gets mad. If I pass to Sid, Larry gets mad. So, I figured I might as well shoot it myself."

Without a true point guard, the Rebels struggled all year, hitting rock bottom with a loss to a poor Air Force team. Danny was playing in a tournament at Dixie that night and was about to accept an All-Tournament award when someone told him Air Force defeated UNLV. He was in shock. He couldn't believe it. Tears welled and he shook his head back and forth, muttering, "How could we lose to Air Force? How could we lose to Air Force?"

After the Air Force loss, Danny made up my mind that he was going to play for UNLV. The Rebels needed a point guard who would pass first and shoot last. This strategy fit him fine as the former was his strength and the latter was his weakness.

There was talent returning for the 1981-82 season, guys like Sidney Green, Larry Anderson, Greg Goorjian, Larry Johnson, Michael "Spiderman" Burns and Richard Box. In addition, UNLV signed one of its all-time great players, Richie Adams.

The previous year, a friend of Jerry's from New York called and told him there was a player in the City who was better than Sidney Green. He said that UNLV needed to recruit him, so Jerry and his assistant rushed to New York to see Adams for themselves.

Adams was raised in a violent area of the projects, aptly named Fort Apache. The neighborhood violence was so legendary that a movie was made about it, showing this dangerous area where murder and illegal drugs were the norm. Adams' neighborhood was so bad that even New York City cab drivers wouldn't drive there at night. So, Jerry and his assistant had to wait until the morning to visit him.

Adams lived in a high-rise on the top floor. The elevator didn't work, so Jerry and his assistant had to walk up the stairs. At every floor, there were people lying around drunk or wasted on drugs. Jerry noticed that they were receiving strange and unfriendly looks, then it hit him. They were two white guys in suits and ties, walking up the stairs of a crime-infested housing project. Could they look any more like law enforcement?

Jerry nervously started running up the stairs yelling, "I am Richie's coach! I am Richie's coach!" He was followed closely by his assistant.

Adams was one of the best jumpers Jerry had ever seen. It was a talent Jerry believed he acquired by having to walk those stairs every day.

Adams had a great career at UNLV. He was a two-time Conference Player of the Year while leading the Rebels to two straight league titles and two NCAA berths.

The 1981-82 season started with great promise. UNLV won its first four games and upset nationally ranked LSU and BYU. After the BYU win, UNLV was nationally ranked for the first time in five years.

Despite the team's early success, there was still divisiveness between some of the players. One day, Sidney Green notified the coaches that someone had broken into his apartment and stolen his stereo. The thief had the nerve to take food out of his refrigerator, sit down at the kitchen table, eat a meal and leave dirty dishes.

Fingerprints were taken from the sliding glass door through which the thief had entered and, to everyone's surprise, they belonged to Michael Johnson, Green's teammate. Green refused to press charges and asked the coaches not to do anything either. He wanted to "handle it" himself.

Midway through the year, UNLV played a game at Madison Square Garden in New York City, Green's hometown. Everyone was worried something might happen to Johnson on the trip.

After practice, several players, including Johnson, got into the elevator with assistant coach Tim Grgurich. Grgurich pressed the up button, but the elevator went down. There was dead silence.

Grgurich later confessed that he was thinking, at the time, that if the door opened and someone was waiting to shoot Johnson, they would all get shot. But when the elevator opened, much to everyone's relief, an elderly couple walked in.

At the game that night, several of Green's "boys" sat directly behind the bench, whooping and hollering. On the floor, Johnson checked the stands every time he heard a loud noise. He kept dropping passes and fumbling rebounds until Jerry finally took him out of the game. UNLV ended up losing, but at least nothing happened to Johnson.

Jerry had been told that when Johnson was young, he had a severe drug overdose which caused him to be slow mentally. Though Johnson was built like a Roman sculpture physically—with huge shoulders, strong chest and a thin waist—that might explain what happened during Michael's first summer job in Las Vegas.

Michael's job was to make change for patrons at the Circus Circus arcade. On the third day, Jerry received a call from security telling him that Johnson was taking people's money and not giving them any change. When Jerry confronted Johnson, he claimed he didn't know he was supposed to give them back any money and, in fact, during the time he worked there, no one had asked for any money back.

Towards the end of the season, UNLV played the University of Wyoming in Laramie. On the way into the arena, Johnson noticed a sign with big bold letters: "Welcome to Laramie, Wyoming, home of the Cowboys, altitude 7,200 feet."

Johnson complained he would tire in this altitude. Using his quick wit, Jerry replied, "The altitude won't bother you because we are playing indoors, not outside."

The season continued with a series of big wins followed by stunning losses. It was obvious there was a lot of jealousy on the team. Several of the players complained that Jerry favored Sid and Larry over the rest. Jerry decided to put a stop to the whining, but not the way most would imagine.

One day after practice, he called the players together. "I hear some of you think I give preferential treatment to Sid and Larry," Jerry began. "Well, I want you to know, that IS true. Sid and Larry are carrying this team and I am going to make sure that they have everything they need. If we were on a desert island and had only one cantina of water, I would make sure Sid and Larry had enough to drink. If there was any water left over, I might give some to the rest of you."

The players sat stunned, not knowing how to respond. Danny thought, "Damn, no water for your own son?" Jerry always felt the best approach with his players was the honest approach.

UNLV finished the season 20-10 and missed the NCAA tournament for the fifth straight year. Although, for three of those years, UNLV was prohibited from participating because of NCAA probation.

Jim Valvano, NC State coach, MC of the 25-year anniversary celebration for JT (1986)

The 1982-83 season revitalized UNLV basketball. Although several of the team's best players graduated or transferred, Sid and Larry returned, along with four important recruits.

Paul Brozovich was a junior college transfer from Pittsburgh who couldn't run, jump or shoot, but he was probably the toughest kid to ever play at UNLV. The team's enforcer, whenever a player got physical with a teammate, Brozovich would say, "Run him down to the baseline, I'll take care of him." This usually resulted in a hard forearm to the defender's chest or face.

The most talented newcomer was Jeff Collins, a transfer from Arizona. At only 6'2", Collins could dunk on anybody, and I mean anybody. Danny would often throw him half court lobs which he would catch on a full sprint and finish with a thundering dunk.

Collins' most spectacular dunk occurred against the 8th ranked Tennessee Volunteers at the Las Vegas Convention Center. The game was a typical sellout, but the crowd was especially animated because of Tennessee's ranking and UNLV's undefeated start.

Just before halftime, Danny threw a pass from the opposite end of the court. Collins, who was streaking down the right sidelines and running full speed, caught the ball in front of the rim. As he did, his defender—who was behind and below him—pushed him under the basket. Collins floated to the other side of the basket, ducked his head so as not to hit the rim, and dunked the ball behind his head. The arena erupted in a deafening ovation.

The players stopped and looked around stunned, not knowing what to do. The noise did not recede. Finally, the players went to their team's benches. Someone must have called a time-out, but no one heard it. The deafening ovation continued throughout the time-out, but the players couldn't hear a single thing the coaches said.

The most heralded recruit for the 1982-83 season was Los Angeles City Player of the Year Eldridge Hudson. Hudson was 6'7" but loved to pass and dribble. He thought of himself as "Baby Magic," though his teammates called him "Baby Tragic."

Hudson was good enough to play at any university in the country; but he scared away most coaches with his antics. He was emotional and sometimes acted before he thought. He was also one of the most loyal players ever.

Hudson attended Carson High School, which was a bitter rival of Banning High. Fans from both sides were crazy. During one of the games between the two schools, Carson fans stood and chanted, "We got spirit. Yes, we do. And you got the monkeys from the L.A. Zoo."

Banning fans responded by chanting "1.6 GPA! 1.6 GPA!" because of Hudson's well-publicized academic problems. During the chant, Hudson stole the ball, raced down court and dunked it. On the way back, he flipped the bird to the entire Banning crowd, who erupted in wild agitation. No one ever knew what to expect from Hudson.

The fourth recruit was Eric Booker, who transferred from the University of San Francisco after USF dropped its program due to serious NCAA violations. Booker was a clutch player who often made big plays at crucial times.

None of these new recruits would make it to the NBA, but all were big time winners with great character and huge hearts. Jerry's favorite line for the season was, "The Rebels are going to win *with* character, not characters." These players were responsible for revitalizing the Rebel basketball program.

UNLV opened the season unranked and expectations were low. That aside, they won their first 24 games, many in dramatic fashion, coming back from double-digit deficits in every road league game.

After the team's 24th straight win, UNLV was ranked number one in the country for the first time in school history. Jerry believed it was the first time in NCAA history that a team started the season unranked and reached the number one spot. UNLV did so despite four coaches not ranking the Rebels in the entire Top 20.

One of those coaches was Marv Harshman from the University of Washington. A frequent critic of Jerry and the Rebels, Harshman told a media outlet that when he was a coach at the 1980 Pan American trials, two UNLV players had carte blanche use of credit cards. Despite Harshman's assertions, UNLV never had any players at the 1980 Pan American trials. Hypocrites like him were the ones who created the false rumors that UNLV paid its players.

In the middle of the season, Hudson came down awkwardly after a rebound and fell to the ground in pain. His knee swelled, but he still played. As the season progressed, he became less and less mobile and his jumping ability diminished. Hudson knew he needed an operation but put it off until the end of the year so he could continue to play in what was, for the Rebels, a magical season.

For the magic to continue, UNLV had to get past a very tough road-trip. The first game was against Cal State Fullerton, led by future Olympian and NBA star Leon Woods. Fullerton played in a small, archaic gym and its seats were within inches from the end line of the court. The place was filled to capacity; the crowd was going crazy and completely out-of-control.

When the players went to the locker room at halftime, fans hung over the railing, spitting on them and throwing beer at them. Late in the game, Danny took the ball out of bounds and felt a repeated sting on the back of his head. He turned around and found this man, who was later identified as a Cal State professor, snapping him in the back of the head with a towel.

The game was tight throughout, but in the closing minutes, Woods took control, making several tough long-range jumpers. Fullerton won 86 to 78.

Two nights later, the road trip shifted to Morgantown, West Virginia, a college town that vigorously supports its team. In the middle of the night, UNLV's players were awakened by loud chants of "Let's Goooo Mountaineeeers! Let's Gooo Mountaineeeers!" West Virginia's student body kept up the chant until the police finally removed them.

By game time, the atmosphere in the gym was wild. Because of UNLV's number one ranking, the game was sold out and the 15,638 fans in attendance were in a frenzy.

The only thing louder than them was the rifle fired by the Mountaineer mascot. This gesture occurred anytime West Virginia made a good play, which was such a regular occurrence in the game, it's surprising he didn't run out of ammunition. West Virginia won by a score of 87-78. The team regrouped after two straight losses and won the rest of its regular season games.

The league tournament was held at the Forum in Inglewood, California, home of the Los Angeles Lakers. Rebel fans poured into town in a festive mood and local hotels fought over which of them would host the Rebels because UNLV's boosters spent so much money at the bars and were extremely generous tippers.

The lobby was a magnificent display, filled with fans all dressed in red, discussing Rebel basketball with a drink or two in hand. It was three uninterrupted days of partying.

In the championship game, UNLV played Fresno State, who had won its last seven games. The winner would earn an automatic bid to the NCAA tournament. Fresno State jumped to an early 17-point lead. The Rebels fought back and forced overtime.

With just seconds left in overtime and the score tied, Sidney Green rebounded a missed shot. He passed the ball to Eric Booker who raced up court, stopped five feet behind the three-point line and launched a high-arching shot. Two Fresno State players flew at him trying to obstruct his view. The ball floated high in the air and straight through the net.

UNLV's bench erupted. Players and coaches stormed the court. Green ran around kicking his knees high in the air and looking for someone to hug. The rest of the players mauled each other at center court. It was a wild celebration.

The Runnin Rebels were going to the NCAA tournament for the first time since being put on probation by the association six years earlier.

March Madness, 1983

UNLV received a first-round bye in the tournament. In the second round, they faced the ACC Tournament champions, the North Carolina State Wolf Pack.

From the opening tip of the game, the Rebels played with great excitement, emotion and energy. They pressured the Wolf Pack players all over the court. NC State couldn't get an open look at the basket.

With 11:40 to play, UNLV was up by 12 points and in complete control. In a last-ditch effort, NC State Coach Jim Valvano instructed his players to foul UNLV's players, hoping they would miss their free throws.

In 1983, after a team committed seven fouls, all non-shooting fouls were one-and-one free throws. This meant that if a player missed the first free throw, there was no second. This rule was later changed and, today, after ten fouls, a team shoots two free throws on all fouls.

At first, NC State fouled Sidney Green, but Green made one free throw after another. Then they fouled other players. First Eric Booker missed, then Danny missed, and, finally, Hudson missed. UNLV missed five free throws in the final two and half minutes of the game.

After Hudson's miss, NC State had the ball. Down by one point with 32 seconds left on the clock, they tried to get an open shot, but UNLV's defense would not allow one. With eight seconds to play, Dereck Whittenburg launched a desperation shot that missed. The ball ricocheted off the rim to Eldridge Hudson.

By this time, Hudson and his deteriorating knee could barely jump. Only his sheer will allowed him to play. As the ball ricocheted off the rim, NC State's Thurl Bailey jumped over Hudson and tipped the ball toward the basket. It missed, but Bailey rebounded the tip and put the ball in.

With four seconds to go, NC State took its first and only lead of the game. The Wolfpack ended up winning the 1983 NCAA National Championship.

NC State had several tough games in the tournament, but none tougher than that fight against the Rebels. Valvano admitted that he felt helpless. He credited UNLV's defense as the toughest his team faced all year.

As part of Jerry's annual contract, a booster provided him the use of an automobile. After the 1983 season, the booster upgraded it from an Oldsmobile to a Cadillac. When Hudson saw the new ride, he shouted, "See coach! We had a great year and got you a new Cadillac!"

"If you had grabbed that last rebound against North Carolina State, I'd be driving a Mercedes," Jerry replied.

Jerry was happy that his good friend Jim Valvano won the national championship. Valvano was one of the funniest coaches in all of college basketball.

In a tournament in Albuquerque, Jimmy V. was asked if his team had bed check. "Yes, we checked last night," he replied, "and all of the beds were still in the rooms."

In another press conference, Valvano told the crowd his wife got excited when she learned the NCAA prohibited recruiting in August. "Jimmy, now I can have sex every night," she said, beaming.

"Put me down for two nights," Valvano panned.

Valvano explained how he tried to fire up his star player, Charles Shackleford. In the locker room before a big game, he shouted to Charles, "Do you want to play? Do you want to play?"

"Nah, Coach," Shackleford replied

Valvano was momentarily speechless before finally responding, "Do you want a minute to think about it?"

The media asked Valvano what he told Lorenzo Charles at the time-out before, in mid-air, Charles caught Dereck Whittenburg's missed shot and dunked it to give NC State the national championship. Valvano responded, "I told Charles to pretend the basketball was a hub cap and he was back in New York. Just go get it!"

The 1982-83 season was notable in many ways. The Rebels had the longest winning streak in school history and was the first team to hold a number one ranking. But most importantly, this team started a ten-year run unmatched by any program not from a major conference.

Over the next decade, UNLV would win 307 games, ten league titles, enjoy ten NCAA tournament appearances, advance to three Final Fours and win one national championship.

The team even had its own music video, the first for a college basketball team. A local singer/songwriter George Dare created "Runnin' Rebel Fever." The video showed highlight clips portraying the excitement of Runnin' Rebel basketball. It was an instant hit throughout the community and was played at all home games.

The 1980-81 UNLV coaching staff—JT, Tim Grgurich, Mark Warkentien, Denny Hovanec, Bruce Victor

CHAPTER 26:

GAME DAY PREPARATION

"Must be mentally, emotionally and physically prepared to play"

—Jerry Tarkanian, preparing teams for games

JT with Diana Ross

THE BEST PART of athletic competition is the anticipation, anxiety and intensity that comes with game day preparation. There is nothing like this feeling.

Jerry always preached to his players that they had to be "mentally, emotionally and physically" prepared to play. The physical part is accomplished in the off-season and in practice, but the mental and emotional part is a game-day affair.

Unlike some coaches, Jerry did not want his players loose. He wanted them focused, tense and concentrating. He compared it to a prize fighter entering the ring: "His eyes are bulging, fixated, and oblivious to everything around him." He wanted his players to have that same concentration.

"Think how you would feel if you just received a phone call from someone who said that they were coming over to your house to kick your ass in front of your family and loved ones," he'd say. "You aren't going to turn on the stereo or laugh and joke around."

Game days started at noon with the pre-game shootaround. The team shot baskets and walked through their plays and their opponent's plays. It was total concentration. Afterward, the players went home or to their hotel rooms to focus on what they were going to do that evening.

Exactly four hours before game time, the team had their pre-game meal. No one was allowed to talk at the meal; there was complete silence. It was pure intensity and concentration. On the drive to the game, there was complete silence as well.

When the team took a bus to the game, Jerry always sat in the front row on the left side. The players boarded the bus and sat in the back. The bus driver was directed to keep the radio off. Not a word was to be uttered. It was total quiet!

In later years, Jerry allowed the players to listen to a Walkman and the only noise you heard on the bus was the low, muffled sound of music. On one occasion, an unwitting bus driver unaware of the directive to maintain complete silence, said something. Jerry lit into him demanding complete silence.

Players were required to be in the locker room an hour before game time, even though they didn't take the court until 35 minutes before tip-off. During the first 25 minutes, they got dressed in total quiet. No one talked—not the players, the coaches or even the trainer. The intensity was unbelievable.

Just before the team took the floor for warmups, the players and coaches gathered in a circle, dropped to one knee and recited the Lord's Prayer.

Diana Ross singing with players at opening of Thomas and Mack Center

CHAPTER 27:

REBELS CONTINUE THEIR CLIMB TO THE TOP

"Don't worry Coach, I'm coming to UNLV. I'll be your great player.
I'm coming with you guys. I give you my word."

—John Williams, high school phenom

Larry Anderson, Sidney Green, Danny Tarkanian and Jerry Tarkanian at the groundbreaking ceremony of the Thomas & Mack Center

UNLV LOST ITS two best players from the 1982-83 team. Sydney Green and Larry Anderson had combined for more than 70 percent of the points and rebounds. Richie Adams returned to UNLV after leaving the team for a season because of family problems.

The Rebels also signed two promising recruits, junior college transfer Frank "Spoon" James and local sensation Freddy Banks. Spoon James quickly became a crowd favorite. Whenever he made a good play, fans waved a huge cardboard spoon outfitted with lights.

Freddy Banks was the most heralded player ever to come out of Las Vegas. He was named Player of the Year three times and his Valley High School team won four straight state championships. No player in UNLV's history won more close games than "Fearless" Freddy Banks. His story is that of one clutch shot after another.

In his freshman season, UNLV played Utah State in Logan, Utah, one of the league's toughest venues. The arena was packed with unruly college students screaming obscenities at the players and the game went into overtime. UNLV clung to a two-point lead and the ball when Utah State's coach sprang from the bench and screamed, "Foul the freshman! Foul the freshman!" With the crowd going berserk, Banks sank six straight free throws to seal the win.

Two years later, UNLV and Utah State played in the highest scoring game in NCAA history. At the end of regulation, Banks hit back-to-back three-pointers to send the game into overtime.

At the end of the overtime, he drove the length of the court and hit another shot to send the game into double overtime. One starter after another fouled out as the game went into a dramatic third overtime. Banks hit big shot after big shot to keep the Rebel hopes alive. UNLV ended up winning, 164-160.

Fearless Freddie hit two free throws with seven seconds left to beat Arizona 60-59 in the Great Alaska Shootout and a jump shot with one second left to beat 14th ranked Alabama. Throughout his career, Freddie won one game after another for his hometown Rebels.

There was a lot of excitement for the start of the 1983-84 season because the sparkling 18,500-seat Thomas & Mack Center became the new home of the Runnin' Rebels. It was the most beautiful on-campus facility in the West.

Jerry wanted to limit the arena to 12,000 seats. He did not think the Rebels could draw more fans than that because Las Vegas was still a small community with a multitude of world class entertainment events. It was a good thing no one listened because UNLV basketball tickets remained the toughest tickets to get in Vegas as the games were always sold out.

The inaugural event held to officially open the doors of the new facility could have come right off the showroom stage of a major hotel in Las Vegas. It was a fundraising event for the basketball program hosted by Frank Sinatra, Dean Martin and Diana Ross. The entire Rebel team attended dressed in black tuxedos and white tennis shoes with Rebel red stripes. Diana Ross sang "We are the World" while holding hands with the players swaying back and forth.

The Runnin' Rebels started the 1983-84 season unranked nationally, but won their first nine games before facing the number one ranked Georgetown Hoyas.

Georgetown had a roster full of high school All-Americans led by future Hall of Famer Patrick Ewing. They were the most feared basketball program of the 1980s and were aptly nick-named the "Beast from the East."

The sell-out crowd in the Thomas & Mack Center was electrifying—a veritable sea of white courtesy of Runnin' Rebel t-shirts provided to fans when they entered the arena.

The game disappointed no one. Both teams played well in a physical, hard-fought game.

Late in the game, UNLV was protecting a two-point lead when Jerry decided to spread the court. John Flowers, a transfer from Indiana who was playing his first game for the Rebels, caught the ball near mid-court. He was quickly covered by Patrick Ewing. Flowers spun toward the sidelines, blew past Ewing, launched himself in the air and threw down a thunderous dunk. The place went nuts, erupting in a boisterous ovation. Fans still talk about that play.

The Hoyas came back to tie the game and the Rebels held the ball for the last shot. Spoon James, a Baltimore native and friend of several of the Georgetown players, drove the baseline, got a step on his defender and took an open 15-foot shot. The ball rolled around the rim dramatically and went halfway down before spinning out.

In overtime, the Hoyas had the ball with less than a minute to play and the score tied. With the clock ticking down, David Wingate made his move, drove to the basket and made a layup to win the game for the Hoyas. It was UNLV's first and only loss in the Thomas & Mack Center for more than two years.

UNLV won its next 14 games and climbed to number three in the national standings before a big game against conference rival, Fresno State. The Rebels had defeated them earlier in the season for the fourth straight time and had already clinched the conference championship.

The team arrived in Fresno with confidence. Too much confidence, in fact. "The Rebels didn't walk into the gym, they strutted," *The Fresno Bee* reported. The players left the gym with an entirely different demeanor.

Fresno State was renowned for its defensive tenacity, but they brought it to a new level that night. Every pass and every shot was contested. The Rebels were completely overwhelmed and Fresno State won 68-43.

UNLV met Fresno State one more time in the finals of the conference tournament. The Fabulous Forum in Inglewood was sold-out and everyone wore red. The only way to distinguish fans was from their pom-poms. Fresno State had all red pom-poms, while UNLV had red and silver.

When the players ran onto the court, Fresno fans erupted, chanting "68-43! 68-43!" UNLV fans responded by chanting "4-to-1! 4-to-1!" which represented UNLV's wins to Fresno State versus its loses.

It was one of the hardest and most intense game ever played. The score seesawed back and forth as neither team led by more than four points the entire contest. Finally, they tied and, with just seconds to play, Fresno's Bernard Thompson hit two free throws to give the Bulldogs the win, the tournament championship and an automatic NCAA bid.

March Madness, 1984

As conference champions, UNLV received an at-large bid to the NCAA tournament. The Rebels defeated the Princeton Tigers 68-56 for UNLV's first tournament win since the 1977 Final Four.

After defeating Texas El Paso in the next round, the Rebels earned a rematch with the Georgetown Hoyas in the regional semifinals. The game gained additional significance when Dayton upset Washington to advance to the Final Eight. Whoever won the game would only have to beat the 11th seeded Flyers to advance to the Final Four.

The game was close for the entire first half, but Georgetown pulled away in the second half, winning 62-48. The school went on to beat its next three opponents to win the 1984 National Championship. For the second year in a row, UNLV was eliminated by the eventual national champions.

In the locker room after the game, John Williams, one of the best players to come out of California in years, tried to console Jerry. "John, this team was special," Jerry lamented, "but it was missing one thing – a great player."

"Don't worry, Coach, I'm coming to UNLV," John replied. "I'll be your great player. I'm coming with you guys. I give you my word."

Jerry was ecstatic. This was the big break UNLV needed. He felt John Williams would surely take the Rebels to the top, but the deal was far from being closed.

CHAPTER 28:

CHANGING THE IMAGE OF LAS VEGAS

"You can't have a great city, without a *great* university."

—Bob Maxson, UNLV President

A FEW DAYS after the 1984 NCAA Tournament, UNLV's recruiting coordinator Mark Warkentien visited John Williams' mother at her home. Toward the end of the conversation, Williams' mom told Warkentien that John loves UNLV and the coaching staff and wants to go there. She also explained that her son was getting cash offers from many schools for large sums of money, some as high as six figures.

John's mother said she had calculated how much money she had spent on John's upbringing and needed to be *reimbursed for her costs*, which amounted to $15,000.

When Warkentien advised Jerry of this conversation, he asked Warkentien to go back and explain to her that they could not do that. He had never bought a player before and wasn't going to now, even for someone as special as John Williams.

When Mark arrived at the Williams' home, there were several cars parked in front. Each contained a coach waiting his turn to speak with Williams' mother. Walt Hazzard from UCLA was in one car, Fat Chance, an assistant at Houston, was in another. Bernie Fine, an assistant at Syracuse, was in a third.

Warkentien decided to have a good laugh. He filled up his briefcase with papers until it bulged and walked up to the house, clutching it tightly, past the other waiting coaches. They probably thought UNLV was offering Williams a small fortune.

Once inside, Warkentien explained to Mrs. Williams that UNLV could not *pay* her for her son's recruitment. "Well, there is no use talking then," she replied.

Before signing day, Jerry went to a high school all-star game in Southern California in which Williams was playing. John put on a tremendous show. It was one of the best performances in the history of that game. While there, Jerry ran into Bob Minnix, the only NCAA investigator he ever liked.

"Who is going to get Williams?" Minnix asked.

"We have right of first refusal," Jerry retorted.

Minnix bellowed in laughter. Jerry didn't know if he was laughing at the joke or if he realized that was how college athletics really worked.

After Williams' performance in the all-star game, Jerry decided to give it one more try. He arranged for a meeting with John's mother at her house. When he arrived, Kenny Fields' father was there. Kenny had been a star player at UCLA.

Jerry told Mrs. Williams that she shouldn't demand money for John to play college basketball. He said it would blow up in her face when the NCAA found out and declared John ineligible.

"We have that figured out," Mr. Fields chimed in. "We will put the money in a relative's name. They will never trace it to John."

Dejected, Jerry left the Williams' home for the last time. John Williams later led the LSU Tigers to the 1986 Final Four. He entered the NBA draft that same year and was the 12th player taken by the Washington Bullets.

Once again, Jerry, the NCAA's "Public Enemy Number One," lost a star recruit by *following* the *same rules* that he was doggedly accused of breaking.

The 1983-84 school year brought a major development to UNLV and its basketball program with the appointment of a new school president, Dr. Robert Maxson. President Maxson approached the job with vigor and enthusiasm and he understood the emotional needs of a city craving legitimacy.

For decades, the Las Vegas suffered from a sullied reputation created by its history of legalized prostitution, gambling and organized crime. For most of the nation, Vegas was known as "Sin City." Despite the fact prostitution was illegal and organized crime had been all but eliminated, its reputation had not improved significantly.

"You can't have a great city, without a *great* university," Maxson proclaimed. He predicted UNLV would become the "Harvard of the West," which was exactly what community leaders wanted to hear.

Maxson soon befriended Steve and Elaine Wynn, who were on their way to becoming the most powerful casino owners in Las Vegas. Maxson also cultivated friendships with other top business leaders— the president of the Howard Hughes Corporation, the publisher of the largest local newspaper and several presidents of the largest banks.

They all agreed that the city needed an image overhaul. Maxson thought that the university's image needed updating as well, which is what he set out to do.

The cover of the 1983-84 basketball press guide featured a picture of the team's five seniors surrounded by scantily clad showgirls. The photo was a huge hit; it even made the cover of *Forbes Magazine*. Maxson disapproved and vowed that UNLV would never use that type of publicity again.

When Maxson arrived, UNLV was known for one thing—its wildly successful basketball program. The face of that program was Jerry Tarkanian but, because of his continual battles with the NCAA and his willingness to recruit inner city kids who had previous off-court problems, Jerry's image was tarnished in the eyes of some. It fit old Las Vegas, but not the new Vegas that Maxson was preaching.

Some people believe Maxson was intent on replacing Jerry as soon as he was hired. UNLV Athletic Director Brad Rothermel recalled that during his first meeting with the new president, Maxson asked if there was anything Jerry had done that could be used as a basis to fire him. Rothermel was stunned. When he replied no, Maxson abruptly ended the conversation. Unfortunately for Maxson, UNLV kept winning and Jerry's local support grew stronger.

In 1984-85, the Rebels won their third straight conference championship and earned their third straight NCAA tournament bid. In the second round, the Rebels lost a close one to Kentucky when Kenny "The Skywalker" Walker came out of nowhere to block a Richie Adams shot in the closing seconds.

After the game, Rothermel grabbed Jerry and put his arm around him. He joked, "Coach, you know that provision UNLV put into your contract two years ago? The one that pays you 10% of the NCAA money UNLV receives by advancing in the NCAA tournament?"

"Yes, why?" Jerry asked.

"Well, Coach, Kenny Walker must have a similar provision with Kentucky."

The 1985-86 team won a school record 33 games and reached the Sweet 16 for the second time in three years. After the season, the boosters held a roast for Jerry, celebrating his 25th year in coaching. Jimmy Valvano was the emcee and had the crowd in stitches, but UNLV President Maxson had one of the biggest laughs.

Maxson displayed to the crowd a street sign named "Tarkanian Way" and said it was in honor of the just-completed 33-win season. After a long applause, Maxson continued, "and Coach, once you win 33 more games, UNLV will actually put it up."

The crowd roared with laughter. One would think the two were the best of friends.

CHAPTER 29:

RUNNIN' REBELS ARE BACK IN THE NATIONAL SPOTLIGHT!

"You know what lost that game Larry? That damn Taco Bell towel!"

—Lois Tarkanian, after a UNLV loss to Indiana

Left: JT with Taco Bell towel during 1987 Final Four game

THE 1986-1987 TEAM led by seniors Freddy Banks, Mark Wade and Armon Gilliam was, up to that time, the best team ever at UNLV. A Junior College transferor, Gilliam was the biggest surprise and only discovered by accident.

In high school, Gilliam was a star *wrestler,* but only a reserve on the basketball team. He wasn't offered any basketball scholarships coming out of high school, so he decided to attend a junior college where he was, again, used as a substitute.

UNLV's assistant coach, Mark Warkentien, was watching Spoon James play in the National Junior College Tournament when he noticed Gilliam, a player on the other team. Warkentien had a great eye for talent so, when he returned home and Jerry asked him what he thought about James, he told him he liked James, but *loved* Armon Gilliam. Jerry had never heard of Gilliam but, based upon Warkentien's recommendation, UNLV signed him.

A preacher's son, Gilliam was big, strong and a tireless worker. There are countless stories of Gilliam shooting baskets in the local gym after midnight, with his girlfriend rebounding for him.

Jerry admits that one of the biggest mistakes in his coaching career was not starting Gilliam in his first game. He didn't even play and UNLV lost to Nevada.

Gilliam started every game thereafter and became one of the greatest players in UNLV history. He was the second player taken in the NBA draft, where he enjoyed a long and successful professional career. Sadly, he died of a heart attack at the age of 42 while playing pick-up ball at a local gym.

While Gilliam and Banks provided the team's scoring power, the glue that held them together was point guard Mark Wade. In his two years at UNLV, Wade established himself as one of the best point guards in school history. And he almost didn't make it into a Rebel uniform.

In the spring of 1985, UNLV had one scholarship remaining and they were trying to sign the Los Angeles City Player of the Year Tommy Lewis. But Lewis kept stalling.

Wade wanted to attend UNLV from the outset because he loved the Rebels' style of play. He was also friends with several players and played on a junior college team coached by one of Jerry's closest friends.

UNLV put Wade on hold, waiting for an answer from Lewis. Fortunately for UNLV, Wade was patient and, when Lewis decided to attend USC, he finally became a Rebel. In his two years at UNLV, the team's record was 70-7.

Wade, Banks and Gilliam were joined by fellow seniors Eldridge Hudson and Gary Graham UNLV added two additional recruits, Gerald Paddio and Jarvis Basnight. Paddio was a tremendous athlete and great shooter. He was also one of the hardest-working players to ever wear a Rebel uniform.

Basnight was a tremendous athlete who, at 6'7", was considered short for a starting center and was best remembered for an incredible slam dunk against Pacific. He stole the ball at half court, dribbled behind his back to get past a defender and raced down the court.

At the basket, a Pacific player stood in Basnight's way, bracing for a charge. He did not slow down or move out of his way; instead, he leaped in the air, spread his legs and jumped *directly over* the Pacific player, smashing the ball through the net. All the Pacific player could do was look up in astonishment as Basnight flew over him.

UNLV's style of play created incredible excitement. The team still played pressure defense, forcing turnovers and easy transition baskets, but the Rebels also made good use of the new three-point rule.

In 1986, the collegiate rule was changed so that if a shot was taken from beyond 19'9", the basket would be worth three points instead of two. UNLV had two tremendous long-range shooters in Paddio and Banks. Jerry encouraged them to take 3-point shots any time they were open.

The players also had their own unique personalities with Eldridge Hudson always testing the limit. Early in the season, Hudson made a steal, drove down court and dunked. Afterward, he did the Pee Wee Herman dance, which was popular at the time. The crowd loved it, but Jerry was furious and benched him on several occasions before he stopped doing it.

UNLV fans were unique as well and often stretched their imaginations to the limit. At that time, it was common for college fans to wave gigantic pictures of bikini-clad girls to distract opposing players who were shooting free throw shots.

Rebel fans took this to another level by raising a real girl—a bikini-wearing blonde named Bambi—on their shoulders when anyone on the opposing team was shooting a free throw.

Though President Maxson put a stop to this practice and Bambi was escorted out of the arena amidst a chorus of boos and hisses, a poster of her in a tight UNLV shirt with the words "Final Four or Bust" was a bestseller throughout Las Vegas.

UNLV's singular style of play, exciting comebacks and unique player personalities created a large and passionate national following. Inner-city kids from all over the country identified with the Rebels as *their team.*

An AAU coach related the following story:

> *Two kids were playing one-on-one on the hard courts of Compton, California. One of them kept taking long range shots. After the first game, the other kid told the 'long-shooter' that it was 'his turn to be Freddy Banks.'*
>
> *The first kid sat down, took off his white Nike shoes with Red stripes, identical to the ones the Rebels wore, and gave them to the second kid, who then put them on.*
>
> *In the next game the second kid shot only long-range jumpers, just like Banks.*

UNLV began the 1986-87 season in the Pre-Season National Invitational Tournament. Late in the semifinals, the Rebels were down by 12 points to Temple but staged a frantic comeback with Freddy Banks hitting two late three-pointers to give the Rebels a 78-76 win.

In the finals, UNLV was down by 20 points in the second half to Western Kentucky before staging another comeback. Gerald Paddio hit a three-pointer as time expired, giving the Rebels a one-point win.

For the second time in school history, UNLV became the country's top ranked team. But this time, they stayed there for almost the entire season. The team's only loss was a road game against undefeated and nationally ranked Oklahoma and it was characterized by controversy.

At the end of the first half, Gary Graham made a long jumper. The official ruled it a two-point shot, but television replays showed it was clearly a 3-point shot.

At the time, officials were not allowed to use TV replays to correct a call. As fate would have it, UNLV lost by a single point.

UNLV finished the regular season 30-1 and rolled through the conference tournament. The Rebels then turned their full attention to the NCAA tournament.

March Madness, 1987

The Rebels entered the NCAA tournament ranked number one in the country and, for the first time in school history, earned a number one seed. In the regional finals, UNLV faced a tough Iowa team led by B.J. Armstrong, Kevin Gamble and Brad Lohaus.

The Hawkeyes led by 16 points at the half, confounding UNLV's switching defense. Iowa ran an offense called the flex that incorporated numerous screens which brought the opposing team's big man away from the basket.

Worried by his team's lack of size, Jerry decided to outsmart the Hawkeyes and had his team switch every screen, allowing his big men to remain inside to rebound. Unfortunately, his players started thinking too much, causing them to play lethargic.

One of Jerry's golden rules was that he wanted his players to just *react* and not have to think about a particular situation. He always said,

"Basketball is a game of habits. And you create habits in practice, through repetition."

When a player develops a habit, it results in quick reactions. Having to think causes a delay in these reaction and Jerry did not believe a team could play hard if the players thought too much.

At halftime, Jerry realized that he violated his own rule. He told the players that the result of the first half was *his* fault and they were going back to "Rebel" defense. There was no more switching. Instead, the team fought through every screen and contested every shot, which was what they practiced every day.

Buoyed by its defense, UNLV staged one of the biggest comebacks in NCAA tournament history. Free to react and not think, Paddio and Banks, who went 1-11 from the 3-point line in the first half, nailed seven 3-pointers in the second half. UNLV outscored Iowa 24-2 over an eight-minute span to win the game and earn the school's second Final Four appearance.

Ten years after NCAA probation, the Rebels were finally back in the national spotlight again.

The 1987 Final Four was held in New Orleans. Bourbon Street was overflowing with tens of thousands of fans from their respective schools, each draped in their school colors.

On each French Quarter street corner, fans shouted "Hoooosiers! Hoooosiers!" for Indiana, "PU! PU!" for Providence or "Orangemen! Orangemen!" for Syracuse. But no chant was louder or longer than "Reeeeebels! Reeeeebels!" It was an unforgettable scene.

In the semifinals, UNLV was matched against Bobby Knight's Indiana Hoosiers. Knight's biggest worry was the Rebels' 3-point arsenal. Before the game, he complained about the new rule, saying he hoped it wouldn't cost his team the win. It almost did as Banks put on a show for the ages.

Fearless Freddie made an NCAA record *ten* three-pointers and finished with 38 points. Gilliam had a tremendous game also, scoring 30 points. For some inexplicable reason, the rest of the team played sluggishly. For years, Jerry questioned why his team was listless that day.

UNLV was down 12 points with 3:40 left to play when they staged another comeback. Banks hit a 3-pointer with 1:10 left to cut the lead to four. UNLV stopped Indiana on their next possession and then the Rebels had three shot attempts to cut the lead to one.

Banks missed. Paddio got the rebound, then he missed. Banks had one final shot, which went halfway down the basket and popped out. Indiana held on for a 97-93 win.

After all tournament games, the NCAA requires the head coach and selected players to speak to the media. Jerry, Banks, Gilliam and Wade, overwhelmed with disappointment, meandered into a large, reporter-filled room in the bowels of the Louisiana Superdome. Television cameras were two-deep. With their heads hung low and close to tears, the players answered questions.

"You made ten three-pointers and scored 38 points. Can you comment on your shooting?" a reporter asked Banks. Banks raised his head and, with swagger, responded, "I was shooting tremendously."

Wade and Gilliam looked up and shook their heads. Banks responded, "Well I was ... they had a hand in my face, and I was shooting tremendously." That was Banks—confident and self-assured, to the very end.

While players and fans all came up with their own theories about what the Rebels could have done differently to secure the win, Lois felt she knew *precisely* what had caused the loss.

Prior to the tournament, Jerry made an endorsement deal with Taco Bell. Despite his well-known superstitions, Jerry instructed the team manager, Larry Chin, to insert a *Taco Bell* logo on his lucky chewing towel. Taco Bell paid him a small fee for it.

After the game, Chin boarded the team bus for the ride back to the hotel. The only open seat was next to Lois. Larry knew better than to sit next to her, but he had no choice.

"You know what lost that game, Larry?" Lois stated authoritatively. "That DAMN *Taco Bell* towel!"

JT and UNLV Athletic Director, Brad Rothermol celebrating big comeback win over Iowa that moved UNLV to the 1987 Final Four

CHAPTER 30:

ACADEMIC SUCCESS

"There has never been a basketball program that has done more to assist its players academically than UNLV did under Coach Jerry Tarkanian."

—Lonnie Wright, PhD, Former UNLV Player

1 986-87 HAD BEEN a memorable season for the Rebels. The team set a school record with 37 wins, had the school's best winning percentage at 95% and was ranked number one in the country for most of the year. They even had their own hit music video, "Walk Like a Tarkanian."

The video was set to the music from "Walk Like an Egyptian" by the Bangles, but the words were changed to reflect Runnin' Rebel basketball, including video highlights of their star players and finishing with Rebel fans walking around campus sucking on a white towel, imitating Coach Tarkanian.

Seldom mentioned was the team's academic success. Five out of the six seniors on the 1987 team graduated, despite the perception around the country was that UNLV players were bad students and that Coach Tarkanian didn't care about their studies. Nothing was further from the truth.

Both of the Tarkanians worked tirelessly to provide the resources necessary for the players to succeed in the classroom. In the early years, there was no money in the budget to hire a full-time tutor so Lois tutored players at her home. After the 1977 Final Four, she persuaded the administration to use some of the money earned from the tournament to hire a full-time tutor for the basketball program. This is common today, but it was rare back in the 1970s.

In 1982, Jerry started the first academic advising program for UNLV athletes. The following year, he started the first fifth-year scholarship program to allow players to remain on scholarship an additional year to complete graduation requirements.

In conjunction, Jerry helped establish the Artie Newman Scholarship which provided over $300,000 to the UNLV Foundation, a funding source that has assisted dozens of former basketball players in returning to school to complete their degrees.

Jerry also worked with Lonnie Wright, who played for the Rebels in the early 1970s, to establish the nation's first Basketball Alumni Association. This organization provided funds for former players to return to school and earn their degrees or gain advanced degrees.

To raise money, Wright created and promoted basketball games between the UNLV alumni and alumni from other marquee schools. Former UNLV stars matched up in charity games against former stars from schools such as Michigan State with Magic Johnson and North Carolina with Michael Jordan.

The alumni games created great excitement within the Las Vegas community and brought a unique closeness to former Rebels. It helped cement the important feeling of "Rebel Pride" and "Rebel Family."

Another goal of the Alumni Association was to assist in community outreach programs. Under Jerry, UNLV basketball was rated number one in the nation in *USA Today* for two consecutive years and was named the national sports program contributing the most hours to *community service*.

A careful analysis of the academic side of UNLV's basketball program provides a very impressive look at what should have been a model NCAA college program. Of the Top 20 teams in 1990, UNLV had the 6th highest graduation rate and it was first in the nation in exceeding the graduation rate of its own general student body.

For four seasons—1982-83, 1987-88, 1989-90, and 1990-91— UNLV was the consensus number one college basketball team in the nation and 13 of the 17 seniors graduated, resulting in an impressive 76% graduation rate.

The men's basketball program was the first UNLV sport to have a Rhodes Scholar candidate (1983-84) and the only sport at UNLV to have two Rhodes Scholar candidates.

It was the first sport to have a player selected to the NCAA Academic All-America team (1982-83 and 1983-84) and also the first to have a student-athlete receive the prestigious post-graduate NCAA academic scholarship.

What makes Jerry's record on academics so impressive is that most of his players came from inner cities with poor educational backgrounds. When they arrived on campus, they were far behind the rest of the student body. Many did not know how to take notes, how to write research papers or how to study for tests. Many could not follow the lectures.

Of course, this problem was not unique to UNLV but, rather, it was and still is a manifestation of a problem endured by many inner-city kids. Our nation's educational bureaucracy has left these kids behind. Many argue they do not belong in college and that college coaches exploit them for their own gain.

Jerry, with Lois's constant support, felt these kids deserved an opportunity to get out of the ghetto, to go to college, to be exposed to higher learning and to be able to earn a life-changing degree.

Even if they didn't get a degree, they were better off than if they remained in the ghetto, where so many promising kids turn to drugs and crime. Even without a degree, these players had opportunities for good jobs in Las Vegas.

It's not fair to compare graduation rates with leading academic institutions such as Notre Dame, Duke and Stanford. Most of their players have strong parental supervision and guidance, have attended good pre-college academic schools and have been provided tools necessary to succeed academically before they get to campus.

They *should* graduate. It is far more difficult for inner-city kids from failing schools in crime-infested neighborhoods with little or no parental guidance to graduate college.

The success of one of these kids is more difficult and, at the same time, more satisfying than graduating a whole class from one of the elite schools. This genuine concern for the future of underprivileged young people is one of the Tarkanians' greatest life attributes.

Jerry didn't threaten his players to go to class. He reasoned with them and inspired them by using real-life examples. He tried to always have a former player, usually in his 30s, as one of the team's managers. That person could then be on a scholarship to finish his degree while helping the team and giving the players someone to talk to who had "been there before."

Jerry appealed to the players to take advantage of their free education. He warned them that if they failed to do so, they would be back at school years later, possibly with a wife and children, trying to get a degree without the benefit of a scholarship or the academic support currently available to them.

The former player always followed Jerry's comments by warning the current players not to make the same mistake he had. "There has *never* been a basketball program that has done more to assist its players academically than UNLV did under Coach Jerry Tarkanian," proclaimed Lonnie Wright.

CHAPTER 31:

BUILDING TOWARD A DYNASTY

"You know Jerry, every year we invite our guest-speaker to join us here for wings and beer. You're the first one who ever accepted our invitation."

—Perry Watson, Coach of Southwestern High School,

speaking for a group of black coaches in Michigan

THE 1987-88 SEASON was supposed to be a rebuilding year after half of UNLV's players graduated. Despite youth and inexperience, the Rebels went on an 11-game winning streak and climbed as high as 5th in the national rankings.

UNLV ultimately won its sixth straight league championship and made its sixth straight NCAA tournament appearance, losing to Iowa in the second round. It was one of the few times that one of Coach Tarkanian's team did not make it to the Sweet 16.

One of the most impressive stats in Jerry's coaching career is that, of the 16 teams that he took to the NCAA tournament while coaching Long Beach State and UNLV, 13 of them made it to the Sweet 16.

In 1988, Junior College All-American David Butler, his teammate Moses Scurry, high school sensation Anderson Hunt and 6' 10" "Jumping Jack" George Ackles all signed with the Rebels. These players formed the foundation of UNLV's greatest teams.

Butler was the top junior college center in the country and close friends with Scurry. Both made it clear that they wanted to continue playing together.

Before Butler and Scurry made their official visit to UNLV, they watched the Rebels play the Soviet National Team on ESPN. When Scurry saw the pre-game fireworks and light show flash across the television screen, he jumped out of his chair and told Butler they were going to UNLV. Both committed without a visit.

Butler and Scurry were tough, physical kids and Rebel fans fell in love with their blue-collar style of play. Many wore hard hats to the games with Scurry and Butler's names inscribed.

At the end of each season, the NCAA produces a training film for the referees to review indicating points of emphasis. Each coach is required to watch it. In 1990, the film was dominated by clips of David Butler knocking people to the ground. Jerry watched the film with Bobby Knight, who could hardly contain his excitement of Butler's play.

In the early 1980s, Jerry spoke at a high school coaching convention in Grand Rapids, Michigan. Afterward, several of the black coaches asked him to join them for some wings and beer.

During the mixer, Perry Watson, the coach of Southwestern High School, told Tarkanian, "You know Jerry, every year we invite our guest speaker to join us here for wings and beer. You're the first one who ever accepted our invitation."

Watson promised him that when he had a great player, he would send him to UNLV. Time and again, the little extra effort exhibited by Coach Tarkanian resulted in huge dividends.

A few years later, Perry called Jerry and told him he had a *great* player, one that was worthy to wear the proud Runnin' Rebel uniform. He was a 6'1" shooting guard named Anderson Hunt.

Jerry told Perry that he had two excellent returning sophomore guards, therefore, he didn't need another. But Perry assured him that Hunt was a difference maker and, whether he knew it or not, Jerry needed this man.

True to his word, Perry delivered Hunt to UNLV. He signed with the Rebels without ever taking a visit to the campus.

Butler, Scurry and Hunt were the prototype kids Jerry recruited and coached throughout his career. They were poor, inner-city kids from fractured families who grew up in tough, crime-ridden environments.

During David Butler's senior season at UNLV, he lost half a dozen relatives. Each was murdered. There were times when he broke down in the locker room before a game and cried.

Likewise, Anderson Hunt's mother told him not to come home for Christmas because too many of his old friends were dying in the city's drug wars. "It's like Saigon here," she described.

These three players—Butler, Scurry and Hunt—were the catalyst for Jerry's ultimate achievement, the national championship. They also proved to be the unwitting agents of his ultimate demise as UNLV coach.

George Ackles played junior college ball at Garden City, Kansas. He was a great athlete with tremendous explosiveness. In his two years at UNLV, he provided some of the greatest dunks and blocks of any player who ever donned a Rebel jersey.

Joining Butler, Scurry, Hunt and Ackles was Greg Anthony, the 1987 Nevada High School Player of the Year. Anthony signed with the University of Portland out of high school but transferred back to UNLV after one season

As it turned out, UNLV signed four of its top six players from the national championship team without a single visit.

Setting the groundwork for this talented group was freshman sensation Stacey Augmon, the greatest defensive player in UNLV history. He was named the NABC Defensive Player of the Year for three straight years, the first person to be so awarded. Augmon was always matched against the opposing team's standout player, and he routinely shut him down.

A great rivalry developed between Augmon and Arizona star, Sean Elliott. The preceding summer, Augmon made the U.S. Olympic team over Elliott, who was a First-Team All-American. Georgetown's John Thompson was the coach of the team and he loved tough defensive kids like Augmon. Arizona fans were furious with his decision.

There was already a bitter rivalry between UNLV and Arizona. These two programs were the best in the West for more than a decade and they were the only western teams to play in the Final Four during this period. UNLV made three trips; Arizona made one.

The programs often recruited the same players. In 1986, Tim Tolbert, a sought-after junior college player, committed to the Rebels. But before UNLV's recruiting coordinator could sign him, Arizona's coach, Lute Olson, paid Tolbert a late-night visit and convinced him to sign with Arizona instead.

Olson asked Tolbert what type of people he wanted as friends when he graduated from college, contrasting Arizona's players with their pristine image and UNLV's players with their noted bad-boy reputations.

With all the negative publicity that the NCAA and certain media outlets were directing towards UNLV and Coach Tarkanian, it made UNLV a difficult "sell" for recruiting. And many coaches, like Olson, were quick to use this misinformation for their own benefit.

Olson used the same tactic with high school sensation, Brian Williams. He convinced Williams that UNLV players were bad people, the kind he would not want to associate with.

Years later, while playing in the NBA, Williams befriended Stacey Augmon and another former Rebel, Larry Johnson. He remarked how great the guys were and he lamented the mistake he made by not going to UNLV.

Even before the recruiting battles, there was acrimony between the coaches. Olson replaced Jerry at Long Beach State and made derogatory remarks about him when the school was placed on probation.

The first game between the coaches was in 1977, when Olson coached Iowa. UNLV beat Iowa in a thriller when Earl Evans caught a length-of-the-court pass, jumped, turned and shot the ball, all in one motion.

The shot trickled through the net just as the buzzer sounded, giving the Rebels the win. After the game, Olson complained about the officiating and vowed never to play in Las Vegas again.

These two coaches met again in 1985 at the Great Alaska Shootout. UNLV was a heavy favorite, but Arizona, bolstered by the scoring of freshman sensation Sean Elliott, fought the Rebels right down to the wire.

Although UNLV won the game, the Wildcats were ecstatic about their performance. Arizona believed that it was only a matter of time before they replaced UNLV as the top power in the West.

UNLV played Arizona again in the 1988-89 season. The bitterness and intensity of the rivalry increased following Augmon's inclusion on the Olympic team over Elliott. Arizona was a big favorite as UNLV was a "young team" that year.

The capacity crowd at the McHale Center wore bright red. They were whooping and howling after every great Wildcat play. Many left the game hoarse as Arizona won 85-76. Elliott had 32 points and 15 rebounds.

Later that year, the teams met in a rematch in the regional semifinals of the NCAA tournament. Arizona was ranked number one in the country and was the consensus choice to win the national championship.

Jerry was worried sick before the game. He didn't think his team had a chance to beat Arizona. Their prospects were so bleak that both Lois and Jerry's best friend, Freddie Glusman, refused to make the trip to Denver.

The game was tight throughout. Neither team could pull away. With Greg Anthony out of the game with an injury, UNLV had the ball and was down two points with just seconds to go. Anderson Hunt dribbled the ball on the right side of the court, guarded closely by future baseball great, Kenny Lofton.

Hunt picked up the ball twenty-one feet out. He spun to his right, but Lofton was waiting for him. Lofton fell down, trying to draw a charge. He had good position and contact was made, but the officials ruled that it was inconsequential.

Hunt turned back to his left and found himself wide open. He nailed the three-pointer. The Rebel bench erupted, mobbing Hunt at mid-court.

That night, Jerry held court in the hotel bar making one toast after another. He had never been so happy. The next day, banners in Las Vegas proclaimed: "Hunt for Mayor!"

Two nights later, Seton Hall beat an emotionally-drained Rebel team and advanced to the Final Four. UNLV would have to wait another year for a shot at the title.

CHAPTER 32:

THE ROAD TO THE NATIONAL CHAMPIONSHIP

"The doctors were telling me that if I could stand the pain, I could play. I figured it would hurt more <u>not</u> to play."

—Greg Anthony, about why he played with a broken jaw

Stacey Augman and Larry Johnson hugging after National Championship game

THE 1989-90 REBEL basketball season was dubbed "The Big Year is Here" in UNLV's media guide. The Rebels returned all five starters, although Ackles was injured during pre-season. In addition, UNLV welcomed its greatest recruit in school history—Larry Johnson.

Johnson was named the National Player of the Year coming out of high school in Dallas, Texas. He originally signed with SMU, but when questions arose concerning his test scores, SMU, which had already endured the death penalty for football violations, refused to admit him. Instead, Johnson enrolled at Odessa Junior College, where he was named Junior College Player of the Year after his sophomore season.

Before the recruiting season started, Jerry told his assistants that *he* was recruiting Dallas and that they could have the rest of the country. He spent the entire summer there recruiting Johnson.

Jerry established a close relationship with Johnson, but so had Kansas coach Larry Brown, who had coached a U.S. Select All-Star team on which Johnson played. As fortune would have it, both Greg Anthony and Stacey Augmon were on that team as well and Augmon ended up Johnson's roommate. Johnson and Augmon developed a special bond of friendship that still exists.

Johnson's recruitment came down to Kansas or UNLV. He appeared to be leaning towards the Jayhawks, but just before the signing date, Brown resigned from Kansas to take the head coaching job for the San Antonio Spurs. This sort of twist of fate can make or break a coaching career. In this case, it helped make Jerry's because Johnson signed with the Runnin' Rebels.

UNLV started "The Big Year" without two of its front court players, David Butler and Moses Scurry. Each needed to finish an incomplete grade in one class to be eligible. The Rebels opened the season with two wins in the pre-season NIT. The semifinals and finals were held in New York City, Scurry's hometown.

UNLV's program was under tremendous scrutiny at the time, not only by the NCAA, but also by the local media. The UNLV professor instructing Butler and Scurry wanted to make it clear that he did not give preferential treatment to the players, so he required both to pass one last test to be eligible. There was talk all over town as to whether the players would travel to New York or not.

When Scurry came out of the classroom, a cameraman asked, "How did it go? Will you be able to travel back home and play in New York?"

"Is Ronald Reagan President?" Moses responded, in his lighthearted manner.

Problem is, Reagan wasn't the President anymore. George H. Bush was. Needless to say, neither Scurry nor Butler passed their tests and neither made the trip to New York.

Without Butler and Scurry, Kansas shocked the Rebels, 91-77. Larry Johnson was horrific. After the tournament, Jerry's brother Myron remarked, "Johnson is not nearly as good as reported."

Myron predicted the Rebels were in for a long year. As usual, Jerry's well-intentioned brother was wrong.

After the NIT, Johnson played like an All-American and UNLV started winning. But before the team could take off, the NCAA decided to intervene and expand its latest investigation of the Rebel program into every conceivable area. Investigators looked for *any excuse* to suspend a player, no matter how absurd, trifling or illogical. *Most* of the suspensions came at the last possible moment before a big game.

Investigators reviewed the team's travel records and learned that some of the players made nominal long-distance calls from their hotel rooms without paying for them. Others had eaten peanuts and other snacks from their mini bars without paying for them. The NCAA ordered UNLV to suspend eight different players for one game each because of these egregious offenses.

On one occasion, the team was *at the airport* waiting to board a plane to Baton Rouge, Louisiana, to play LSU on Super Bowl Sunday when the coaching staff was notified that Augmon and Chris Jeter were suspended from the game because they had made long distance calls on a road trip. The two were not even allowed to travel with the team, so the airline had to pull their bags off the plane. The players were humiliated. LSU beat the Rebels 107-105.

On another occasion, Greg Anthony and David Butler were walking to the locker room to get dressed for a big-league game against UC Santa Barbara when they were notified that they were suspended for unpaid hotel incidentals. Despite playing at home, UNLV won the game by only two points.

NCAA investigators examined each player's scholarship records and source of tuition payments. They learned that Anderson Hunt received a scholarship check his first year before he dropped a class and became a part-time student. As a part-time student, Hunt could not be on scholarship and, thus, he had to repay the first monthly check he had received.

When the NCAA learned that Hunt had not yet repaid it, they ordered UNLV to suspend him. The coaching staff was notified of the suspension at 11 p.m. the night before a game with Temple. The NCAA continued suspending Rebel players, reaching a climax the following year with the most ridiculous violation ever charged.

After a game against the University of Nevada, Reno, Jerry was interviewed by the media. "They [UNR's coaching staff] were saying that their players were as good as we were...," Jerry said. "It was the damndest thing... So we went out and bought a bunch of newspapers, and passed them out. We didn't have to get them [our players] fired up after that."

The NCAA ruled that since "the newspapers were purchased by coaching staff members and placed in each student-athlete's room, such an arrangement would be considered an extra benefit..." Each player was suspended until he paid 25-cents in restitution.

There was nothing the players, coaches or school could do but obey the NCAA's directives. Instead of letting the suspensions rattle them, the players banded together and derived strength from their shared adversity. They developed an "us against them" mentality and redoubled their efforts

Over the next year and half, the Rebels didn't lose a game. Paradoxically, the NCAA investigators who had promised to run Jerry out of coaching actually assisted him in winning the national championship.

UNLV faced two more crises during the season. The first occurred at the end of the Utah State game when Chris Jeter took an elbow from a Utah State player that was unobserved by the referees. In retaliation,

Jeter head-butted the Utah State player. Jerry immediately removed him from the game.

When the game ended, Jeter walked toward the tunnel. Utah State's Kendall Youngblood grabbed him by the shoulder and yelled, "If you want to hit somebody, hit me Mother Fu#%&*! Hit me Mother Fu#%&*!" So, Jeter turned and punched Youngblood squarely in the face.

Players from both teams stormed the court. Coaches, managers and security guards intervened to break up the fight. Utah State's Coach Kohn Smith, wearing his trademark sweater, grabbed Scurry who instinctively turned and punched him. After the game, reporters asked Scurry why he punched Coach Smith. "I didn't think he was a coach because he wasn't wearing a suit," Scurry replied.

A couple of games later, North Carolina State played UNLV. Before the game, Coach Valvano grabbed Jerry and asked to be introduced to Scurry, who he started to joke with. "See, I am wearing a suit," Valvano said. "I am a coach. Please don't hit me."

The fight video was played on all the local and national sports shows. Although it was only the second fight in Jerry's 17 years at UNLV, the players were portrayed as hooligans and thugs. This perception gained force when UNLV's president Robert Maxson wrote a letter apologizing to the Utah State president.

"The behavior of our players involved in the disturbance ... was inexcusable," Maxon's letter stated. "I am ashamed and embarrassed. On behalf of all of us here at UNLV, I apologize ... for that behavior. Such acts do not represent the more than 16,000 law-abiding, decent students here, who are as appalled, as I am."

Maxson disseminated the letter to the media to generate more publicity. It infuriated the players. They understood that the fight was wrong, but they felt it was equally wrong for the school president to claim they were not "law-abiding, decent students" because of one fight in which it could be fairly claimed that *both teams* had a hand in starting.

After a home game against Louisville, Maxson went into the locker room to speak with the team. At the time, Jerry was doing a television interview. When the players saw Maxson walk in, several scattered to the showers, while others hid in the toilet stalls. When Maxson spoke, one of the players repeatedly flushed the toilet. The already strained relationship between Maxson and the basketball team only got worse.

Toward year's end, UNLV traveled to Logan, Utah, for a rematch with Utah State. Emotions were so high, police asked UNLV not to practice or stay in Logan the night before the game, which was standard. Instead, UNLV stayed overnight in Salt Lake City, traveling to Logan on game day.

When the team arrived in town, their bus had a police escort. As the Rebels took the arena floor for warm-ups prior to the game, Utah State fans hurled *racial epithets* and *personal insults* at the players.

When the team returned to the locker room before tip-off, Jerry thought he was going to have to settle the players down, fearing they might be intimidated by the tough environment or angry at the insults being hurled at them by the crowd. But when he walked into the room, he found the players pounding their lockers, slapping each other on the back and exhorting each other to play hard. Jerry knew he didn't have to say a word.

Just before halftime, blue-dyed water (Aggie colors) spurted from a vent under Jerry's chair, soaking him. Utah State's student body erupted with amusement. Jerry, who was quite the prankster himself in his younger days, thought it was ingenious.

UNLV went on to win a tough, hard-fought game by two points. After, the Rebel players gave Coach Tarkanian an ice water shower in the locker room. On the bus ride back to their hotel, they donned cardboard "Tark masks" worn earlier by the Utah State student body.

The second "crisis" occurred on February 12, 1990, during the Fresno State game. While driving hard to the basket, Greg Anthony had his legs cut out from under him and fell face first several feet to the floor.

Anthony's jaw was the first part of his body to hit the court. A loud thump was followed by complete silence as the stunned crowd watched Anthony in agony, lying on the floor holding his mouth. He was taken immediately to the hospital for x-rays.

Anthony had suffered multiple jaw fractures. It was devastating news. A doctor said he would be out a minimum of three to four weeks. Whether he would be back in time for the NCAA tournament was still unclear.

The next two games on the schedule were against New Mexico State, the league leader, followed by UNLV's most bitter rival, the Arizona Wildcats.

The next day, before practice, Anthony, with a protective mask on his face and a wired mouth, walked onto the basketball court. There was dead silence when he entered, as if a ghost had risen from the dead.

Less than 24 hours after breaking his jaw in multiple places, Anthony was back practicing with the team. He was interviewed by *USA Today*.

"The doctors were telling me that if I could stand the pain, I could play," he said. "I figured it would hurt more *not* to play." With Anthony leading the team onto the court, UNLV beat New Mexico State and Arizona.

Because of the character of the players, UNLV was already a close team. Jerry stated often that Larry Johnson was a better *person* than he was a basketball player and he was a *great* basketball player. After every big play, Johnson hugged a teammate. Augmon soon followed, as did the rest of the team. Pretty soon, UNLV was leading the nation in hugs.

The team became even closer after the NCAA began its run of player suspensions. And with Anthony's display of heroism, the team was united with a determination and strength of mind that would prove to be unbeatable in the upcoming NCAA Tournament.

JT at NBA draft with UNLV stars, Larry Johnson, Stacy Augman, and Greg Anthony. All three players with lottery picks

UNLV team enjoying visit to the White House with President George H. Bush after 1990 NCAA Championship

CHAPTER 33:

REACHING THE PINNACLE OF COLLEGE BASKETBALL

"This win was not only for UNLV and Las Vegas, but for the whole State of Nevada."

—Jerry Tarkanian, on winning the 1990 NCAA
Championship game

IN ADDITION TO their basketball prowess, these Rebels were also trendsetters. In preparation for the upcoming NCAA tournament, Butler and Scurry decided to wear all black tennis shoes to illustrate that they were going to war. At that time, players typically only wore white tennis shoes with their school colors as trim. Today, colored shoes are the norm.

When Scurry came down with a rebound, he let out a big growl. When Johnson finished with a big dunk, he let out a monstrous scream. Soon, college and professional players were copying Scurry's growl and Johnson's screams.

The following season, the team started the trend of long, baggy shorts. From its inception, basketball players had worn tight, high-cut shorts. When the team first broke out the baggy shorts, there was universal disapproval from the fans. Now, every team at every level wears the long, baggy shorts started by Johnson, Augmon and company.

UNLV entered the tournament as the number one seed. After easily winning the first two rounds, the Rebels survived a scare in the Sweet 16 against an unlikely opponent, the Ball State University Cardinals. Ball State had the ball and was down by two points with 12 seconds left when David Butler intercepted a pass to preserve the win.

In the regional finals, UNLV faced the winner of the Alabama v. Loyola Marymount game. Alabama was the favorite, led by future NBA stars Robert Horry, Keith Askins and Melvin Cheatum. The Loyola Lions, however, were the sentimental favorites.

The Lions star player, Hank Gathers, had a seizure and collapsed during a game in their conference tournament. He was rushed to a hospital, but was pronounced dead on arrival of hypertrophic cardiomyopathy, a heart condition.

Loyola was the run and gun team of the early 90s. They led the nation in scoring and broke numerous NCAA scoring records, many of which had been held by the Rebels.

Alabama, with its great athletes, made the crucial mistake of not running with Loyola. When Alabama broke Loyola's full-court press, they refused to attack the basket, instead choosing to slow down the game.

This strategy played right into Loyola's hands. The Lions were able to create turnovers and easy baskets from their full-court press without having to give up easy baskets when their press was broken. Loyola won the game by two points.

In the press conference following the game, Loyola players boasted, "The 'Runnin' Rebels' can't run with us. They will need oxygen tanks if they try!"

Jerry had no intention of changing his team's style of play as Alabama had. The night before the game, he told his wife that he was sure the Rebels were going to win. He had *never* made that statement before.

Also the night before the game, Stacey Augmon received a special gift that many of us take for granted. Augmon's father, whom he had not seen since childhood, showed up unexpectedly at the hotel. The two embraced in Augmon's room and both cried.

On the drive to the arena, UNLV's bus passed Loyola's hotel. A large banner carrying Loyola's mantra "Living the Dream" hung from the wall. Greg Anthony broke Jerry's code of silence on the bus and bellowed, "We're going to wake Loyola up tonight."

When the Rebels took the court, they not only ran with Loyola, but defended them as well. UNLV beat their press, attacked the basket and scored easy layups. On the flip side, UNLV beat Loyola back on defense and stopped their fast breaks.

The Rebels were up 38 points with five minutes to play before settling for a 30-point win, and their second Final Four appearance in four years.

After the game, Loyola's coach, Paul Westhead, told Jerry that his team "played with great dignity and great class."

In post-game remarks, Loyola's starting guard Tom Peabody told the press, "I think those guys get a bum rap... I think they're a class act through and through, from the coaches all the way down to the players. They were cordial with us, and were nice, and sympathetic to what happened."

The Final Four

The 1990 Final Four was held at the McNichols Arena in Denver, Colorado. UNLV opened with Georgia Tech, led by freshman sensation Kenny Anderson.

When the team took the court for warm-ups, Georgia Tech fans chanted "Thugs! Thugs! Thugs!" and "Hoodlums! Hoodlums! Hoodlums!"

Instead of letting the taunting get to them, the Runnin' Rebels used it as motivation. Before tipoff, they huddled and chanted, "Hoodlums! Hoodlums! Hoodlums! Let's go!" and broke the huddle.

During the game, Georgia Tech's mascot ran around the court waving play money at the UNLV players. One fan barked, "Butler, your GPA matches your number!" Butler's number was 00.

The Yellow Jackets led 53-46 at the half, and when Larry Johnson picked up his fourth foul early in the second half, Rebel fans got worried. Moses Scurry replaced Johnson and played like a man possessed. He grabbed nearly every rebound and propelled the Rebels to a nine-point win, 90-81.

UNLV's first-ever national championship game was against the Duke Blue Devils, who were participating in their third Final Four in the past four years. The contrast between the images of the two programs could not have been greater.

Duke had a pristine image. Most of their players were from solid middle-class families with strong parental influence. Most graduated and few had problems off the court. The NCAA never visited their campus.

The media portrayed Duke as everything wholesome in college basketball and portrayed UNLV as a manifestation of everything *wrong* with college sports. The media and the fans came up with several clever pre-game tag lines: "Tark the Shark vs. Mr. Clean," "Preppy vs. Gaudy," "Saints vs. Sinners," "Good Guys vs. Bad Guys," "Law Students vs. Law Breakers," and perhaps the most fitting descriptor: "The Establishment vs. the Rebels."

After the Georgia Tech win, Jerry headed back to his hotel to prepare for the Blue Devils. Dick Vitale, a close friend of his, asked him to do an interview with another *ESPN* commentator. Jerry didn't want to go, but Vitale insisted until he finally relented.

One of the first questions the reporter asked was, "Coach, people are billing this game as good versus evil. What do you think?"

"I don't think that is fair at all," Jerry responded. "I know those kids on Duke's team and I think they are fine young men. People shouldn't talk that way about them."

When the focus wasn't on the players' images, it was on NCAA investigations. The day before the game, Ted Koppel interviewed Jerry on *Nightline*. One of the first questions he asked was about the newest NCAA investigation involving former Rebel recruit Lloyd Daniels.

"This year's team is 34 and 5," Jerry replied, "and [we're] playing for the school's first national championship. These are great kids with great stories. Don't you think we should talk about them?"

There was one true distinction between the Duke players and the UNLV players. While most of the Duke players had family members at the game cheering them on, not one family member from any of UNLV's black players were able to attend. They simply could not afford it.

When this was made public, several large companies offered to pay the family members' expenses. The players had to decline as it was against NCAA rules. After the avalanche of bad publicity, the NCAA received for this decision, they changed the rules and now allow a school to pay for the immediate family of players to attend the Final Four.

Chalk up yet another rule change brought about by the Tarkanian legacy. On the drive to the game, Jerry commented to his wife, "We've come a long way from Riverside Junior College, haven't we Lois?"

Before the game, legendary Chicago Bears player Walter Payton asked if he could speak to the team. The Hall of Famer was a big UNLV fan. "I see so much of myself in the way they play," Payton said. "They're aggressive and they're misunderstood. They're really a bunch of genuinely nice guys."

Payton gave an emotional and inspiring pre-game speech, one of the best Jerry had ever heard. Afterward, each player walked up to Payton and gave him a big hug before they took the court.

Nearly two thousand Rebel fans made the trip to Denver. Seven thousand more watched on two big screen TV's in the Thomas & Mack Center in Las Vegas while millions more watched the televised broadcast. On April 2, 1990, they all witnessed UNLV play the finest championship game in college basketball history.

Unlike previous big games, where it was obvious the players were fueled by emotion and caught in the moment, the players in this game had a methodical and determined look throughout.

The Rebels pressured the Blue Devils until Duke cracked, extending a 12-point halftime lead to 28 points early in the second half. The Blue Devils appeared helpless, turning the ball over again and again while showing obvious frustration at the constant pressure applied by UNLV.

"There was a moment in the second half when Bobby Hurley, Duke's point guard, appeared as if he wanted to cry," the *San Jose Mercury News* reported later. "And you couldn't blame him."

With the Rebels up by more than 30 points, Jerry slowed the action and substituted freely. The final score was 103 to 73, which remains the largest margin of victory in an NCAA Championship Game. To put it in perspective, the previous *five* national championship games were decided by a *total* of 11 points.

"Never has a team been as totally and utterly dominated in an NCAA Championship game," was the commentary in *The Denver Post*. It was the *third* 30-point win for the Rebels in the NCAA tournament. No other team has ever done this before or since.

A lasting memory from that game, one captured by *CBS* and shown throughout the years, is Moses Scurry and David Butler hugging Jerry on the sidelines, celebrating the accomplishment. Moses had his coach in a head lock. Jerry looked like a man in obvious pain, but he clearly was enjoying the moment.

The presentation of the championship trophy was an awkward scene. On a podium high above the ground, with a national television audience watching, Jim Delaney, the Chairman of the Division-I Basketball Tournament for the NCAA—the same organization that had persecuted Jerry for decades and harassed his championship team with spurious and petty suspensions—was forced to present the trophy to Coach Tarkanian and his band of Rebels.

Jerry, with his voice cracking, told the national television audience, "This win was not only for UNLV and Las Vegas, but for the whole State of Nevada!" For decades, residents of Nevada had been branded with an unfair stigma. This national championship, by the Rebels, brought a newfound sense of pride to the entire state.

On the floor of McNichols Arena, the Nevada contingent celebrated and praised their team. "What the Rebels accomplished by winning the national title was to bring instant, positive recognition to the state," Governor Bob Miller declared. "They really have a lot of character."

"This will bring a tremendous amount of prestige to the city," UNLV booster Leo Diamond stated. "We've been bad-rapped as 'bad boys' because we're Las Vegas; that we have no culture and no civic pride. We showed we have pride tonight." All the while, UNLV's president Bob Maxson shook hands with everyone within reach.

In the press conference after the game, Larry Johnson commented, "You can call us bad guys. You can call us thugs. You can call us hoodlums. But at the end of that, please call us national champions too!"

Coach Krzyzewski was gracious in defeat. "That's the best any team has ever played against me," he said in a post-game interview. "It was an incredible display of great basketball by UNLV. Their half-court defense is the best in the country—and it dictated the whole basketball game. I don't know if you realize how good they were defensively... Incredible. We could not function out there all night. They would not let us."

Coach Krzyzewski also complimented the UNLV players by saying, "Las Vegas has classy kids... Augmon and Johnson are two of the class basketball players in the United States."

The New York Times wrote, "The Runnin' Rebels will... be respected for ushering in a new decade of college basketball, by establishing a new standard for execution, discipline, uncompromising tenacity and single-mindedness of purpose."

A letter to the editor in *Sports Illustrated* stated, "They won in true Rebel style—with flash, flair, excitement and class."

Jeff German of the *Las Vegas Sun* wrote: "The Runnin' Rebels, despite the machinations of their detractors in the Eastern media, proved to the nation they aren't the 'bad boys' of college basketball. They're the class of the league. UNLV's basketball players were gentlemen on the court. They were selfless during press conferences...Their actions *contradicted* all the negative stereotypes of UNLV basketball players."

Reserve guard and future Rebel coach David Rice stated it best, 'I think if you look at all we endured, it really dispels the myth that the media tried to paint about the team. They tried to say we had no character. But, any group of guys *without* character would have folded two seasons ago. Instead, we received pressure from the NCAA, the media, the administration and because of the kind of people we are, we were able to draw closer and be even more successful."

The morning after the victory, Jerry, a first-generation Armenian-American raised during the Great Depression and whose only real interest in life was sports, was interviewed on the *Today Show* and *Good Morning America.* Only in the United States of America could this happen.

The newly crowned national champions returned home for a parade down one of the most famous streets in the world, Las Vegas Boulevard, also known as "The Strip." Ten thousand wild, enthusiastic fans filled the sidewalks. Players, coaches and family members rode in convertible cars and waved to the fans. Player's names flickered across casino marquees.

The parade ended at the Thomas & Mack Center on the UNLV campus, where a ceremony was held to honor the team. More than 19,000 fans wearing red and white T-shirts jammed into the home of the Runnin' Rebels to celebrate.

The championship game was replayed on two huge television screens. When the team walked onto the stage, they received a thunderous standing ovation that lasted for several minutes.

When Jerry followed, the players engulfed and hugged him. The "Walk Like a Tarkanian" video played while Chris Jeter imitated his coach storming the sidelines, stomping his foot. David Butler gnawed on a white towel. The crowd went nuts. The happiness was explosive.

Jerry told the deafening crowd that not only was this Rebel team number one in the country, but that the Rebel *fans* were number one as well. He proclaimed that what the Rebels did the previous night would go down in history as one of the greatest basketball performances of all time.

Butler took the microphone and told the crowd, "Next to my family, I love the hell out of the UNLV fans!"

"If the Thomas & Mack Center isn't Heaven, it sure isn't far from it!" Travis Bice declared.

When Larry Johnson took the podium, the crowd chanted, "One more year! One more year!"

"From the bottom of our hearts, we really, truly love you," Larry responded. "This championship is for you."

In that glorious moment, it was hard to imagine that these were the same kids that were so maligned by the media. Hoodlums? Very gracious winners and complete gentlemen were more like it.

President Maxson had the final say at the microphone. "I think this is wonderful," he said. "This is another step in the development of this university. The team has put the national spotlight on the city, and the university, and opens a window for us. I just love it."

After the excitement of the national championship wore off, the question was whether Larry Johnson and Stacey Augmon would return for their senior season. Most draft experts pegged Johnson one of the top two picks and Augmon as a lottery pick. The consensus was that Johnson would turn pro. The amount of money was too great to turn down. And if Johnson went, Augmon would follow as they were close.

Johnson made his announcement in Washington D.C., during the team's trip to the White House. Each player was provided blazers, but, Johnson's was too small. His large build burst through the jacket.

Larry was so embarrassed, he didn't want to visit the White House. One person after another talked to him. They told him it was a chance of a lifetime to meet the president of the United States; that he would regret missing the opportunity.

"I will make the trip next year, when we win another title," Johnson replied. That was exactly what the Rebel faithful wanted to hear.

Johnson finally relented and joined the rest of the team for the visit to meet President George H.W. Bush. It was an amazing experience for the players considering most came from poor inner-city families with bleak futures. Now they were heralded as champions, enjoyed a tour of the White House and meeting the president of the United States.

The trip was perhaps most special for David Butler, who had grown up in the projects of Washington D.C., just a few minutes away but in a whole different world. The day finished with a ceremony in the Rose Garden, where the Runnin' Rebels proudly represented UNLV, the city of Las Vegas and the State of Nevada.

CHAPTER 34:

THE BATTLE WITH THE NCAA RAGES ON

"No one was more eager than the University of Nevada, Las Vegas to end the 13-year old controversy between the NCAA and Coach Tarkanian. With all due respect, however, we think that the case was wrongly concluded."

—Robert Maxson, UNLV President

AFTER THE NATIONAL championship game, former Bruins great and current basketball analyst Bill Walton enthusiastically grabbed Jerry's son Danny and said, "Your father is going to go on a run of consecutive national championships just as John Wooden did at UCLA." With Johnson and Augmon returning, the possibility certainly existed.

The NCAA quickly made it clear that they were not going to allow that to happen. With its unlimited resources, generated mostly from proceeds derived from the men's basketball tournament, the association appealed the Nevada Supreme Court decision that barred Coach Tarkanian's 1977 NCAA-ordered suspension to the United States Supreme Court.

The NCAA boasted it had never lost a case once it was concluded and they had the legal bills to prove it. At the time of this case, the association was spending more than $1.5 million per year on litigation.

The United States Supreme Court declined to review the case on the merits, leaving in place three lower court rulings that held that the NCAA investigation and hearings failed to provide Jerry both procedural due process (procedural safeguards necessary to assure a fair hearing) and substantive due process (that the final decision is not arbitrary and capricious).

There is another element necessary to the due process clause—state action. The 14th Amendment requires only *state actors* to provide due process before it imposes disciplinary sanctions, not private organizations. Since UNLV was a state institution, it was required to provide due process before it disciplines its employees. Therefore, UNLV could not suspend Jerry, even at the direction of the NCAA. This decision was final and permanent.

The Supreme Court agreed to rule on whether the NCAA enforcement proceedings were, in fact, state action. The association's position was that it was a private organization like the Elks Club or Boy Scouts. They contended that if you don't like their rules and procedures, you are free to leave and join another similar organization.

Following this argument, although UNLV was legally prevented from suspending Jerry, the NCAA was free to sanction UNLV for failing to do so. If UNLV didn't like it, the school could drop out of the NCAA and join another organization.

The fallacy of this argument is obvious. The NCAA has a monopoly on major college sports. There is no alternative organization to join if UNLV wanted to participate in major college sports.

On October 5, 1988, the United States Supreme Court heard oral arguments in the case *Tarkanian v. NCAA*. For this, the NCAA hired one of the best attorneys in the country, former U.S. Solicitor General Rex Lee. Money was no object to the NCAA. Sam Lionel, the preeminent attorney in Las Vegas, represented Jerry.

Lionel made the logical argument that if UNLV is prevented from suspending Jerry because of the Due Process Clause of the 14th Amendment, then the NCAA should be prevented from penalizing UNLV for failing to suspend him. If this were not the case, the NCAA would be penalizing UNLV for failing to violate the United States Constitution.

Astonishingly, Justice John Paul Stevens argued that UNLV had a choice; it could withdraw from the NCAA. Lionel responded, "That would be a hollow victory, your Honor, because if UNLV withdrew from the NCAA, it would not have a major college basketball program and Tarkanian would essentially be out as a coach."

Justice Stevens shot back, "I graduated from the University of Chicago and the University of Chicago does not have major college sports and it is doing just fine." How could a person be so intelligent and so badly miss the point? Months passed with no word from the Supreme Court.

Then the decision that would change the Tarkanians' lives forever. Lois burst into her attorney son's room with tears in her eyes and her voice cracking. She stuttered, "Danny, we lost. We lost, Danny. The Supreme Court ruled against us."

In a 5-4 decision, the Supreme Court ruled that the NCAA was a private organization that did not have to afford due process to its members, even if its members are public institutions. Justice Byron White, a former running back at the University of Colorado and the only Supreme Court justice familiar with the NCAA, wrote the dissenting opinion. Surprisingly, Justices Stevens and Blackman, two of the Court's most liberal judges, ruled against the protection of individual liberty. Stevens even wrote the majority opinion.

The Supreme Court decision in *Tarkanian v. NCAA* was not a true triumph for the NCAA. The organization claimed it provided Jerry a fair hearing and ordered UNLV to suspend him. The Supreme Court concluded that this was not the case and that UNLV could not suspend him. The NCAA won the shallow victory that it is not required to provide fair hearings in its disciplinary proceedings, hardly something to boast about.

Duke University's sports law professor, John Weistart, crystallized it when he said, "Some people might pose the general theoretical question to the NCAA of, 'Well, why don't you provide due process?' And the NCAA doesn't have a good answer."

The Supreme Court decision posed a serious dilemma for the NCAA. It wanted Jerry removed as coach, but it couldn't force his ouster. What would be their next move?

On May 1, 1990, *twenty-nine* days after UNLV's national championship, Stephen Morgan, Executive Director of Enforcement for the NCAA, sent UNLV a letter requesting it to "show-cause why additional penalties should not be imposed upon the University, if it does not make complete severance with its relationship with Jerry Tarkanian" as originally ordered in 1977.

UNLV responded that it *had* suspended Jerry, but that it could not *enforce* the suspension because it is permanently barred from doing so by the final court order.

Incredulously, on July 19, 1990, the infractions committee concluded otherwise and banned UNLV's team from post-season play. With four starters back, UNLV was the consensus number one team in the country and the odds-on favorite to win back-to-back national championships.

With UNLV banned from postseason play, all of the seniors— Larry Johnson, Stacey Augmon, Greg Anthony and George Ackles— could have transferred to another school and been eligible immediately. Several schools contacted them in an effort to get them to transfer. None of them even considered it. Each remained loyal to UNLV, to their coach and to each other. Their loyalty stunned the pundits, but not the people who knew their unimpeachable character.

Loyalty was the most important human quality to Jerry. He often stated he would rather have a kid who steals than a kid who is disloyal. He reasoned, "You can always teach a kid not to steal, but you can't teach a disloyal kid to be loyal."

He also understood that loyalty was a two-way street. He knew it was imperative for a coach to show loyalty to his players before he could expect loyalty from them. Throughout his career, Jerry supported his players under tough circumstances, often to his detriment. Many times, he was vilified for his unwavering support. His players always showed loyalty in return.

There was widespread condemnation of the NCAA decision banning UNLV from postseason play. Former UNLV players rushed to Jerry's defense.

"I am sorry he lost because I know he did absolutely nothing wrong when I was there," Glen Gondrezick stated.

"It's a personal thing, the accusations against UNLV are 'shabby,'" Reggie Theus declared.

"I never got any money or any car from anybody," Billy Cunningham said, "and, as far as I know, neither did anybody else when I played there."

UNLV *fans* expressed their outrage too. Forty students dropped their pants during a mass photo shoot and then sent the dubious "mooning" image to the NCAA to protest the decision.

Kansas Coach Roy Williams had the rare courage among coaches to speak out. "It is obvious that a vendetta exists against UNLV Coach Jerry Tarkanian ... They're after Tark; there's no doubt about it," he deduced.

Even media members, who were often anti-Tarkanian, blasted the unfairness of the decision and the impact it had on current players.

"The NCAA... is supposed to be fair and credible and, above all, not let personal vendettas get in the way," *Orlando Sentinel* columnist Brian Schmitz wrote. "The case against Tarkanian reeks of vindictiveness."

As a result of the Supreme Court decision, several states introduced bills requiring the NCAA to provide due process in its enforcement procedures involving their state institutions. In response, the NCAA commenced a smothering lobbying blitz to stop the legislation. Schools were threatened with expulsion from the NCAA *if their state passed the law*. As a result, most states dropped the legislation.

Nevada was an exception. It passed the bill into law. The NCAA challenged the constitutionality of the bill and restated its threat to expel UNLV.

Nevada's Attorney General Frankie Sue Del Papa cowered under the threat and refused to defend the bill's constitutionality. The attorney for the university system, Donald Klasic, backed down as well, stating: "It will do us the least damage." The NCAA had *everyone* running scared.

With no support from the state itself, U.S. District Judge Howard McKibben declared the due process bill unconstitutional. As a result, there is no law in America requiring the NCAA to provide fair hearings in its enforcement proceedings.

Just when it appeared that there was no hope and that the defending national champions were going to be denied an opportunity to defend their title, Larry Johnson and Stacy Augmon made the NCAA blink. They retained lawyers who notified the NCAA that if it did not lift the ban on the Rebels, it would face a multi-million-dollar personal lawsuit from these players.

The players' argument was that the NCAA indicated (in previous testimony to Congress) that it would *not* further penalize UNLV for failing to violate a valid court order. Johnson and Augmon had relied upon those statements made by the NCAA in making their decision to return to UNLV to repeat as national champions, and possibly improve their positions in the draft.

The time to enter the draft in 1991 had already passed by the time the NCAA banned the team from postseason play. Without the chance to participate in the NCAA tournament, there was a strong likelihood that Johnson and Augmon's *value* would drop in the draft and they would lose millions of dollars in inherent value. The legal theory is called "Tortious interference with prospective economic advantage" and, apparently, it frightened the NCAA.

The NCAA was presented with a real dilemma. They didn't want the Rebels to win another title and start a dynasty under the guidance of Jerry Tarkanian. They also realized that they could lose a very expensive lawsuit which would result in a public relations nightmare. The NCAA concluded it could not stop the team from repeating, but it *could* stop the dynasty from materializing.

On November 19th, the eve of the season opener, the NCAA reversed its decision and lifted their ban so the Rebels could play in the 1991 NCAA Tournament. But the ban from tournament play and an additional ban from appearing on television would be enforced *the following year*.

In addition to this most recent penalty imposed upon UNLV, the NCAA enforcement staff was in the fourth year of yet another Tarkanian investigation—regarding the recruitment of New York City legend, Lloyd Daniels. In their exhaustive search, the NCAA investigation had expanded into every aspect of the UNLV basketball program.

Almost twenty years earlier, the NCAA declared it was going to run Jerry out of coaching. It was obvious they were not going to let up until they finished the job.

At some point, President Maxson decided he needed to get rid of Coach Tarkanian. The reason and timing of this decision has been fiercely debated in the Las Vegas community.

One possible theory is Maxson felt the University could not continue to do battle with the NCAA *and* create the new image of Las Vegas he wished to promote. Maxson realized that the only way to get the NCAA off of the University's back was to get rid of Jerry.

With the success of the basketball program, removing Jerry was not going to be easy. Maxson and his cohorts needed a plan that would make it seem the university *had no choice* but to fire him. And the university had to come out looking like the "good guys" while Jerry and his program would play the role of "bad guys."

The strategy was simple. Maxson would make it a choice between academics or athletics. For the university to survive, academics had to prevail. It is hard to argue against that.

Maxson, with the help of others, was going to look like the brave university president facing the wrath of a community absorbed by its widely successful basketball program, but one that had run off course and was out of control.

Bob Sands, from the *Las Vegas Review Journal*, reported:

> *Now the battle cry is: We've got to clean up this mess in the UNLV athletic department and project UNLV as a growing, viable educational institution... Make no mistake about this.*

Maxson is perceptually wearing the white hat in this one...Look, Tarkanian is a helluva guy, and a helluva coach. But he carries considerable baggage from the past indiscretions, perceived or real. Maxson wants to present what he believes is a cleaner image.

For Maxson's strategy to work, the basketball program had to be perceived as corrupt and out of control. The NCAA was doing its part in creating this image, but more was needed.

After the 1990 season, Brad Rothermel, a close friend and ally of Jerry, stepped down as athletic director. Maxson quickly replaced him with Dennis Finfrock, a former wrestling coach with no experience in athletic administration. Within days after his appointment, Finfrock scheduled a meeting with Jerry and asked him to resign.

"Jerry, you can be a hero," Finfrock implored, but Jerry angrily refused. He told Finfrock he had fought the NCAA for decades. He had done nothing wrong and wasn't about to quit now.

When Jerry refused to "be a hero," Finfrock enlisted the aid of his Assistant Athletic Director Sheila Bolla and her husband, Women's Basketball Coach Jim Bolla. This covert team commenced a clandestine public relations campaign designed to weaken Jerry in the eyes of community leaders.

Over the next two years, the terrible threesome met with the power brokers of Las Vegas, fabricating stories and providing misinformation concerning Coach Tarkanian and his program.

The *Miami Herald* wrote:

UNLV once was a happy and defiant family, proud of its refusal to wilt under the NCAA's full-court press of Tarkanian. But out of obvious fear of more NCAA retribution, the family has left the side of the patriarch...UNLV's hierarchy has done everything except enter an NCAA witness protection program...Considering what Tarkanian has provided for UNLV, you'd think school officials would share the blindfold.

Nevertheless, there remained one huge obstacle: the success of the basketball team. The Runnin' Rebels entered the 1990-91 season as the favorites to repeat as national champions. It would be difficult to remove Jerry if they did.

Big UNLV boosters, Irwin and Susan Molasky with JT before UNLV game

CHAPTER 35:

THE QUEST TO REPEAT

"Everywhere you go, it's Rebels, Rebels, Rebels—the supermarkets, the workplace, the taverns."

—from the *Las Vegas Review-Journal*

THE 1990-91 RUNNIN' Rebel team was a juggernaut. It included Final Four MVP Anderson Hunt, three future lottery picks (Johnson, Augmon and Greg Anthony) and the return of George Ackles, who had been a starter two years before. Given this lineup, the Rebels were everyone's pick to repeat as NCAA champions.

When the season began, the team proved worthy of their many accolades, destroying one good team after another. They beat Michigan State in Detroit by 20 points. They beat a good Princeton team by 34. They beat Fresno State by 49, Alabama Birmingham by 41, Rutgers by 42, Florida State by 32, Louisville by 12...the list went on and on. The pundits started to compare the Rebels to the greatest teams of all time.

The biggest game of the regular season was against the University of Arkansas in Fayetteville. Arkansas was ranked number 2 in the country and UNLV was number 1. As with the Rebels, Arkansas returned most of its starters from its previous Final Four team. The game was billed as the biggest regular season game since UCLA, when

Lew Alcindor (Kareem Abdul Jabbar) played in Houston, and with Elvin Hayes.

The game was so big and the hype so strong that the Fayetteville airport was littered with private jets of Vegas boosters. Arkansas provided UNLV with only 59 tickets, none of which were good seats. UNLV couldn't satisfy the ticket requests for many of its most important boosters.

Finfrock allocated the best tickets to people close to Maxson and himself, providing the worst tickets to boosters close to Jerry. This included Irwin Molasky, one of Las Vegas' largest real estate developers and Freddie Glusman, the owner of one of Las Vegas' most popular restaurants.

Finfrock and Glusman hated each other. The night before the game, Finfrock mocked Glusman about the bad seats he was provided. "No matter where you're sitting, I guarantee you, we'll have better seats," Glusman responded. Finfrock stormed out of the restaurant.

Irwin Molasky knew the top people at CBS, who were televising the game, from his days as owner of Lorimar Productions. CBS arranged for extra chairs to be placed behind UNLV's bench for Molasky and his friends, which included Glusman.

There was tight security at the game, which was attended by the future President Bill Clinton. A pass was required to enter the team's locker room and a security guard was stationed outside the door checking passes. Molasky and Glusman were provided passes by CBS.

Molasky went in first, Finfrock was right behind. The security guard stopped Finfrock and asked for his pass. He told the guard he didn't have one, but that he was the school's athletic director. The security guard refused to allow him in.

Suddenly, Glusman bumped into Finfrock and showed his pass to the security guard. Glusman apologized to Finfrock and smugly said, "Dennis, if you need a pass, I have extras," flashing a handful of extra passes at him. A furious Finfrock never got into the locker room.

Fuming, Finfrock waited for the team to exit. As the team re-entered the court for the last two minutes of warm-ups, Finfrock grabbed Jerry and angrily scolded him, demanding to know how Glusman had seats behind the bench and passes to the locker room.

Jerry was stunned. He was about to play the biggest regular season game in school history and, seconds before tip-off, he was being chastised by his athletic director about seating arrangements.

Arkansas started the game with a vengeance, leading by four at the half. UNLV, however, used one of its patented runs in the second half to open up a 23-point lead with 6:23 left before Jerry freely substituted, allowing the Razorbacks to close within seven points. It turned out to be the only regular season game the Rebels didn't win by double digits.

After the game, the *L.A. Times* asked Coach Richardson what he learned from the loss. "I didn't learn anything I didn't already know..." Richardson responded. "[The Rebels] should be ranked second in the country . . . *in the NBA.*"

Although they were not ranked 2nd in the NBA, UNLV did retain its number one *collegiate* ranking for the entire season. The Rebels finished the regular season 30-0.

There was tremendous excitement throughout Las Vegas for the upcoming NCAA tournament. The Rebels had a chance to create history, to be the first team to repeat as national champions since UCLA did it in 1973. And to be the first team to finish the entire season undefeated since Indiana in 1976.

The *Las Vegas Review Journal* wrote, "Runnin' Rebel fever—that highly infectious but benign, communitywide phenomenon—is upon us with a vengeance. Everywhere you go, it's Rebels, Rebels, Rebels—the supermarkets, the workplace, the taverns."

March Madness, 1991

It was no surprise that UNLV was the top seed in the NCAA tournament. However, Jerry was shocked when he learned the Runnin' Rebels' second round opponent would be the powerful Georgetown Hoyas, led by future NBA all-stars Alonzo Mourning, Dikembe Mutombo and Hall of Fame Coach John Thompson. Normally, the top seed has a relatively easy second round opponent. To make matters worse, the game was played in Tucson, Arizona, where the hatred for the Rebels permeated the entire community.

When the starting lineups were announced at the game, a deafening roar erupted for the Georgetown Hoyas. The Runnin' Rebels got hissing and booing from the same crowd. Coach Thompson remarked that, for the first time in his coaching career, the Hoyas were the crowd favorite *on the road*.

The game was less entertaining than the atmosphere. Georgetown slowed the pace while trying to maximize the talents of its two seven-foot players. They kept the score close, but UNLV prevailed 62 to 54.

After the game, the Rebel players decided to have some fun with their arch rivals, the Arizona Wildcats. A trophy with half of a basketball was hanging from the wall of the locker room. The players decided it would be a nice gesture to autograph the ball.

On the next day of practice, Arizona players were furious when they entered their locker room and saw Larry Johnson, Stacy Augmon and the rest of the Rebels' signatures on the ball.

UNLV breezed through its next two games to earn its third trip to the Final Four in five years, and a semifinal rematch with the Duke Blue Devils. The media continued its comparison of the teams as "good versus evil" – all that was good in college basketball against all that was bad.

Before the game, Bill Benner of the *Indianapolis Star* wrote that his 8-year-old daughter asked him who was going to win the Final Four. He told her that UNLV would probably win. "The kids at school say they cheat," she replied. "They say they buy their players."

Jerry had four teams participate in the Final Four. Each was dogged by these same types of malicious misperceptions.

Duke had a better team than the previous year. They returned most of their key players, including center Christian Laettner and guard Bobby Hurley. Plus, they added freshman sensation, Grant Hill.

Jerry was one of the few people who worried about the rematch. He noted that several of the Duke players were from successful athletic families. He knew that they were competitive, that they had waited a year to prove the previous season's thrashing was a fluke and that they would play with boundless determination and emotion.

Jerry was also concerned about a key matchup. The previous year, Laettner, a great shooter for a power forward, was guarded by Johnson, who had the quickness to defend him on the perimeter. The second year, Laettner moved to the center position and UNLV's center, George Ackles, did not have the agility and quickness to guard him on the perimeter.

Duke also made a key defensive assignment. Instead of guarding Ackles away from the basket, Ackles' defender stayed down low to double team Johnson. Ackles was not a good outside shooter and was not generally a threat to score from there.

Jerry did not want to keep Ackles inside because it would have prevented Johnson from posting up. He countered by having Ackles set ball picks for Anthony at the top of the key. Since no one was guarding Ackles, there was no one to step out and stop the ball pick. Anthony either had a clear shot or a drive to the basket. Duke, however, believed it had a better chance winning with Anthony shooting than Johnson scoring down low.

Duke was also better prepared for UNLV's amoeba zone defense. The previous year, Duke had no idea how to attack this defense because no other team in the country had played it. In the rematch, Duke had a year to prepare.

As Jerry had predicted, the game was close. Everyone expected the Rebels to go on one of their runs and pull away, but they never did. With 3:51 to go, UNLV was up by three points when Anthony drove to the basket and lifted a high arc shot off the backboard. Just as the shot left his hand, a Duke player stepped in front of him. There was a collision and the whistle blew just as the ball went into the basket.

The referee's decision was critical. If the call was ruled a block, the score would count and Anthony would shoot one free throw. If the call was ruled a charge, the basket wouldn't count and Duke would be given the ball with Anthony fouling out of the game.

There was hushed anticipation for the call, and then, referee Ed Hightower whistled *a charge*. The Blue Devil fans exploded in wild celebration. Instead of a possible 6-point Rebel lead, Duke would get the ball back with only a three point deficit to overcome...and Anthony was out of the game.

With 2:16 to play, Hunt, who replaced Anthony at the point, failed to cover the top of the key in the amoeba zone, leaving Hurley wide open for a three-point shot that tied the game.

Duke got the ball back with less than a minute to play and the score tied. Grant Hill drove the lane, but missed a running layup. Laettner grabbed the rebound and was fouled. He calmly sank both free throws.

Duke now had to protect a meager 2-point lead. With 12.7 seconds to play, UNLV inbounded the ball under the Blue Devils' basket while Duke full-court pressed.

With the court spread, Johnson received a pass in the front court. Instead of driving to the basket to tie the game, he passed to Hunt at the three-point line to go for the win.

Anderson Hunt, last year's Final Four MVP, caught the ball and went up for a game-winning shot. Two Duke players ran toward him contesting his shot and forced him to put more arc on the ball than he had intended. The ball ricocheted off the backboard, just out of reach of the outstretched hands of UNLV's Evric Gray.

The horn sounded and the game was over. Duke upset UNLV, ending their 45-game winning streak which was the fourth-longest ever.

ESPN reported that after Hunt missed what would have been the Rebel's winning shot, NCAA enforcement chief and Jerry's nemesis, David Berst, who was watching the game in the stands, jumped up excitedly and thrust both of his arms into the air. "The drinks are on me!" he cried joyously.

Berst later tried to deny the story, but several other reporters confirmed that he had made the statement.

Jerry was heartbroken from the loss. He felt pain for the players who had sacrificed so much, endured so much and given so much. He spent the night in his hotel room with his good friend Mike Toney and cried. It was the only time Jerry ever cried after a loss.

JT with Santa Barbara coach Jerry Pimm

CHAPTER 36:

FORCED TO RESIGN

"One man cannot beat a bureaucracy. I don't care how wrong it is... this is what they [the NCAA] have been fighting for, all along."

—Lonnie Wright, quoted from *the Las Vegas Sun*

THE RUNNIN' REBEL family was devastated from the loss—the players, the coaches and the fans. The city of Las Vegas was like a morgue. Las Vegans were searching for answers—any answers—something, anything that would make sense of this most devastating loss. From this atmosphere of despair, of failing to win a second national championship, a specious rumor emerged.

An "anonymous source" claimed that Stacey Augmon had thrown the basketball game and was seen crying in the locker room afterward. Jerry was later told that Dennis Finfrock was the source of this information.

Augmon had a bad game, certainly, but he was matched against future NBA All-Star Grant Hill, who caused a lot of people to have bad games. The rumor was preposterous, of course, but as with even the most outrageous rumors, many people believed it as truth.

Augmon had already passed up millions of dollars from the NBA to return to UNLV with the hope of repeating as national champions. Why would he throw the Final Four game and deprive himself of the reason he returned? He could have never made enough money throwing a game to offset his losses by passing up the NBA and coming back to school.

Further, there was no unusual movement in the betting line. Had there been an unusual surge of money bet on Duke, the line would have changed. The story was ridiculous and nothing ever came of it. But, at the time, with everyone reeling from the loss, it was both devastating and heartbreaking.

This rumor proved to be the first in a wave of ridiculous and malicious stories leaked to the media to discredit Jerry and his players. Emotions and passions ran high. Logic had no place for what transpired. Flames were fanned by rumors, most of which were started by UNLV administrators.

Following up on the point shaving allegation, several news stories focused on contacts UNLV players had with a man named Richard Perry. Perry was from New York and coached a summer league basketball team on which Moses Scurry played. The two established a friendship. When Perry moved to Vegas, he re-established his relationship with Scurry.

Unbeknownst to anyone at the time, Perry had been convicted of point shaving Boston College games in 1978-79. He soon thereafter acquired the nickname Richard "The Fixer" Perry. To distance himself from his past, Perry changed his first name to Sam.

When Perry's past was made public in Vegas, Jerry warned his players not to socialize with him anymore. After the Duke loss, a seed was planted in the public's mind that maybe, *just maybe*, UNLV players had thrown the game and Perry was somehow involved.

The local media ran one story after another linking Perry to the basketball program. Most, if not all, came directly from the UNLV administration led by Finfrock, at the behest of Maxson.

A local newspaper ran a front page story on Perry with a picture of him sitting at a UNLV game in seats assigned to Jerry. The night before the story ran, the reporter called Jerry for comment. He swore he didn't know how Perry got the tickets and that he did not give them to him. As part of Jerry's contract, he was provided a substantial number of tickets to UNLV home games, which he distributed to coaches, their families, casino personnel, a variety of charities and other people who supported the program.

Sitting next to Perry at the UNLV game was local attorney, David Chesnoff. After the story ran, Jerry called him and asked how he got the tickets. Chesnoff told him that he had <u>won</u> the tickets at a charity event. He asked Perry to accompany him to the game because Perry was his client. The facts were innocent enough but, with the frenzy engulfing the program, once the story was printed, the damage was done.

It was later disclosed that Dennis Finfrock ordered his staff at the Thomas & Mack Center to search through *thousands of pictures* of fans at UNLV games in an effort to find Perry at one of the games. Finfrock even provided magnifying glasses to his staff to help in their search.

Incredulously, Nevada tax dollars, which paid the salaries of Finfrock and his employees, were spent in an effort to destroy the most successful and profitable athletic program the university has ever had.

And there was more to it than just leaking photos and misinformation. The stories were *timed*, usually a couple of days apart, and always at the end of the day so Jerry did not have time to discover the true facts or prepare a rebuttal.

The foundation for this assault was laid in advance. Maxson, Finfrock and Sheila and Jim Bolla had spent the previous year cultivating relationships with the Las Vegas power brokers; the bank presidents, real estate developers and casino owners.

These power brokers were told that what was being made public was only the tip of the iceberg; that there was much more out there that would destroy Jerry if it were made public and that it was in the best interests of the university, and even for Jerry, for him to be removed as coach.

The behind-the-scenes whispering and continual stories planted in the media by the administration were effective. Although the typical blue collar sports fans still supported Jerry, he was losing the support of the city's most influential citizens, including the most powerful casino owners at the time, Steve and Elaine Wynn.

In the midst of this barrage of salacious stories, rumors and outright lies, Jerry met with long-time friend Irwin Molasky. For years, Molasky had been one of the most influential persons in Las Vegas.

At the meeting, Molasky warned Jerry not to get into a fight with the Wynns, that it was a fight he could not survive. He did not tell Jerry, however, how to defend himself in a fight which he did not choose. Jerry left the meeting with the impression that Molasky did not think he could survive the onslaught.

Next, Jerry called long-time friend and supporter, Sig Rogich, for his opinion and advice. Rogich assured Jerry that he would do everything he could to make the *transition* as easy as possible for him. That was not exactly what Jerry wanted to hear.

On May 26, 1991, the *Las Vegas Review Journal* printed an undated picture of Moses Scurry, David Butler and Anderson Hunt in a hot tub with Richard "The Fixer" Perry. The players have maintained that the picture was taken <u>before</u> Perry's background became known, and before Jerry warned them not to associate with him.

Coming on the heels of the ridiculous point shaving allegation and the benign story of Perry's basketball tickets, the "Hot Tub" story resulted in an astonishing barrage of condemnation of Jerry, despite its lack of relevance.

There was never any indication or *even an allegation that* Scurry, Butler or Hunt was involved in point shaving or any other illegal or improper activities. In fact, Butler and Scurry had already graduated and were not even *on the team* when Duke upset UNLV; Hunt was the leading scorer for the Rebels in that game. At worst, these players were hanging out with an old friend who had an unsavory, but also unknown, past.

Late one night, after the story ran, UNLV's legal counsel, Brad Booke, called Jerry and asked him to come by his office to go over the university's response to the NCAA's latest allegations. When Jerry arrived at the meeting, he was told President Maxson would be joining them. When Maxson arrived, he told Jerry the hot tub picture was a big problem. "You ought to resign Jerry," Booke implored. "Be a hero. Go out on top."

"If you don't resign…it could reach the point I'll have to fire you," Maxson added.

Jerry was stunned by the ambush of these two. He realized that there was an ongoing effort to discredit him and to force him to resign. But he didn't think "the movement" had yet reached that critical point, particularly over the meaningless hot tub picture.

On the drive home, Jerry called his son Danny. His voice cracking and with long pauses, Jerry said, "Danny, I just left a meeting with Maxson. He asked me to resign."

Danny's heart raced and he started to hyperventilate. He couldn't breathe. He jumped in his car and drove as fast as he could to his parent's home.

When he arrived, his parents were meeting with their close friend and attorney, Chuck Thompson, to discuss the situation. Thompson felt there was no way Maxson would make a move without the support of the Board of Regents. He suggested they wait and see how the story played out.

As expected, Maxson called an emergency session of the board to discuss the basketball program and, more particularly, Jerry's future. Thompson was right. Maxson was going to ask the Regents to support his decision to fire Jerry.

It was immediately clear that two Southern Nevada Regents, Joe Foley and Carolyn Sparks, were firmly in Maxson's corner. Two others, Lonnie Hammargren and Shelley Berkley, were firmly in Jerry's. Jerry had no idea how the Northern Regents lined up, but he was not optimistic.

After much contemplation, Jerry reached the conclusion that he would not survive the Regents meeting. He decided, instead of being fired, to offer his resignation effective the end of the following year.

He made a good decision. The closed-door Regents meeting was a complete ambush. UNLV's legal counsel Brad Booke, who had defended the basketball program in the past, now claimed it was out of control and had committed serious NCAA violations which could possibly lead to the death penalty. So thorough was the misinformation campaign, Jerry commented that he wouldn't have faulted any of the Regents for wanting to fire him after Booke's presentation.

As word spread about the troubles, it was heartwarming to see the response of so many former players. Sidney Green and Armon Gilliam flew to Vegas to support their coach and asked to speak at the Regents meeting. Both were denied.

"He's [Tarkanian] probably helped out his players more than any coach I know," Lonnie Wright told the *Las Vegas Sun*. "But one man cannot beat a bureaucracy. I don't care how wrong it is…this is what they [the NCAA] have been fighting for all along."

Assistant coach Tim Grgurich and many Rebel players lobbied outside the conference room for Jerry. Though, all of the lobbying in the world couldn't change the outcome.

On June 8, 1991, a mere 14 months after winning the national championship, Jerry announced his resignation as UNLV's coach effective the end of the following season. "I hope my teams and staff will be remembered as being hard-working and dedicated," Jerry said with humble pride, "having great love for each other and *great loyalty* to the university and the Las Vegas community."

Steve Carp of the *Las Vegas Sun* wrote, "Fifteen months ago, Tarkanian was on top of the world. Today, he looks to end a fabulous career with a modicum of grace and dignity."

JT with UNLV greats, Stacey Augman and Larry Johnson, on night UNLV retired the players' jerseys

295

CHAPTER 37:

TARK'S FINAL SEASON AS A REBEL

"The University cut off his balls and then threw him a party."

—Myron, Jerry's brother

A LITTLE OVER a year before, the Governor of Nevada, the president of UNLV and everyday Nevadans were praising Coach Tarkanian and his band of Rebels, exalting their character and the accomplishments of the basketball program. The city of Las Vegas held a parade to honor the same coaches, players and program that were now being branded an "embarrassment to the university." What changed?

They failed to repeat as national champions and three players were caught socializing with an old friend who had an unsavory past. Old Las Vegas would have understood, but times were changing.

Northern Regent Jill Derby, whom Jerry had never met, called him to apologize for what had happened. She was in tears. Southern Regent Joe Foley, on the other hand, said, "If Jerry leaves without a fight, we will build a museum and honor him. But, if he fights us, we will eliminate any memory of him."

Over the next 15 years, UNLV did just that. The school made no reference to the great tradition Jerry built. There was no picture of him hanging in the Thomas & Mack Center. There was no *Jaws* music, nor was there an accompanying shark clap at Rebel games. There was no longer anything related to Jerry Tarkanian—nothing. It was as though the man who had placed UNLV on the national athletic map had never existed.

The events caused a dramatic rift within the former UNLV family. You were either with Tarkanian or you were with Maxson, and the division affected players, fans and friends alike. Four of the six senior players graduated, but all four refused to walk at graduation ceremonies because they didn't want to shake Maxson's hand.

Johnson, Augmon and Anthony did their best to distance themselves from the university. For years, none of the players attended a UNLV event and they refused to have their numbers retired. Larry Johnson even made sure his NBA basketball card listed his college as Odessa Junior College, not UNLV.

All three players changed their jersey number in the NBA to number 2, in honor of Jerry, who had worn that number when he played college ball at Fresno State. Jersey numbers are given almost a sacred regard by athletes, so it was a deeply meaningful gesture to Jerry and one he never forgot.

Jerry's forced resignation also divided the city's two newspapers. Maxson had the support of the largest one. Sherman Fredericks, publisher of the *Las Vegas Review Journal,* wrote: "The nation…saw a young school stand up, and in effect say, 'a good university is more than a good basketball team.' That bravery surprised the country… Because people were willing to stand up for the ultimate integrity of the University, UNLV became a national symbol of academic fortitude."

Tarkanian had the support of the smaller, *locally owned* newspaper. Ruthie Deskin of the *Las Vegas Sun* wrote: "I find it repugnant that [Coach Tarkanian] has been treated so savagely."

The community itself was also divided. Maxson had the support of many of the city's power brokers. Jerry's supporters, for the most part, had less money and less influence, but they were determined and tenacious. They began a grass-roots campaign to try to get him restored as head coach.

More than 30,000 people signed a petition asking the Board of Regents to rip up Jerry's resignation. Local attorney, Pat Clary, and a group of blue collar citizens formed the Committee to Save Tarkanian. Nevertheless, there was nothing anyone could do to restore him as coach of the Runnin' Rebels.

Despite the "civil war" raging throughout the city, Jerry still had one last season to coach. But his resignation wasn't going to end the administration's attacks. During the summer, Finfrock tried to catch Assistant Coach Tim Grgurich working out with current players, which was an NCAA violation.

Grgurich was considered the premier development coach in the country, largely credited with turning Sidney Green and Armon Gilliam into top draft picks. His workouts were so intense that former Rebel Greg Goorjian termed the phrase "Grg-outs" instead of workouts because Grg-outs were much tougher.

During the summer, Finfrock notified a local television station that Grgurich was training current UNLV players at Bishop Gorman High School. A film crew went to the school in an effort to catch him but, much to their embarrassment, they found Grgurich working out *former* players from several different colleges preparing for the NBA camp. This was not a NCAA violation.

In the fall, UNLV's basketball team participated in a conditioning course. It was open to the student body in general, but usually only scholarship players and students attempting to walk on the team joined the class. It was too demanding.

The class consisted of three weeks of running outside on the track and three weeks of conditioning inside the gym. Virtually every day on the track, at least one player threw up. After one running session, Spoon James complained that, "even the cops in Baltimore don't chase you that long!"

Many credited the conditioning class as a key instrument in turning the Rebel program around. It was so grueling and demanding that it brought the whole team together and instilled Rebel Pride in each player. Rebel Pride meant that no one outworked the Rebels. No one!

Grgurich supervised the class and, in the fall of 1991, varied its structure because there were so many new players on the team. He finished the indoor part of the class with the team running a simulated fast break using a rolled up towel as a basketball. This type of activity was not allowed under NCAA rules.

In order to catch Grgurich committing this most egregious offense, UNLV's legal counsel Brad Booke hired a student worker to go in a back room, climb a twenty-foot ladder, enter an air conditioning duct, crawl another 15 feet on his belly and secretly film UNLV's conditioning class through the grill.

When the student worker filmed the simulated fast break, Booke was ecstatic. He had finally caught the basketball program red-handed violating an NCAA rule. The NCAA declared the workout a secondary violation and reprimanded Grgurich. The covert action backfired as the public was repulsed by Booke's tactics.

Entering the 1990-91 season, UNLV lost one of the great senior classes in college basketball history when Larry Johnson, Stacey Augmon, Greg Anthony and George Ackles all graduated.

In addition, Anderson Hunt decided to forgo his senior season since the Rebels were under NCAA sanctions and could not participate in the NCAA tournament or in televised games and entered the NBA draft. As a result, the Rebels started the season with a whole new lineup.

Because of the program's recent success, the Rebels started to attract some of the best players in the country. In 1991, the number one high school player in the nation, Ed O'Bannon, and fellow high school All-American, Sean Tarver, committed to UNLV.

When UNLV forced Jerry to resign, both players backed out of their commitments and signed with UCLA. With O'Bannon and Tarver, the Bruins won the 1995 National Championship, its only title since John Wooden's retirement.

In addition to O'Bannon and Tarver, future NBA All-Star Jason Kidd announced as a freshman in high school that he was going to attend UNLV. After Jerry's departure, he attended the University of California at Berkley, leading the Golden Bears to its greatest season in 30 years.

Michigan's Fab-Five member Jalen Rose attended the same high school as Anderson Hunt and idolized him. Rose told everyone he wanted to be a Rebel. Instead, he led Michigan to two straight national championship games.

UNLV, from the paltry Big West Conference, was on the verge of an improbable dynasty. Great high school players all over the country wanted to join the Rebels. "We may not have dominated the suburban kids," UNLV's recruiting coordinator Mark Warkentien said, "but we *owned* the urban kids. They all wanted to be Rebels."

Even without signing any new players, Jerry entered his final season with a formidable crew. The 1991-92 Runnin' Rebels were led by scoring phenomenon Isaiah J.R. Rider, swingmen Dexter Boney and Evric Gray, as well as 7'0' center Elmore Spencer. But because the Rebels were banned from televised games and postseason tournaments, few basketball fans ever saw this great team play.

Jerry tried to make light of the situation. He told a gathering at a booster luncheon that "our administration felt so bad we weren't on TV, they decided to videotape our practices."

UNLV opened its home season with a huge win over nationally ranked LSU in front of a capacity crowd at the Thomas & Mack Center. Spencer thoroughly outplayed LSU's great center, Shaquille O'Neal.

Then the team lost two of its next three games on the road. After the second loss, Jerry gathered the players in the locker room. "I know you guys are down..." he said sincerely, "but if you want, and you work hard, you can win all of the rest of your games."

Jerry's son Danny thought his dad had lost it, that the stress had finally gotten to him. But Coach Tarkanian did what he did best. He made bold adjustments, including scrapping his pressure man-to-man defense and returning to the 1-2-2 zone he made famous at Long Beach State. UNLV responded by winning its last 23 games and finished the season 26 and 2, ranked 7th in the country with two first place votes.

The team was playing so well at the end of the season, the coaching staff was convinced that they could have won the national championship. Unfortunately, no one will ever know because of the NCAA sanctions. Jerry finished second for AP Coach of the Year honors.

UNLV's final home game was against Utah State. Before the game, the university hosted a ceremony for Coach Tarkanian. His entire family, former players and former coaches attended. "The University cut off his balls and then threw him a party," Jerry's brother Myron wryly remarked.

When Jerry's name was announced, the sell-out crowd of 18,944 fans gave him a standing ovation that lasted more than 10 minutes. You could see the tears swell up in his eyes. It had an indelible effect upon the entire Tarkanian family.

The team ran onto the court wearing jet black warm-up shirts with the name "Tark" on it and "#2" on the back. Susan Molasky and other long-time fans from "Gucci Row" wore black shirts with "Tark" on the front.

"I feel terrible," Susan said sadly. "I've been following Jerry's teams on the road for 19 years and this is one of the saddest nights of my life. I think it's terrible what they did to the program."

"This night is one of the saddest moments for this community," Sig Rogich commented.

A banner hanging from the rafters stated: "Axe Max."

Hundreds of fans wore "Keep Tark, Fire Maxson" t-shirts. Beach balls imprinted with the same slogan were batted around the arena.

During the game, two students carrying a "Fire Maxson" banner ran around the floor to a deafening cheer until security officers confiscated it. They wrestled the students to the ground while the crowd booed.

At halftime, a sign was displayed in the outer concourse stating "Bob, Be a Hero, Resign." Security guards tried to take it away too but stopped after being loudly booed by spectators.

The fans again booed loudly when UNLV officials announced after the game that they were retiring the biggest banner. The one that proclaimed: "Welcome to Tark's Shark Tank."

Jerry finished his coaching career at UNLV with a 509-105 record for a .829 winning percentage. His overall major college record was 630-125 for a .834 winning percentage, the highest in the history of the NCAA.

To put those numbers in perspective, Claire Bee had the next highest winning percentage at .826, John Wooden was only at .804 and the next highest active coach, Roy Williams, was at .783.

The Tarkanian Era at UNLV was really over.

CHAPTER 38:

CLEANING UP THE BASKETBALL PROGRAM

"There is no way any student athlete will ever embarrass this university – EVER."

—Rollie Massimino, new UNLV head basketball coach

TWO DAYS AFTER Jerry's last game at UNLV, Maxson, Finfrock and Booke met in the University Student Union to discuss the pending announcement of the next UNLV basketball coach. Booke boasted that the new coach had won a national championship, graduated 100% of his players and had never had an NCAA problem. "The program won't miss a beat," Maxson proudly proclaimed.

On April Fools' Day 1992, Rollie Massimino was named the head basketball coach at UNLV. "We became a better university as soon as Massimino stepped on campus." Maxson declared.

"There is no way any student athlete will ever embarrass this university – EVER!" Massimino stated, his voice rising in an obvious slight to his predecessor.

One of Massimino's first actions as UNLV coach was to convince its star player, Isaiah "J.R." Rider, to withdraw his name from the NBA draft. But there was a problem.

Rider had stopped going to class after he put his name in the draft and didn't pass any courses in the spring. Massimino scrambled to get him 15 units over the summer to be eligible for the upcoming season.

It didn't matter the course, where it was taught or how he passed. One course was a videotaped English course while others were taken at Nellis Air Force Base.

Nevada Regent Carolyn Sparks praised Massimino's work. She told a UNLV journalism class that Rider was academically rehabilitated by the new coach, referring to the player as a perfect example of a "scholar-athlete" while describing athletes under Jerry as "spoiled kids...they didn't even have to go to class..."

Steve Carp, a long-time writer for the *Las Vegas Sun* was incensed by her remarks. "Sparks, who is given to flippant remarks without consulting her brain, declared that Rider went from a throwaway student to one of the brightest on the team," he wrote. "As someone who teaches at UNLV, and someone who has taught some of Tarkanian's players, the facts are, they went to class regularly, they did the work on their own, and they earned the passing grade they received."

During the basketball season, it was reported that one of the classes Rider passed was Prevention & Management of Premenstrual Syndrome, which prompted the *Seattle Times* to ask: "1. What is a man doing taking this course? 2. What is a University doing giving that course? 3. Are you kidding me?"

The problems mounted when an instructor of another class came forward claiming academic fraud. "Rider had not completed half the course work and [I] was going to give him an incomplete..." Vicki Bertolino claimed. "But [I] felt pressured into giving a grade by repeated phone calls from UNLV Compliance Officer Jaina Preston, and UNLV basketball administrative assistant Tom Pecora."

Bertolino said she "was called repeatedly, including in the hospital room of her husband who had suffered a heart attack." The university denounced her claims and tried to discredit her. "I find it unimaginable that any instructor would let anyone pressure them into giving a grade," Maxson declared.

"Pressure was subjective," reasoned UNLV's Compliance Officer David Chambers.

"He [Rider] did his work," Massimino avowed, "and we know he did his work. I'll vouch for him."

In response to the publicity generated by the allegation, UNLV announced it would conduct an internal investigation and then named Patricia Wright, the wife of UNLV assistant basketball coach Jay Wright, to be a part of it. You couldn't make this story up!

Two days after the story broke, UNLV issued a press release stating it had "completed its investigation and is satisfied that the certification of Mr. Rider's eligibility was proper..."

"The investigation has not shown any wrongdoing on the part of the basketball staff," stated UNLV's new Athletic Director Jim Weaver.

The quick cover up backfired when it was disclosed that "three of Rider's papers had his first name, 'Isaiah,' spelled incorrectly" and that "two pages of Rider's work for the course, were each done in different handwriting." After those revelations, UNLV had no choice but to suspend Rider.

"The suspension came three days after UNLV president Robert Maxson said that the school had investigated Rider's academic performance and found 'no impropriety whatsoever,'" wrote *Sports Illustrated*. "It's hard to see how UNLV could have been so quick to dismiss the charges in the face of such damning evidence."

Maxson told the magazine, "The athletic department has handled all of this properly ... There is nothing embarrassing about this." *Sports Illustrated* concluded, "UNLV has simply lost the capacity to be embarrassed."

"First, it was who shot J.R. Now it's who taught J.R.?" wrote the *Pittsburgh Post-Gazette*.

Massimino was fired after producing one lackluster team after another. Several coaches followed, all with little success.

The Rebels did not win another NCAA tournament game for 16 years, but the NCAA violations continued. In the late 1990s, high school All-American Lamar Odom received more than $150,000 from a UNLV booster. The NCAA commenced a short investigation and additional instances of cash payments and other major violations were disclosed. So much for cleaning up the program!

CHAPTER 39:

LLOYD DANIELS INVESTIGATION

". . . at the university's request, a preliminary inquiry of the men's basketball program at the university will be undertaken by the NCAA enforcement staff . . ."

—David Berst, NCCA Enforcement Chief

AFTER JERRY RESIGNED from UNLV, the NCAA finally concluded a 5-year-old investigation into the program. And investigation which started by the recruitment of New York City legend Lloyd Daniels.

Daniels was considered by many to be the best high school player in the country; however, he was a poor student who was severely handicapped by dyslexia. He was recruited by many of the top programs before finally deciding to attend UNLV.

Daniels' only chance of becoming eligible was to graduate from junior college. To do so, he would need a lot of tutoring and hands-on assistance, which would result in NCAA violations.

UNLV's recruiting coordinator Mark Warkentien and his wife Maureen became close with Daniels. Warkentien analyzed the NCAA rulebook and determined that a *legal guardian* was exempt from the extra benefit and contact rule.

Since Daniels did not have parents and was not close to any surviving family members, Warkentien requested permission to petition the court to become his legal guardian. UNLV's athletic director checked with the league office and President Maxson. Neither had an objection to the guardianship, so Warkentien filed formal papers with the court.

Based upon Daniels' learning disability and absence of assistance from immediate family members, the Warkentiens were granted legal guardianship over Daniels. With the guardianship established, Warkentien paid for Daniels to be tutored, assisted him in attending a junior college, paid nominal living expenses for him and bought him a motor scooter for transportation to school and back. He didn't buy Daniels an expensive car, clothes or give him large sums of money, just some of the basic things any parent might provide.

When the guardianship was made public, New York's *Newsday* wrote a salacious and misleading story alleging major violations. As a result of the adverse publicity, UNLV, along with the league office— both of whom had no objection to the guardianship when originally asked—formed an internal committee to investigate.

After six months, the committee concluded that they could not determine if any violations occurred. The university then made the fateful decision, requesting the NCAA to take over the investigation.

On October 23, 1987, NCAA Director of Enforcement and Tarkanian nemesis David Berst notified President Maxson that, "at the **University's request**, a preliminary inquiry of the men's basketball program at the University will be undertaken by the NCAA enforcement staff..."

Inviting the NCAA onto campus to investigate Coach Tarkanian's program was tantamount to providing the hangman a rope. The NCAA took full advantage of the invitation, interviewing every player at UNLV, and the majority of the players they recruited.

Despite the fact that the NCAA's manual specifically exempts legal guardians from the extra benefit rule and that the league office advised UNLV's athletic director that it was acceptable, the NCAA nevertheless determined that Warkentien's guardianship was a rules violation.

In a November 24, 1986, letter, Bill Hunt, the same NCAA investigator who boasted that "the NCAA was going to run Tarkanian out of coaching," advised UNLV's athletic director that the guardianship must be with a relative or long-time family friend. Hunt did not provide any basis or supporting documentation for this conclusion because none existed.

The opening provided by Daniels' guardianship issue, the NCAA investigated the UNLV basketball program for *five* years and concluded that 28 violations occurred. Most were so ridiculous, it is inconceivable that they were even put into writing. One violation was called "administering a fund for student/ athletes."

There were times certain players did not pay their bills on time and the coaching staff received complaints, mostly from landlords. As a result, the coaches put a hold on the delinquent player's scholarship check, preventing that player from picking up his check without a staff member present. The staff member would then accompany the player to the bank to cash his check, taking the money owed for rent and any other items and making sure they were paid on time.

Another violation was for excessive hotel expenses incurred by recruits on their official visits. NCAA rules allow a university to pay for reasonable expenses incurred by a recruit on his official visit. What is "reasonable"? Is ordering room service reasonable? Is calling home reasonable? Is eating at the steakhouse reasonable?

The total charges incurred by UNLV players deemed to be unreasonable included: $14 for Bobby Joyce, $26 for Larry Johnson, $40 for Barry Young, $43 for Everett Gray and $46 for George Ackles.

The NCAA found another violation when members of UNLV's academic support staff admitted that, on occasion, they drove student-athletes from their apartment to school. The association determined that a car ride to class was "providing free transportation to a student-athlete."

Another violation was the unauthorized use of office telephones by four student-athletes to make long distant calls. James Jones made four calls totaling $6.87; David Butler made nine calls totaling $17.74; Barry Young made 12 calls totaling $21.15; and Moses Scurry made 36 calls totaling $67.18. It took two investigators weeks to comb through several years of telephone records to reach this conclusion.

Other trivial violations included a recruit receiving a free pair of tennis shoes on his official visit, Jerry commenting publicly about a recruit's athletic ability and a tutor paying a $50 library fine for a student-athlete so he could participate in his graduation ceremonies.

After an intense internal investigation by UNLV and the Big West Conference, and five years of NCAA investigations, there were no violations of cash payments, cars, expensive clothes, jewelry or anything else of substantial value besides the guardianship issue.

Somewhere during the midst of this investigation, Maxson decided the university needed to make friends with the NCAA. In a July 18, 1990 letter to Rick Evrard, UNLV's legal counsel, Brad Booke, wrote, "Unfortunately, all of this leads nowhere, except perhaps to get UNLV crossways with NCAA staff, which is the last thing in the world I want to do."

On October 27, 1992, after Jerry resigned, Booke wrote Mark Jones, Director of Enforcement: "This is just to let you know how much we appreciate both the support you give us institutionally and personally... we feel we have a good relationship with the Association now and that you contribute much to that fact... We also enjoyed our time over beer and chicken wings the evening we left town."

After forcing Jerry to resign as its coach, UNLV had the enforcement staff in its corner. At the Committee on Infractions hearing, the enforcement staff advised the committee that UNLV had cooperated fully in the matter and assisted the staff with its efforts to determine the truth.

The Committee on Infractions praised Maxson and rewarded the university's efforts in its final report on the case:

> *The University's president, Robert C. Maxson, determined that for the University to grow as an academic institution, the athletics program must become an integral part of the university, and must be subject to appropriate institutional control by the president... It is never an easy task for a University to change the direction of its athletic program, but that has been accomplished by the University of Nevada, at Las Vegas... The president was advised that, but for the actions he had taken at the university,*

309

*the penalties that would have been imposed, in a case as serious
as this one, would have been much more severe...*

In a November 9, 1993, press release, the NCAA discussed
UNLV's penalty: "Because of the age of this case [six years], the
Committee said it wanted to impose penalties that had the least
possible effect upon the present student/athletes, while at the same
time imposing meaningful sanctions." For these reasons, the
committee continued, "no limitations were placed on post-season
competition, and the televising of games was not totally prohibited."

Just three years earlier, most of the same committee members
banned UNLV's basketball team from postseason play and television
based upon a 14-year old infractions case.

There is no reconciling those two decisions and the Committee on
Infractions never even tried. The only difference was that Jerry was no
longer the coach at UNLV in the latter decision.

CHAPTER 40:

SHORTEST COACHING STINT IN NBA HISTORY

"If you can't win with this line-up, you should leave as coach."

—Red McCombs, owner of the Spurs

UPON HIS DEPARTURE from UNLV, Jerry received several offers from NBA teams. One was from the Philadelphia 76ers. Jerry was close friends with their general manager, Jim Lyman, and had a great relationship with their owner, Harold Katz. He also loved the Sixers' superstar, Charles Barkley.

Jerry was ready to announce his acceptance of the 76ers coaching position when Red McCombs, owner of the San Antonio Spurs, contacted him. Jerry was intrigued by the Spurs job because they had one of the best rosters in the NBA. The consensus was they could compete immediately for the NBA championship, so Jerry accepted McCombs' offer.

The entire Tarkanian family took a trip to San Antonio, Texas. They stayed on the River Walk, toured the Alamo and bought bags full of San Antonio logo apparel. Their wardrobes changed from scarlet and grey to black and silver.

Before the season started, the Spurs lost three-fifths of its starting lineup. Shooting guard Willie Anderson had operations on both legs and power forward Terry Cummings blew out his knee. The Spurs also released their talented point guard, Rod Strickland, because he was causing them problems on and off the court.

Spurs General Manager Bob Bass promised to replace Strickland with a comparable point guard, but instead signed Vinny Del Negro, a shooting guard from North Carolina State. Jerry's teams had great success with quick, athletic point guards who could defend the ball. Del Negro did not fill this bill.

Jerry pleaded with Bass to sign Greg Grant, a pure point guard from Michigan who was a great defender. Bass declined. Jerry suggested a trade for Mookie Blaylock who was, perhaps, the best defensive point guard in the NBA, but Bass declined that as well.

Jerry kept pleading with Bass to trade for another point guard. Weeks passed and losses mounted. It was a difficult environment for a coach who was used to having the final word on recruiting.

Danny surprised his father with a visit to Dallas to watch the Spurs play the Mavericks. Walking onto the court, he noticed his father looked sad and dejected but, when he saw Danny, his face lit up and he gave his son that great big smile of his. It was painful to witness.

Unhappy with the player roster and Bass' refusal to improve it, Jerry *complained publicly* that the Spurs needed a point guard to compete for the championship. This is a no-no in professional sports and Bass and McCombs were infuriated. After 20 games and a 9-11 record, McCombs invited Jerry into his office.

"If you can't win with this lineup, you should leave as coach," McCombs told him. Jerry was shocked at the quick timing, but relieved to be out of the situation. The Spurs lost more games in a month than he had lost in his final three years at UNLV. His NBA career may have been the shortest in league history.

After leaving the Spurs, Jerry planned to return to Las Vegas and retire for good. His departure from San Antonio was so sudden, there was no chance he would get another NBA job. Given his contentious NCAA battles and his nasty departure from UNLV, he thought there was little chance any college would hire him.

Jerry was settling into retirement when it was announced that Gary Colson had been fired as Fresno State's basketball coach. Jerry had many ties to the Fresno community. He was a Fresno State alum, he met his wife in Fresno, had many close friends there and there was a large Armenian-American population in Fresno. Armenians are a loyal ethnic group and they are very influential in the San Joaquin Valley.

The groundswell of local support to hire Jerry was already spreading by the time he learned the position was open. He fielded one call after another encouraging him to take the job. Fresno State's president, John Wetly, was overwhelmed by the pressure to hire Jerry. As a result, Welty offered him the job.

Jerry was touched by the community support. He had great memories of his time in Fresno and great respect for Fresno fans.

On April 6, 1995, at an unlikely press conference held on Fresno State's campus, Jerry donned a Bulldog baseball cap and told the audience that he was thrilled to be the new basketball coach at Fresno State. He said he had one goal for his team: to be able to compete against the best programs in the country. And the Bulldog-loyal loved it! "Tark the Shark" was back.

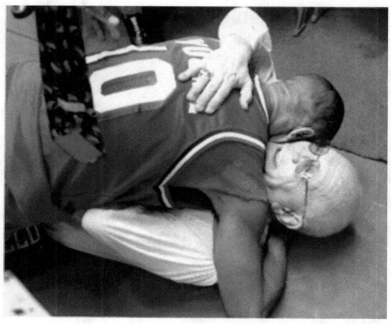

Dominick Young hugging Tark on the gym floor after the big upset win over Utah in the 1995-96 season

CHAPTER 41:

THE DAWGS ARE BARKING AGAIN

"You have nothing to be down about, you played your hearts out and you should walk out of the arena like winners because that is how I view you."

—Jerry Tarkanian, to his team after a heartbreaking loss

HE WALKED INTO a plush, Fresno restaurant and the piano stopped. People stood and cheered. With a huge smile on his face, Jerry approached the excited Bulldog fans, or the "Red Wave" as they are called in the Central Valley, and began shaking hands.

Jerry had not received this type of reception in a very long time. After three years of disappointments, he was in a place where he could start over. He was energized at the prospect of building another program that would create the excitement and memories few people have the opportunity to experience.

The anticipation and expectations created from Jerry's hiring were incredible. During the previous decade, the city of Fresno had agonized over the dismal performance of its basketball program. Now, it was about to hire the winningest coach in college basketball history. Best of all, he was one of theirs—a 1955 graduate of Fresno State and two-year basketball letterman.

The *Fresno Bee* wrote numerous front-page stories about the hiring. It was called the biggest news story to hit the Central Valley since the end of World War II.

Even with all his victories, titles and accomplishments, Jerry had never experienced anything like the media attention he received when he was hired at Fresno State. *The Bee* built him up to be bigger than life, even hiring two additional sportswriters just to cover the basketball team.

Jerry was aware the Bulldog program was in dismal shape. During the past decade, the basketball team had only two winning seasons and one postseason appearance, which was at the NIT in 1993. But there were bigger obstacles of which he was not yet aware, that he would also have to overcome.

The president at Fresno State, John Welty, had just survived a vote of "no confidence" from the Faculty Senate. He could not afford another scandal, so he put the basketball program on a tight leash to minimize any controversies.

Face it, the reality was, where Coach Tarkanian went, NCAA investigators were soon to follow. It had been that way for his entire Division-1 coaching career. No one really believed it would change at Fresno State.

Despite the obstacles, Jerry was excited about his new job. The people of Fresno were great and the potential of the basketball program was unlimited. He hit the recruiting trail signing Northern California Junior College Player of the Year Kendric Brooks with one visit.

The next new talent Jerry signed was junior college transfer James Gray, a vagabond from Los Angeles who for several years had either lived on the streets or with a friend. Gray had never lived in an apartment of his own and didn't understand how apartments worked. When he came to Fresno, Gray moved into his first. When he didn't pay rent in January, the apartment manager called complaining. Jerry confronted Gray about the missing rent payment.

"Coach, you know we have hardly been in Fresno the whole month of January," Gray said. "We have been on the road playing games. Why should I pay rent if I haven't stayed there?"

The top two recruits that first year were high school All-Americans Terrance Roberson and Chris Herren. Neither was eligible to play the first season, but both generated great hope and excitement for the future.

Although expectations were low his first year, Jerry was confident that the Bulldogs would surprise people. He loved returning point guard Dominick Young who was a great defender and the focal point of his famed "pressure defense."

Young was a great talent and the team was built around him. Throughout the preseason, the Bulldogs practiced pressure defense and fast break offense. Jerry wanted Fresno State to play like his old Runnin' Rebel teams.

On November 15, 1995, Fresno State opened the season in the Preseason NIT against Weber State, on national television, in front of a sellout crowd that was buzzing with excitement to witness the magic "Tark the Shark" would bring to their town. The national audience was curious to see if Jerry could turn Fresno State into a powerhouse like UNLV.

The day before the big game, Fresno State's Vice President, Ben Quillian, notified Jerry that Young was suspended. Apparently, Young had failed to repay donations he received in order to participate on a college all-star team, which he later missed due to a family illness. Jerry was stunned. There was so much excitement and enthusiasm throughout the city, yet his team was forced to open the season without their star player.

Just like old times. Yes, it was beginning to seem more and more like UNLV. Jerry had had to deal with a lot of last minute suspensions of key players there.

Without Young to pressure the ball on defense and run the fast break offense, Fresno State dropped back into a zone defense and tried to slow things down. They had never practiced a zone or a slow-down offense and it showed. Weber State embarrassed the Bulldogs, winning 102 to 86.

Fresno State lost two more games without Young. When he returned, the team came together, creating great excitement and hope throughout the city.

In early January, Fresno State traveled to Salt Lake City for a game against the 13th ranked Utah Utes. The Bulldogs entered the game as *19-point* underdogs.

From the opening tip, the team played with great passion and kept the score close. Those kids played their hearts out, but it looked like it wouldn't be enough. Fresno State was down by six points, had 45 seconds left to play, and three starters had fouled out. But the players never quit. They battled back and cut the lead to just two points with seconds left.

In a scene that will never be forgotten by the Fresno State faithful, Young raced the ball up the court, blowing past one defender after another. He stopped suddenly, just behind the three-point line and, with two Utah defenders running towards him, launched a high arcing shot that fell softly through the net.

With the team in wild celebration, Young ran to the bench and tackled Coach Tarkanian. There was this 20-year-old kid rolling on the ground, bear hugging a stunned 65-year old coach while screaming, "Coach... Coach... Can you believe it?"

Jerry walked into the locker room and jokingly shouted, "Never in doubt."

"This is one of the biggest games I ever had...the best one ever," Jerry told the media.

Six weeks later, Utah played Fresno again. This time, they had "revenge" on their minds! The 8th ranked Utes jumped to a big lead and led by 12 points with ten minutes left to play. Dominick Young was shooting poorly, having made only 1 of 11 shots.

During a time-out, Jerry's son Danny, an assistant for Fresno State, grabbed Young and looked him in the eyes. "If you have a big heart, you will take this game over!" Danny shouted passionately, hoping to inspire Young.

And did he ever! Young scored 14 points in the final 9 minutes, including three straight 3-pointers. With three Utah players surrounding him and a minute to play, he hit his last 3-pointer, ensuring a 71-68 victory. Afterward, all Jerry could do was mutter, "Unbelievable. Simply unbelievable."

Over the course of the season, Young continued to hit one big shot after another, securing <u>five</u> last-second wins for the Bulldogs. Jerry had never seen anything like this in his entire career.

Fresno State finished the season with a great chance of making the NCAA tournament. A win over New Mexico in the semifinals of the WAC tournament would assure the Bulldogs their first NCAA bid in 12 years. But that would be no easy task!

In what was one of the hardest fought and most thrilling games in WAC tournament history, Fresno State led by three points with only seconds remaining in the second overtime. New Mexico missed a shot, but the ball ricocheted back to the shooter. He dribbled backward to get behind the three-point line and took another shot.

Fresno State's Darnell McCullough leapt straight up in the air and cleanly blocked the ball, causing one of the officials to call a foul. The New Mexico player went to the free throw line and made all three shots, sending the game into an unbelievable third overtime. New Mexico finally prevailed, 104-99.

The players walked up the long tunnel to their locker room. There they sat in disbelief, some crying, some speechless. No one thought that they would get to the NCAA tournament that first year, but to have come so close and fought so hard only to have it taken away so suddenly was unbearable.

Jerry entered the locker room sad and disappointed, but positive with the team. He told the players they had nothing to be down about, that they played their hearts out and should walk out of the arena like winners because that is how *he* viewed them.

With the NCAA tournament denied, the Bulldogs accepted an NIT bid. Even though it was not "the big dance," at least it was postseason play and the Red Wave was thrilled. Fresno State won three games before losing to the eventual champion, the University of Nebraska. This ended Fresno State's best season in more than a decade. And the Red Wave knew that this was only the beginning.

CHAPTER 42:

BULLDOGS HIT ROCK BOTTOM

"It's okay. I will give you a second chance, just like I give my players."

—Jerry Tarkanian, to *60-Minutes* anchor Mike Wallace

JT coaching with son, Danny, at Fresno State

AMONG THE RED Wave, there was a great deal of excitement and hopeful expectations for the 1996-97 season. Chris Herren and Terrance Roberson joined four returning starters for the Fresno State Bulldogs.

The Bulldogs started the season 5-0 but, after playing nine of ten games away from home, fell to 8-6. Dominick Young went into a horrendous shooting slump, missing those same last-second shots he had made the previous year.

By league season, the team started to gel. They clinched the division championship with a road win at San Diego State. It was Fresno State's first championship in 15 years.

Afterward, the players stayed on the court and cut down the nets in celebration. President Welty joined them in the locker room, congratulating the team and telling them how proud he was.

The following week, the WAC tournament was held in Las Vegas. One win and Fresno State would, in all likelihood, earn an NCAA bid. The Bulldogs opened the tournament as the top seed against TCU.

The morning of the game, Fresno State had a shootaround on UNLV's campus. When the team walked into the gym, there was a buzz in the air and a media swarm. Initially, no one knew what was happening; however, they quickly learned.

The *Fresno Bee* had printed a front page story claiming Chris Herren and Dominick Young were involved in a point shaving investigation. The story blindsided the team. Although there had been rumors, no one took them seriously. The rumors started when Young shot an air ball at the free throw line late in a game and Fresno State did not cover the betting spread.

Apparently, *Bee* reporter Andy Boogaard was a big sports bettor with the local bookies and one of *them* had told him that Young and Herren were throwing games. *Bee* reporters reviewed game tapes trying to find something suspicious.

They interviewed Jerry and others around town, but came up with nothing. They assured Jerry there wouldn't be a story unless there was corroborating evidence. Weeks passed and nothing was written. Everyone thought the matter had ended.

Without warning, the *Bee* broke the story the morning of the first WAC tournament game, and they did so *without* corroborating evidence, but at the optimum time for maximum exposure.

The shootaround was a circus. People ran in and out of the gym talking about the story. The players all discussed it. Jerry was furious. He was so mad that he told the coaches that, for the first time in his life, he didn't want to coach.

The whole team felt the way he did. The players took the court with no emotion or energy. They played lethargically and TCU destroyed the Bulldogs, 106-81.

The *Bee* was bombarded with criticism from the Fresno community, questioning the timing as well as the story's lack of substance. The article never named a source. Everything was anonymous.

At the insistence of the *Bee*, a grand jury was convened, not once, but twice. For two years, witnesses were called. Every time a new witness testified, the *Fresno Bee* ran a new front-page story.

When it was finished, both grand juries came back with no indictments. But the story kept reappearing for many years to come.

The start of the 1997-98 season was ushered in with glowing optimism. Jerry felt he had the most talented roster he had ever coached. Returning were Chris Herren, Terrance Roberson and JUCO All-American Damon Fortney. In addition, high school All-Americans Avondre Jones and Winfred Walton joined them.

Pac-10 Freshman of the Year Tremaine Fowlkes transferred to Fresno State, as did New York City street legend Rafer "Skip to my Lou" Alston.

The Bulldogs did lose one top recruit who had committed to them, Kenny Brunner. In the spring, Danny went to an all-star game to watch

Brunner play. Brunner told Danny how excited he was to play for Fresno State. Then he asked if Danny would help him get a car.

"Sure, come to Fresno over the summer and we will get you a job," Danny replied. "You can save some money and put it down on a car." Brunner went stone silent.

After the conversation, Brunner decided not to attend Fresno State. Danny advised his father of the conversation and Jerry said, "You can't blame him. He grew up in Southern California and he knows those kids at UCLA are getting new cars, so he thought he should get one too."

Fresno State began the season ranked 14th in the country, the first time the school had been nationally ranked in 13 years. There was even talk of a Final Four appearance.

In anticipation of a memorable season, *ESPN* had a documentary crew follow the team the entire season recording all of its activities. One of the more benign but humorous memories the crew recorded was a bed check conducted by assistant Johnny Brown. With cameras rolling and the documentary crew following him, Brown knocked on Rafer Alston and Larry Abney's door two minutes before the designated time. Brown heard girls giggling.

When Abney finally let Brown and the documentary crew in, everything was quiet. Brown asked where the girls were, but the players denied that there were girls in the room. Brown looked everywhere— in the bathroom, under the bed—until he found the stunned girls hiding in the closet. The documentary crew caught their embarrassing response and the players' mea culpa.

Afterward, Brown advised Jerry of the incident thinking he would impose some disciplinary measure. But Jerry, who never wanted to suspend his star players, didn't miss a beat. "So, the girls were out of the room two minutes before curfew, right?" he asked.

The Bulldogs would encounter far worse problems throughout the season. That year, Fresno State implemented one of the most stringent drug testing programs in the country. Players with past drug problems were tested weekly. If they tested positive, they were suspended until they finished a drug treatment program.

The first casualty was Damon Fortney, whose mother had a drug addiction when he was born. He said he had started smoking marijuana when he was 11 years old. Fortney tested positive for marijuana before the season even started.

Despite Fortney's suspension, the Bulldogs began the year with resounding wins over UMASS and LSU. After the LSU game, Herren tested positive for drugs and checked into a rehab center. his loss was devastating to the team.

Fresno State went on a five game losing streak, the longest in Jerry's coaching career. After, he was asked about Fresno State's chances of making the NCAA tournament. "We shouldn't even be invited to the *YMCA* tournament," Jerry remarked.

As the year continued, so did the suspensions. Fortney returned to the team, but after several weeks of passing his drug tests, he tested positive again and was suspended for the remainder of the season. Avondre Jones was suspended, and then so was Tremaine Fowlkes. It got to the point that every time Athlete Director Al Bohl called, the coaches would simply ask, "Who is it this time?"

During the season, *60 Minutes* contacted Fresno State concerning a story they were doing about universities accepting kids with troubled pasts and using them to generate successful athletic programs.

Jerry was well known for taking troubled youths and giving them a second chance. Throughout his career, many kids used this opportunity to turn their lives around and make a good living. Some continued to get into trouble. *60 Minutes* wanted to do a story on the latter. They picked the perfect year to do it.

60 Minutes brought in its top man, Mike Wallace, to do the story. Wallace was one of the most feared investigative reporters in the country. Jerry, who spent his entire adult life working in a gymnasium, mostly with inner-city kids, went toe-to-toe with Wallace in his interview and clearly held his own.

On his departure, Wallace complimented Jerry on how well he handled his interview and told him, "you won't be disappointed in the segment." He also told the media he "was impressed by the coach's willingness to answer questions without side-stepping issues."

As in the two previous years, the Bulldog team came together at season's end. However, they dug themselves into a hole with the early losses and needed to <u>win</u> the WAC tournament to get an NCAA bid.

The semifinal game was against UNLV, which faced suspensions of their own. Their star center, Keon Clark, was also suspended for flunking drug tests. Clark was a great player, the eventual 13th player taken in the NBA draft.

In his second year with the Denver Nuggets, an assistant coach tried to motivate him. "If you work as hard as Raef LaFrentz [the Nuggets star player], you will make $3 million a year just like LaFrentz," he told Clark. "You are *that* talented."

"Coach, I am happy with my $800,000. I don't want to work any harder," Clark replied. It is hard to argue with that logic.

The game was played on UNLV's home court. The atmosphere was electrifying, with both teams needing to win the tournament to get an NCAA bid. The crowd was boisterous in their support of the hometown Rebels, who thrived on the atmosphere and played a nearly perfect game. UNLV won 76-67 and advanced to the NCAA tournament.

Danny acknowledged that it was the most disappointing loss he had ever experienced. He could not imagine the hurt and pain it caused his father.

It was the NIT again, for the third straight year. After all the pre-season hype, the NIT was an emotional letdown for the team, and the Red Wave.

The night before the second round NIT game, *60 Minutes* aired its piece on Fresno State. Despite Wallace's assurances of a positive spin, the story was devastating. But it got even worse.

The following night, Tremaine Fowlkes sank a half-court shot at the buzzer to beat highly regarded Memphis State. Selland Arena erupted as the fans stormed the court celebrating. But the celebration would be short-lived.

In his apartment after the game, Fresno State's starting center, Avondre Jones, escalated a teasing incident into a national story by pulling a Samurai sword on his friend. After getting hit several times with the sword, his friend sprinted out of the apartment and called the police.

Coming on the heels of the *60 Minutes* story, the sensation caused by the sword incident was unfathomable and Jones was dismissed from the team. It mattered little that he was later found innocent of the assault charges. The damage had been done.

A few days after Jones' arrest, the Bulldogs traveled to Hawaii to play the Rainbows in the NIT quarterfinals. The atmosphere in Hawaii was incredible, the place was a sellout. Fans yelled insults and waved signs about Samurai swords and drugs. One sign stated "FSU— Firearms, Samurai-Sword University."

Hawaii led the game until Tremaine Fowlkes made a key steal and dunk that preserved a two-point win. The players celebrated with tremendous relief and satisfaction. After all they had faced together, they were going to New York for a chance at the NIT championship.

Before they arrived in New York, the Manhattan media crucified Jerry and his players. He had experienced malicious articles in the past, but these were the worst he had ever seen.

There was one unexpected fan at the game, and he sat on the bench next to Jerry as the Bulldogs warmed up. It was *60 Minutes'* anchor Mike Wallace. He tried to explain to Jerry why the show had been so negative after he promised it would be positive.

"It's ok, I will give you a second chance, just like I give my players," Jerry quipped.

Late in the semifinal game, Fresno State was up by one point when a Minnesota player hit a three-point shot. Rafer Alston took the inbounds pass, raced up the court and hit Larry Abney for a chance to tie the game.

The 15-foot shot rolled around the rim and went halfway down before it fell out. It was a fitting ending to a most disappointing season.

CHAPTER 43:

TARK IS BACK IN THE BIG DANCE

"It is time to sit back and consider that, maybe, Jerry has been the one who has been wronged and that maybe his courage, tenacity and stamina in this battle ought to be more appreciated."

—Attorney Chuck Thompson, on the NCAA lawsuit

Fresno State winning the WAC Tournament Championship. (need to find year)

IN APRIL 1998, Jerry finally received some good news. Years earlier, he had filed a civil lawsuit against the NCAA claiming defamation of character, among other things. Before trial, the association conducted a series of mock trials and were convinced they could not win, so the organization settled by paying the Tarkanians $2.5 million. At the time, this was the largest settlement ever paid by the NCAA in a lawsuit.

The *Fresno Bee* reported, "Tarkanian's settlement cracks the image of the NCAA as invincible."

"After 25 years of battling the NCAA …Tarkanian can declare himself the winner," the *Las Vegas Sun* added.

Chuck Thompson, a Las Vegas attorney who was involved in the NCAA case from the beginning, said, "It is time to sit back and consider that, maybe Jerry has been the one who has been wronged, and that maybe his courage, tenacity and stamina in this battle ought to be more appreciated."

Jerry didn't feel victorious or gratified. "They can never, ever, make up for all the pain and agony they caused me," he said. "All I can say is that, for 25 years, they beat the hell out of me… I've learned you are much better off being their friend than their enemy… I want to finish my career as their friend… If we didn't have those problems, we would have had one of the greatest runs in history."

Before the *60 Minutes* story, samurai sword incident and *ESPN* documentary, Fresno State was on course to have the greatest recruiting class in Jerry's coaching career. After the stories came out, one recruit after another backed away.

Brandon Kurtz, whose family lived an hour and a half from Fresno's campus and whose sister attended Fresno State, signed with conference rival Tulsa. He earned First Team All-Conference honors two years in a row.

DeAndre Hewitt, who led the junior college team coached by Jerry's son George to the State Final Four while averaging 32 points and 21 rebounds, decided to put his name in the NBA draft instead of signing with the Bulldogs. He was not drafted and bounced from one minor league club to another, never making the NBA.

The top high school big man in the country was Leon Smith. Smith endured severe personal problems growing up. He was placed in a foster home when he was five years old because of parental neglect and sparingly saw his twin brother, who was placed in a separate foster home. He was shy and rarely spoke.

Jerry visited Smith and, when he finished speaking, Smith got up, shook his hand and walked out without saying a word. Jerry was discouraged because he thought the visit went poorly. The director of the foster home assured him it went great.

The director told Jerry that when Lute Olson of Arizona visited, Smith stared at the ceiling and failed to acknowledge him. He said Smith got up and walked out before Olson even finished.

Danny visited Smith on several occasions. After one of those visits, he received a telephone call from a person close to Smith. This person told Danny he wanted Smith to sign with Fresno State, but Smith had been offered money from other schools and wanted to get paid. He promised to deliver Smith to Fresno State if they paid him $5,000. Danny was stunned.

There are always people befriending star athletes hoping to cash in on their success. They are called "handlers," "street agents" or a variety of other names. Danny knew this happened all the time, but it was the first time he personally experienced it. He called his father and told him of the conversation.

"Absolutely not!" Jerry told him. "I have never paid for a player before and I am not going to start now."

Smith ended up entering the NBA draft, where he was the last player taken in the first round. He did not, however, last in the league. He was not mature enough to handle professional life and, over the next several years, bounced around from one minor league to another like Hewitt.

Smith ended up playing overseas in Puerto Rico and Argentina, never making it in the NBA even though he had the potential to be the best center Jerry ever coached. The best player to *ever* sign with Fresno State was unknown and not recruited by any major program.

Because of family and grade problems, Jamal Crawford had played only one year of high school ball. Jerry's former assistant at UNLV, Tim Grgurich, who was then an assistant with the Seattle Super Sonics, told his former boss that he had to recruit Crawford.

Jerry took a trip to Seattle and met with Crawford and offered him a scholarship. Crawford was so excited, he immediately committed to Fresno State and even had a large Bulldog tattooed on his arm. The greatest player was the easiest to sign. It seemed too good to be true. And it was.

That summer, Crawford participated in his first summer basketball circuit, where the best high school players in the country face each other in tournaments all over the nation during the course of 20 days. Every major college coach attends these games.

Crawford destroyed the best guards in the country. He went from not being rated in any scouting service to being rated one of the top guards in his class. Crawford ended up signing with Michigan, was chosen 8th in the NBA draft and was a top guard in the NBA for many years.

Despite losing every major recruit they targeted, Fresno State still had two of the greatest players in school history enrolled at the school and eligible to play for the upcoming season, Courtney Alexander and Melvin Ely.

Alexander had transferred from Virginia the previous year. He was a tremendous talent but had a lot of personal problems and was subject to mood swings. When he was focused though, there was no one better.

After his successful career at Fresno State, Alexander was selected 13th overall in the NBA draft. His parents thanked Jerry and told him he was the only coach their son ever responded to, and that he wouldn't have made it into the pros without him.

Melvin Ely was a high school All-American from Chicago. He didn't have the grades to be eligible out of high school, so he sat out his first year. After four great years at Fresno State, he was drafted 12th by the Los Angeles Clippers in the NBA draft.

With a little luck, the Bulldogs would have started three lottery picks—Jamal Crawford, Courtney Alexander and Melvin Ely—and a possible fourth in Leon Smith, who was drafted in the first round without playing college ball.

Nevertheless, they still had a formidable lineup and, by mid-season, they put together one of the most impressive runs in school history, beating three nationally ranked teams: Georgia, Temple and New Mexico. *Fresno Bee* reporter Bill McEwen remarked, "The city was the most excited it had been, since Tarkanian's hiring."

There was hope among the Red Wave that the program had turned the corner and overcome two straight years of adversity involving the point shaving allegations, the drug suspensions, the *60 minutes* piece, the *ESPN* documentary and the samurai sword incident.

Just when Fresno State's star was rising, the team fell flat on its face, losing to a poor San Jose State team. The loss led to a fourth straight NIT appearance. Frustration was building. Could Jerry ever get the Bulldogs into the NCAA tournament? There were many doubters.

Fresno State began the 1999-2000 season with a group of solid, dependable players. Jerry knew that if they were going to make it to the "Big Dance," he needed to build his team around Alexander and Ely, two great players, and the rest would have to accept their roles. However, bad breaks seemed to follow him every year at Fresno State, and the "Millennium Season" would be no exception.

Both Alexander and Ely developed stress fractures in their legs, resulting in several missed games early in the season. The team suffered one disappointing loss after another.

The low point for Jerry was a loss to Utah State in a lackluster effort. After the game, former Las Vegas sportswriter and good friend Mike Fitzgerald told him, in as gentle a way as possible, that this team did not resemble the coach's UNLV teams of old. They didn't play hard. That was the worst possible assessment a person could give Jerry.

Danny was to fly to Barton County, Kansas, the next day to recruit, but his father told me not to go because he wasn't coming back to Fresno State next year. He told Danny he would have resigned that night were it not so embarrassing.

Entering league play, the Bulldogs knew that they had to win either the league title or league tournament to make the NCAA playoffs. Standing in the way was Tulsa.

Tulsa had one of the best teams the WAC ever produced, led by former Bulldog recruit Brandon Kurtz. The Golden Hurricanes were *destroying* teams playing the way Jerry's teams played at UNLV – with great defense, speed and effort. Tulsa was coached by Bill Self, whom Jerry considered one of the best in the country.

Before the teams' first game, Jerry's brother Myron asked Danny if the Bulldogs had any chance of winning. Danny told him his fiancée, who was in acting school at the time, had a better chance of winning an Oscar.

The first game was played in Fresno. Tulsa led by 13 points with 12:26 to play before the Bulldogs staged a fervent rally. The score was tied with 5.6 seconds left when Bulldog Demetrius Porter, a walk-on and the most unlikely of heroes, dribbled into the paint and lifted a running shot just over the outstretched hands of Kurtz and into the basket. Bulldog players stormed the court, celebrating like they hadn't in a long time.

The regular season rematch was in Tulsa. The Golden Hurricanes entered the game as a 14-point favorite. Playing with great emotion, Tulsa led by seven points with 3:51 left to play.

At that point, Alexander took over the game. He fed Porter for an open three-pointer then hounded Tulsa's point guard until he dribbled the ball out of bounds.

Down by one point with one possession left, all 8,355 fans in the sold-out arena knew who was going to take the final shot. Tulsa put their best defender, Eric Coley, on Alexander.

In true Hoosier folklore fashion, Alexander dribbled the ball at mid-court, waiting for the clock to count down. As it ticked to 8 seconds, he dribbled toward Coley and crossed over to his left, exploded off the ground, rose above Coley and released an 18-foot jump shot. The ball left Alexander's hand and went high in the air before it swished the net.

Bulldog players stormed the court, celebrating and mobbing one another in front of a shocked Tulsa crowd who stood staring in silent disbelief.

After the game, Jerry told the media that "Some of our boosters told me we going to win. I said, we need St. Jude [the patron saint of lost causes] and St. Jude came through for us."

Even though Fresno State had beaten Tulsa twice now, they were still one game behind them in the league standings. No one else was going to beat the Golden Hurricanes. This meant that the Bulldogs were left with the improbable task of having to beat Tulsa *a third time* in the WAC tournament.

The one thing going for the Bulldogs was that the tournament was held in Fresno. Selland Arena was completely sold out; it was standing room only. The grand old arena was more electrifying than it had ever been. One can only dream of this kind of sporting atmosphere.

Tulsa jumped out to a lead, but Alexander brought the Bulldogs back and kept it close. The lead changed several times. With less than a minute to go, Tulsa led by one point, but the Bulldogs had the ball.

Jerry called time-out. For the third game in a row, it had come down to one final shot. Alexander was exhausted and had missed several of his last shots. In the huddle, Terrance Roberson implored, "Give me the ball! I will make it."

Jerry called the play for Roberson, who got open on the right side of the court. Roberson fulfilled his promise, knocking down a three-point shot with 11.4 seconds to go, giving the Bulldogs the win, the tournament title and their first trip to the NCAA tournament in 16 years.

As the buzzer sounded, Bulldog fans swarmed the court. Players hugged one another and were mobbed by their fans. "Fifteen years of heartache, frustration and jilted expectations came crashing down in one rapturous afternoon," Marek Warszawski wrote in the *Fresno Bee*.

"People stood by us," Jerry said emotionally. "They had heartbreak after heartbreak, but they stood by us."

March Madness, 2000 – The Shark Returns!

The next day was selection Sunday, when the NCAA announced the pairings for the "Big Dance," the NCAA tournament. The team, cheerleaders, members of the band, over 500 fans and several university administrators, including President Welty and Athletic Director Al Bohl, met at a local restaurant to watch the pairings. Every television station was there.

This was a huge event for Fresno and something the community had expected much earlier, but something they cherished, nonetheless.

With all the cameras on the players and coaches, the selection committee announced each team. When Fresno State's name came across the screen, the entire restaurant erupted. Players high-fived and hugged each other. Welty and Bohl shook boosters' hands, and the cheerleaders and fans cheered. It was pure pandemonium.

Fresno State had been to the NCAA tournament only three times in its 60-year history and had won only one game. Could this year's team, at such a low point only two months earlier, achieve more than any team in school history?

The Bulldogs had won their last eight games and were playing the best ball since Jerry arrived. Expectations were high.

Jerry had great respect for their first-round opponent, the University of Wisconsin, and its coach, Dick Bennett. Wisconsin also had the two-time Big 10 Defensive Player of the Year Mike Kelley, who would guard Alexander.

Alexander had been carrying the Bulldogs on his shoulders and any hope of advancing was in his hands. Fresno State led for most of the first half even though Alexander played horribly. He could not get an open look and he was getting frustrated.

At halftime, Jerry pleaded with his players to pick it up. He knew they would not win if they did not play better in the second half. He was right. Wisconsin pulled away in the second half and won the game 66-56. The Badgers would advance all the way to the Final Four.

With the great run at the end of the season and the team's first NCAA tournament appearance, Jerry was rejuvenated and excited about the following year. He asked his attorney to contact Fresno State and request an extension of his contract. The university agreed but, as a condition to the extension, they demanded that he announce his *retirement* at the end of the following season.

No one could understand the timing. Two years previous would have been an appropriate time to make this demand, not now. Not after the program had just finished one of its most successful seasons ever, creating tremendous excitement within the community. It had no off-court problems and the players were excelling in the classroom. The timing made no sense.

Jerry was left with no choice. He signed the contract extension without argument and started to prepare for his sixth and final year at Fresno State.

Right: Lois cheering

335

CHAPTER 44:

SOME THINGS NEVER CHANGE WITH THE NCAA

"I had heard about the vendetta the NCAA had against you, but I never believed it. However, I now know the vendetta is real; the NCAA has it in for you."

—Compliance Officer Jon Fagg,

after Tito Maddux suspension

FRESNO STATE HAD two terrific players who sat out the previous season, Tito Maddux and Chris Jefferies. Maddox was the type of point guard Jerry had great success with at UNLV. He had the ability to break the defense down off the dribble and create opportunities for his teammates to get wide open shots. He made everyone on the team better.

Jefferies was one of the most talented kids to ever come out of Fresno. He signed with Arkansas out of high school, the same year as Fresno State's string of public relations debacles. But he was unhappy at Arkansas and transferred back to the Bulldogs.

Fresno State also strengthened its front line by signing Mustafa Alysaad from Sudan. The previous summer, Danny went to Spain to watch the Junior World Games and fell in love with a big kid on the Qatar team, Hashim Basheer. He was 6'11" tall, blocked every shot within range and took a charge on anyone. He was Coach Tarkanian's type of kid.

The Qatar coach told Danny that several college coaches had already inquired about Basheer, but he didn't think Basheer wanted to play in America. At that point, the team's power forward, Mustafa Alysaad, tapped Danny's shoulder.

"I am coming to America," Alysaad stated. "Watch for me."

Danny smiled politely, but just wasn't interested. He didn't think Mustafa was big enough. He was only 6'5", which was short for a power forward.

The following year, while reading a recruiting service publication, Danny noticed that a "Mustafa Alysaad, from Sudan," was listed as one of the top ten power forwards in the country. He was attending a prep school in Tennessee.

Danny hopped a plane to watch him play. There he was, now 6'9", with long arms and dominating everyone on the court.

After the game, Danny reintroduced himself and told Alysaad that he was from Fresno State. Mustafa told Danny that he had two cousins in Fresno and he wanted to visit there.

Alysaad came to Fresno the weekend of the 2000 WAC tournament, so he witnessed firsthand the thrilling win over Tulsa and the ensuing celebration. He loved the excitement and enthusiasm and decided that Fresno was where he wanted to play.

When Alysaad notified his prep school coach that he was coming to Fresno, his coach became agitated and warned him that if he did so, he would be *deported*. Western Kentucky had also been recruiting Alysaad and the prep school coach had promised to deliver him to them. This is how recruiting works.

When a four-year coach finds a player who is not eligible, he places the player in a "friendly" junior college or prep school on the condition that the junior college or prep school coach "deliver" the player back to the four-year school. Dennis Felton, the Western Kentucky coach at the time, had persuaded Alysaad to come to America and placed him in the prep school.

Alysaad did not pay for his air fare to America, or for his classes, or for room and board at the prep school. In addition, during his term at the prep school, Felton and his assistant visited often, playing basketball with Alysaad and providing him small amounts of pocket money. *All of these* were potential NCAA violations.

After being threatened by the prep school coach, Alysaad called and said he was not coming to Fresno. He did not want to be deported.

Danny arranged for one of Alysaad's uncles to call him and explain to him that the threat made by his coach was not true, that he would *not* be deported. After their conversation, Alysaad agreed to leave the prep school.

The morning he was scheduled to leave, the prep school coach waited for him. He directed Alysaad into a room where two NCAA investigators waited. For the next two hours, they drilled Alysaad about Fresno State, attempting to find a recruiting violation. Of course, they never asked one single question about Dennis Felton or Western Kentucky.

The NCAA investigator also warned Alysaad that if he left the prep school for Fresno State, he could be deported. She told him he "seemed like a nice kid" and "didn't want to see him get hurt."

The investigator said Fresno State was "a bad place" and that Alysaad should look at other schools. These were the same types of comments NCAA investigators had made to recruits when Jerry was still at UNLV. The association's tactics never changed!

Because of Jerry's many battles with the NCAA, a few changes had been made to the investigative procedures. All interviews by NCAA investigators are now taped, with a copy provided to the witness upon request.

Alysaad's uncle obtained a copy of the tape and played it for Coach Tarkanian. He couldn't believe the investigator was so blatant. Danny sent a letter to the NCAA complaining about her conduct. The NCAA ultimately removed her from the case.

Danny knew that Felton was behind the NCAA interrogation, so he had Alysaad's uncle call Felton. After making the call, his uncle called Danny back laughing hysterically. He told Felton not to worry about all the money Felton had spent on Alysaad, that he would pay him back. Felton, who was driving at the time, pulled over.

"No, no, no we didn't give Alysaad anything," he stammered. "You, you, you don't owe us anything."

Interestingly enough, Felton was later hired as the head coach at the University of Georgia. His main mission there was to clean up the NCAA violations committed by Jim Harrick and his son.

As the new season approached, everything looked great. When practice started, Maddox was better than anyone expected and with him in the lineup, all of the other players were better also. The coaching staff was ecstatic. They felt this would be their best team yet.

Before their first game, the NCAA requested a meeting with Maddox. No one knew what it was about, but when the NCAA came to town, it had to be bad.

During the summer, Maddox and a USC player took a trip to Vegas to visit a friend of theirs from Compton, UNLV player Dalron Johnson. On that trip, they met with, but *did not receive anything* from, a sports agent. The NCAA ordered Fresno State to suspend Maddox until the case was resolved.

Weeks passed and games were played, but there was still no word from the NCAA. Each week, the administration was told they should have an answer by week's end. And at the end of each week, there was only silence.

After the eighth game, the NCAA concluded that "no violation occurred" and cleared Maddox for competition. The Bulldogs had already lost three games without him.

Fresno State's compliance officer, Jon Fagg, remarked that he heard about the vendetta the NCAA had against Jerry Tarkanian, but he never believed it. After the Maddox episode, he told Jerry that the vendetta was real. The NCAA had it in for him.

With Maddox back in the lineup, Fresno State started destroying opposing teams. They beat NCAA tournament-bound Georgia by 19 points. They beat the second-best team in the league, Texas El Paso, by 52 points. That was a particularly satisfying victory as it was Jerry's 700th career win.

The Bulldogs won 13 straight games, tying the school record. For the first time since he was hired, Jerry had the whole team together with no distractions. The players played like "Tarkanian teams," a trademark which signified that they played hard.

Basketball gurus marveled at the level of intensity Jerry's teams always exhibited. The assistant general manager of the Portland Trailblazers wrote an internal memo after watching one such practice that year:

> *First of all, this is not the same type of college basketball practice/program that I have seen in my travels the past year. There are no stretch outs, no towels and jerseys nicely laid out for the players, water not rushed over by managers to the players. Some guys had different shorts on, the assistant coaches are not decked out in polo shirts and nicely pleated shorts, they have t-shirts and baggy shorts on and they get after it. I mean get after it! Once Coach Tark blows the whistle at 2:30, they start to ball, no three-man weave or 3 on 2, 2 on 1. THEY START TO BALL! There is no half-stepping, if you do you get called out and everyone in the gym knows it. If you get injured and are lying on the court they say get the hell up or roll over to the side because they are not stopping. This is blacktop hoops and if you can't hang, then the door is right there. It is great!"*

Jerry never worried about the small stuff. If a player showed up with different practice gear, he didn't go ballistic. If a player lost his temper on the court, he wasn't benched. The players had latitude, except when it came to playing hard and competing.

The assistant general manager told Jerry he had seen every top team in the country play and, besides Duke, Fresno State was playing better than any of them. Fresno State ended up winning the conference championship by four games and entered post-season play on a roll!

The league tournament was held in Tulsa, Oklahoma. At 7:30 a.m., the morning of their semifinal game, Jerry was awakened by a telephone call from President Welty. Welty demanded that Melvin Ely be brought to Vice President Ben Quillian's room immediately. Danny woke up Ely and took him to Quillian's room.

Quillian told Ely that the NCAA had received an "anonymous tip" claiming he had received money from a street agent. Ely denied it, but Quillian didn't seem to believe him.

Quillian told Ely to sign several releases of personal information for the NCAA, including a release of his bank records for the previous four years, or he would be finished at Fresno State. Ely did as requested and was ultimately cleared of the "anonymous" charge.

Frustrated, offended and probably a little tired, Ely played the worst game of his career. The conference Player of the Year went scoreless for the entire first half, as Hawaii prevailed 76-67.

Just when it seemed the momentum was finally going the Bulldogs' way, the NCAA reappeared to create more distractions. That was how they played. Even after paying Jerry millions of dollars to avoid a defamation of character lawsuit, it continued its relentless persecution of him.

March Madness, 2001

Jerry awaited Selection Sunday with apprehension. Although a 25-7 record and WAC regular season championship assured a bid, Fresno State's hopes for a high seed was hurt by the Hawaii loss. They paid dearly for that loss as the NCAA Selection Committee designated Fresno State a 9th seed.

The Bulldogs played brilliantly in its first-round game beating Cal-Berkley by 10 points. The win matched them up with the defending national champions and number one seed, Michigan State.

Jerry had tremendous respect for Michigan State and its coach, Tom Izzo. He knew Fresno State would have to play a near-perfect game to have any chance of winning. With great emotion, Fresno State played their hearts out.

The Bulldog guards constantly harassed Michigan State ball handlers, forcing numerous turnovers. Early in the game, Ely scored at will against Michigan State's strong front line, before picking up his 3rd foul in the first half and having to go to the bench. With Ely benched, the Bulldogs had a difficult time scoring.

Coach Izzo implemented a brilliant defensive game plan for Michigan State. In the preceding Cal game, Maddox had continually beat his man off the dribble. When Cal defenders moved to help out, Maddox passed to Demetrius Porter for uncontested jump shots.

Izzo decided he was not going to let Porter have an open shot and forced Maddox to beat them with tough drives to the basket and shots over Michigan State's huge front line. The plan worked.

Porter did not make a basket until the last minute in the game and Maddox forced numerous errant shots. The final score was 81-65 and the Bulldogs were headed home.

In the post-game press conference, Jerry was more than just saddened. He was subdued His demeanor and answers were almost melancholy and he appeared to not want to leave the stage.

Danny had seen almost every post-game press conference his father had in the NCAA tournament, but this one was different. Watching him, Danny felt disheartened thinking this might be his father's last NCAA tournament press conference. His father must have felt the same way. How sad it was for it to end in this environment. It just didn't seem right.

Although disappointed in the loss, Jerry was proud of the team. They won 26 games, the second-most in school history. They won the school's first outright league title in 19 years, and they matched the total number of NCAA tournament wins in school history.

The only question remaining was whether Jerry and his three-star underclassmen would return for another year. His contract stipulated that he was to retire, but no official announcement had been made.

CHAPTER 45:

TARK'S FINAL YEAR OF COACHING — 2001-2002

"I don't know if I feel like a legend. I've always felt more like a fugitive."

—Coach Jerry Tarkanian, at his retirement ceremony

JT with wife, Lois

A FTER THE RECORD breaking 2000-01 season concluded, Jerry's attorney contacted Fresno State and requested a contract extension. Fresno State agreed, but again demanded that he retire at the end of the season. The school gave no explanation for the requirement. It was a real slap in Jerry's face.

After it was announced that Coach Tarkanian was returning to Fresno State, Melvin Ely, Chris Jefferies and Tito Maddux announced their intentions to return as well.

All of the elements were in place for a final glorious closure to Jerry's fabulous career. The Bulldogs had three future first-round NBA draft picks in the 2001-02 lineup. The supporting cast was good enough to make a run at the Final Four and, if things went well, a possible national championship.

Just before school started, the NCAA declared Maddox ineligible for accepting an airline ticket from an agent over the summer. Fresno State dismissed the player from the team and notified him that he could never play at Fresno State again.

Jerry scrambled to find another point guard. Since it was the end of the summer, few players were available. His son George, who was a junior college coach, insisted that he had a great kid who was eligible right away. Jerry remembered that he had seen the kid play a few years back and he had loved him.

Antonio Gates was the high school football Player of the Year in Michigan. He signed a football scholarship with Michigan State, but transferred after his first semester to Eastern Michigan so he could play basketball. After one year, he was dismissed from school.

Gates enrolled at the College of Sequoias. He was ineligible to play, but was able to practice with the team. George said he was the best player on the floor.

Jerry called Gates and offered him a scholarship, which he accepted. Gates was home at the time and needed money to pay for his flight back to Fresno. His AAU coach said he would pay for it, but it would take a day or two for him to get the money.

Gates was close to his high school coach, who recently had been hired at Kent State. Before the AAU coach could buy Gates an airline ticket to Fresno, his high school coach picked him up at his house and took him to dinner. At dinner, the coach persuaded Gates to attend Kent State.

Not wanting to give anyone a chance to change Gates' mind, the coach drove him from the restaurant—in the middle of the night— directly to Kent State, where he enrolled the next day. All of these actions were NCAA violations. Losing Gates was devastating to the Bulldogs, but it was not Jerry's style to turn a school in.

Two years later, Gates would lead Kent State to the Elite Eight. He went on to become an All-Pro tight end for the San Diego Chargers.

Fresno State had one last point guard on scholarship, Chris Sandy. Sandy was a solid leader for a successful junior college team and he was also a great kid. Over the summer, Fresno State learned that Chris Sandy was short academic credits to be eligible.

Fresno State's academic advisor scrambled to put together a class schedule that would give him a chance to pass the requisite courses, regaining eligibility. Included in the class schedule were some correspondent courses.

Jerry did not want another player declared ineligible right before the season, so he requested Fresno State's NCAA faculty representative Pete Simis approve the schedule. Simis reviewed the courses and approved them, and Sandy worked hard during the summer, passing them all.

The day before practice started, Simis inexplicably declared Sandy ineligible for competition. He acknowledged that he had approved the courses and even admitted that he had approved similar courses for other student-athletes in the past. Since then, he said he had "changed his mind on the interpretation of the NCAA regulation" with regard to the correspondent courses.

Jerry showed Simis an NCAA regulation that appeared to *allow* for the courses. Simis agreed with this interpretation, but said another regulation appeared to disapprove of them. Simis said he would check with the NCAA and get their interpretation.

"If you check with the NCAA and tell them you are from Fresno State and it deals with a basketball player, they will rule against us," Tarkanian declared flatly. Simis laughingly assured him that was not the case.

The next day, the first official day of basketball practice, Simis entered the coaches' office and told them that the NCAA had made a ruling. They concluded that the correspondent classes *did not* count and that Sandy was ineligible to play. The only one surprised was Simis.

Losing Sandy left Fresno State no choice. They would have to start a freshman walk-on at point guard. Jerry decided the team could not play pressure defense without Sandy or Maddox, so he brilliantly created a new zone defense.

This new defense was part amoeba, the zone he'd made famous at UNLV, and part match-up. Jerry hoped no one would know what it was and not know how to attack it. He was right. The new zone thoroughly confused opposing teams.

Fresno State started the season by upsetting two nationally ranked teams, USC and Michigan State. After an 8-1 start, the Bulldogs were ranked 14th in the country. The NCAA was still not finished!

In the middle of a pre-game walk-through, Vice President Ben Quillian informed Jerry that the school was suspending its star player, Melvin Ely. Apparently someone told the NCAA that, over the summer, Ely had stayed in a Budget Suites hotel room in Las Vegas which was paid for by an agent.

Ely denied it. He admitted he went to Vegas over the summer, but said he stayed with two friends from Chicago at the Barbary Coast Hotel.

Quillian told Ely the school had a copy of the hotel registration with his signature. Ely claimed that wasn't true and assured Quillian that he never stayed at the Budget Suites, nor did he sign the hotel registration. Quillian got up from his seat, quite agitated.

"I can't believe I am wasting my time listening to this stuff," Quillian mumbled. "You guys need to leave."

Ely was in tears. He told Quillian he came back to Fresno State for his senior year to do all the right things, that he had never been in trouble before and that Quillian's story was wrong. Nevertheless, Quillian dismissed him from his office.

Another innocent victim, roadkill on the NCAA highway. But this was so obviously a mistake. Surely they would reinstate Ely when the truth was proven?

The next day, Quillian provided Jerry a copy of the hotel registration form with Ely's name on it. Ely proved it wasn't his signature. Jerry suspected the signature was actually from Nate Cebrum, one of the agents involved with Maddox.

Cebrum had been working secretly with Quillian and two former NCAA employees hired by the university to assist the NCAA in its investigation of the Fresno State basketball program. So, the plot thickens.

Ely was reinstated, but suspended again while the investigation continued. Jerry had no idea when the suspension would end. The Bulldogs lost several games. A season that started with promise and excitement spiraled out of control. The losses caused morale to sink and the team roiled in dissension.

Ely's mother issued a public statement blasting Fresno State. She pointed out that her son had passed up a multi-million-dollar NBA contract to return to Fresno State, to get his degree and be a good example for future student-athletes. What did he get to show for it, for making the morally correct choice? He was turned into NCAA roadkill.

The NCAA finally concluded its investigation of Ely, acknowledging that he had *not* stayed at the Budget Suites and that he was telling the truth about his actual accommodations.

In perhaps the most *outlandish* decision in the history of the NCAA, they also ruled that Ely <u>had</u> committed a violation. Not because he had received anything free, indeed not even because of any personal conduct on his part. But because *a friend of his (and Tito Maddux)* stayed in a Budget Suites hotel in a room that was paid for by an agent.

You can't make this stuff up to be any more *unbelievable* than it actually is! And yet, the NCAA determined that, for a rule infraction *as serious as this one,* the penalty would be a <u>suspension</u> for 20% of the season for Ely.

Jerry was shocked and outraged by the decision. Ely was in disbelief. He was ready to pack his bags and go back to Chicago.

Surely, the NCAA would not get away with this. Certainly, the local and national press would crucify them? Ely was a great kid. He was an example of everything that was *right* in college sports. To impose this penalty on him was outrageous.

So where was the outrage?

The incident barely received any press. The national media ignored it. The *Fresno Bee* reported the suspension, inferring only that Ely was *guilty* of some wrongdoing.

The NCAA walked away unscathed by its decision, having damaged yet another promising athlete. Even for the vindictive and arbitrary NCAA, it was a cruel and soulless decision.

Without Ely, Fresno State opened league play with a devastating loss to Hawaii. After Ely was reinstated, Chris Sandy joined him, having finally *again* passed his required courses to become eligible.

The Bulldogs were at full strength for the first time all season and ready to make a run for the NCAA tournament, *the Big Dance*. They won five of their next six games, losing only one one-point heart breaker at Nevada.

Just as it looked like the Bulldogs might turn things around, Chris Jefferies injured his knee and was out the remainder of the season. The team went into a tailspin, losing games at an alarming rate.

Jerry made some late adjustments, trying to fit the remaining players into the correct defense and offense to take advantage of their strengths. The adjustments paid off.

Playing their best game of the year, Fresno State beat 14th ranked Oklahoma State 58-52. Sandy was phenomenal. The players' confidence grew. The Fresno community regained hope in the team and it appeared there might yet be a chance to salvage the season.

Then, out of nowhere, right after his great game against Oklahoma State, the NCAA struck again. It ruled Sandy ineligible because his church had paid for one of his correspondent courses.

The pastor at Sandy's church provided documentation to the association showing that the church had made similar gestures for other members of the church who were *not* student-athletes. The NCAA simply ignored the pastor's documentation. Sandy was suspended and ordered to pay the cost of the college course to a charity.

Sandy made the payment and expected to be reinstated immediately. But he was declared ineligible again. This time because his godfather from New York, with *no ties* to Fresno State, had paid for Sandy's airfare to Fresno.

The NCAA suspended Sandy for the rest of the regular season. He was yet another innocent victim, just a casualty of war—the NCAA's *war* against Jerry Tarkanian.

The momentum the team had created with its third upset win over a nationally ranked opponent, ended with Sandy's suspension. The team was devastated and limped through the rest of the season.

The team did earn a bid to the NIT, but neither the coaches nor the team wanted to play and it showed. Fresno State lost to Temple in the first round. The once mighty Bulldogs were finished!

With speculation that this might be Jerry's last game, Temple's coach, John Chaney, grabbed the microphone and hollered, "Tark, I love you!"

The season that began with so much promise, so much hope, ended as Jerry's worst ever in his major college career. After spending millions of dollars and investing thousands of man-hours to get rid of this "Armenian rug merchant" as NCAA investigator David Berst once called him, they had finally figured out a way to beat him on the basketball court.

All they had to do was take away his players, one at a time.

With the season over, Jerry set up a meeting with university president, John Welty, to discuss his future. On a beautiful Saturday morning in the Central Valley, he and his son Danny went to Welty's home.

Welty listened patiently while Jerry explained his desire to coach one additional season. He explained his disappointment over what had transpired during the past season, and how the NCAA suspensions had destroyed their chances.

Jerry told Welty that he did not want to leave under *these* circumstances. He asked to coach one final year, so he could leave on a positive note. He also made a point that the NCAA was investigating the basketball program and he wanted to be the coach to defend the charges.

After Jerry finished, Welty, without explanation, declared that he wanted to make a change with the coaching staff, and that his decision was final.

A Sad Good-Bye

On March 15, 2002, in a teary-eyed press conference held on Fresno State's campus, Jerry announced his retirement from coaching after 44 years. He was eloquent and gracious, but also very honest about his treatment at the hands of the NCAA.

"I think every coach eventually has to head for the pasture and I stayed longer than usual," he began. "Nobody wants to end their career the way we ended the season... The NCAA dismantled this team... I thought after I won the settlement in 1998, things would change, but they haven't."

He went on to say, "What started out as a season of great promise that should have been my best at Fresno State, has turned out to be the most frustrating year of my career. I've been dodging bullets for 20 years, and it's been difficult. The NCAA has harassed me my whole career... I fought them every time, because they were wrong... It's been hard on me, hard on my players and hard on the university." Fellow coaches, former players and associates were complimentary in their remarks.

Duke Coach Mike Krzyzewski said, "He's had an amazing career...Jerry had consistent high levels of success, because his teams played hard defensively. He's one of the truly remarkable defensive coaches."

UNLV Coach Charlie Spoonhour added, "Anybody who has ever played against [one of] his teams, has to respect how hard they played... But they also played *together*, and that's what made them so tough to beat."

Utah Coach Rick Majerus commented, "His teams played with great passion, and defended extremely hard. They played so well together. That was the biggest challenge you had, to try and match their overall intensity."

David Rice, former UNLV player and future UNLV coach, said, "I don't think he gets enough credit for being a great coach in terms of X's and O's. He revolutionized modern basketball with the man-to-man pressure defense, and the transition offense his teams in the 1970s played."

Former UNLV player Glen Gondrezick said, "He was so great at adapting to the players he had, and changing ... He was always willing to change, if it meant he could win. Had the NCAA left him alone, he'd be the second-best college coach ever, after John Wooden."

John Welch, assistant coach at Fresno State, said, "Humility is his strongest trait ... It's amazing being around him every day, all these years. He's the most humble man I've ever been around."

Brad Rothermel, the former athletic director at UNLV, said, "Jerry was a regular guy. He would be down in the hotel lobby and talking to fans. He was great with the press. He really liked being around people."

Diane Pucin of the *L.A. Times* made a poignant observation, "Tark has always wanted to take rough-edged basketball players and make them winners. He wanted kids who wore tattered jeans and worn sneakers, to *beat* the other kids, the ones at the fancy places, the ones wearing designer suits and alligator shoes."

That is one of the things Coach Tarkanian was most admired for. He took the downtrodden, the disadvantaged and the underdog, and routinely beat the wealthy, privileged, establishment schools. This is probably the thing that the NCAA, and many in the media, *disliked* most about him.

Sports Illustrated's Alexander Wolff wrote that he would miss Tark because, "He detested hypocrisy. He was, in a roguish and bracing way, honest." This is another trait of Coach Tarkanian's that people admired, but it also put him at odds with the NCAA and many in the media.

In response to a fan's remark that he was a legend, Jerry replied, "I don't know if I feel like a legend. I've always felt more like a fugitive."

CHAPTER 46:
TARK'S FINAL NCAA HEARING

"Your son missed his calling; he should have been a trial attorney."

—John Welty, Fresno State President

IT ONLY TOOK the NCAA three years with Jerry at the helm to start investigating the Fresno State basketball program. It began when the local newspaper reported that basketball players received free rice bowls—which cost $4.95 each—from a Japanese restaurant.

The NCAA used "Rice Gate" to commence an investigation into every aspect of the Fresno State basketball program. Every player, including many former players, was questioned by investigators. Many repeatedly, such as Melvin Ely, who was questioned seven times.

Wanting to exhibit full cooperation with the investigation, Fresno State president, John Welty, made the fateful decision to hire two former employees of the NCAA, Richard Evrard and Mike Glazier, to represent the university in the process. In fact, Evrard was involved in several of the questionable suspensions of UNLV players in the early 1990s.

For obvious reasons, Welty's decision to retain Glazier and Evrard sealed Jerry's fate, and the school's fate. The NCAA had been after him for almost 30 years.

Jerry fought and won the suspension they tried to impose upon him. He helped initiate two congressional inquiries into their enforcement practices, which proved extremely embarrassing for the organization. He forced the NCAA to spend millions of dollars fending off federal and state legislation requiring due process in their enforcement practices. And he forced them to pay him $2.5 million dollars to settle a case for malicious and fraudulent actions perpetrated against him by the organization.

A former NCAA director of enforcement called Jerry a "rug merchant," a well-known racial slur against Armenians. The former executive director claimed he had manipulated the system to stay in coaching. Did anyone really believe that hiring two former employees of the NCAA to represent the university was going to result in a fair investigation and hearing?

When the interviews with the players provided no serious violations, the NCAA turned its attention to an ex-felon and sports agent, Nate Cebrum, who had run afoul of the NCAA with football players at Florida State and Auburn.

Cebrum had been friendly with Jerry at UNLV, but became bitter after he failed to sign any players at Fresno State. He was particularly upset with Jerry's son Danny, after he had warned Terrance Roberson and Larry Abney not to trust Cebrum and to sign with another agent.

In four separate interviews with Glazier, Evrard and the NCAA, Cebrum claimed he was a born-again Christian, who couldn't tell a lie and wanted to clear his soul. He claimed numerous major violations were committed by Coach Tarkanian and Danny. In each interview, he described these violations.

The problem was that in, each interview, he also told conflicting facts about the same violations. He contradicted his story on each allegation.

After five years of investigating every aspect of Fresno State's basketball program, the NCAA issued an official inquiry on July 24, 2002, which listed nine allegations. Jerry learned of the official inquiry and its contents in the newspaper. Fresno State never notified him and refused to provide him a copy of the charges.

Five minor infractions were alleged, including basketball players receiving free rice bowls from Tomodachi's. There was only one *major* allegation against the men's basketball program, and it was based solely upon Nate Cebrum's testimony—that Cebrum provided cash and travel expenses to two student-athletes and their families.

Much to Welty's consternation, there were three major allegations against the *administration*, two dealing with the certification of players and the catch-all "lack of institutional control" by the university. Danny Tarkanian represented his father in the investigation.

On August 27, 2002, Danny sent Mike Glazier a letter requesting 16 different items to help formulate his father's response to the inquiry. Glazier refused to provide any of the items and replied that the university would handle the response.

Danny followed up with a call to the NCAA, requesting a copy of the evidence the association collected against the basketball program. Investigator Stephanie Hannah advised Danny that the NCAA would provide only evidence concerning the two allegations in which Jerry Tarkanian was named.

Danny appealed her decision to the chairman of the infractions committee, Thomas Yeager. Yeager denied Danny's request stating, "The only pertinent material which applies to your father is the information relating to those allegations in which he was named." Obviously, the NCAA wanted Glazier and Evrard to defend the basketball program, not the Tarkanians.

Since Cebrum's allegation was the only serious one against the program, Danny concentrated on those interviews. After reviewing the tapes, he finally understood why Welty refused to extend his father's contract. The university had already determined his guilt years in advance.

The transcripts of the four interviews with Cebrum and his girlfriend, Colleen Preiss, were frightening to say the least. Either Evrard or Glazier told Cebrum "We have a story we believe to be true. The question is how to prove it."

The vice president of the university, Ben Quillian chimed in. "You gave us good solid leads we can pursue," he said. "There will be some action taken against Tarkanian." All of this was said before Jerry had a chance to respond. It only got worse.

Preiss asked, "Do you want me to go in there and take all of the hard drives?" After Quillian, Glazier and Evrard failed to respond, the NCAA investigator stated, "We can't tell you to do that."

Neither the vice president of Fresno State nor its two licensed attorneys advised Colleen Preiss that it was illegal to steal information off a hard drive and, incredibly, the NCAA investigator's response was one of arms-length encouragement.

Later in the interview, Cebrum and his girlfriend discussed setting up basketball players to commit a violation. Preiss stated, "You can buy a player and set him up and use it… You can take a kid who needs money, but he will be working for you all [the NCAA]."

Cebrum replied, "It's happened before."

Danny got chills from what he read. Not only had the university, its attorneys and the NCAA investigators already determined guilt based upon the testimony of a bitter ex-felon—before interviewing any other witnesses—but they were also part of a conversation to commit grand larceny and the entrapment of innocent athletes, all to nail Jerry Tarkanian.

All of the horror stories of past NCAA investigations came rushing through Danny's head. He had to do something to stop it.

He wanted to go public with this information. He believed the statements in the transcripts would greatly embarrass the university and reveal the sham that was about to occur.

Instead, his father asked him to keep quiet and work with the university. Jerry did not want another public fight with a university president.

Danny scrutinized Cebrum's different statements and started piecing together all his irreconcilable declarations, the number of which was truly incredible. Glazier himself acknowledged Cebrum's voluminous inconsistencies, but stated that some of his statements appeared true.

Danny thought to himself, "Isn't this amazing? With all of the inconsistencies clearly exposed in the taped interviews, the university attorney still gives him credibility. Boy, we are in trouble."

The only allegation at issue at the infractions committee hearing was Cebrum's, since Fresno State admitted the rest. When it was Danny's turn to speak, he pointed out statements showing Cebrum's bitterness towards Coach Tarkanian and his motive to lie. Danny listed an abundance of factual inconsistencies in Cebrum's statements, and only time preventing him from continuing. Incredulously, Glazier and Evrard failed to bring any of this to the attention of the committee.

Afterward, everyone was confident Fresno State would prevail in this allegation. There was a sigh of relief and an air of excitement in the downstairs bar after the hearing. It appeared that Jerry and his program would emerge unscathed from the NCAA hearing. Not quite. The *Fresno Bee* had one last bombshell.

After the investigation was closed and the hearing finished, the *Bee* reported that Stephen Mintz, a former student at Fresno State, claimed he wrote papers for three players at the request of Fresno State's academic adviser. As a result of Mintz' claims, the NCAA issued a supplemental official inquiry alleging academic fraud by the academic adviser and three former basketball players.

Glazier, Evrard and the NCAA investigators questioned the individuals involved in the allegation. Danny was denied permission to be present at the interviews. Glazier did allow Danny to come to his office and review the transcripts and take notes, but he could not make copies.

Before Danny had a chance to review any transcripts or evidence, the university admitted the academic fraud violation based upon Evrard and Glazier's recommendation. This was a devastating blow. There was little chance the infractions committee would rule against an allegation in which the school had admitted wrongdoing.

Danny knew the allegation wasn't true, so he spent hundreds of hours scanning the different transcripts, looking for falsehoods and inconsistencies. He put together an impressive list of facts and felt good about their chances of prevailing at the hearing.

On June 14, 2003, President Welty, Athletic Director Scott Johnson, Compliance Officer John Fagg and Jerry and Danny Tarkanian joined Glazier and Evrard at the Fairmont Hotel in Kansas City, Missouri for the last Committee on Infractions hearing attended by Coach Tarkanian.

That night, Danny shared a room with his father and wondered what was going through his mind. He had been down this road before. In past hearings, his father and his attorneys provided overwhelming evidence refuting the charges, but the infractions committee still ruled against him.

Naively, Danny hoped this time would be different. Because his father had won a multi-million-dollar lawsuit against the NCAA, he hoped the association would be more cautious in rendering an insupportable decision.

Investigators opened the hearing by presenting testimony from two witnesses whom they claimed supported Mintz' assertion that the academic advisor was involved in the academic fraud. Mintz's best friend, Chris Lavagnino, claimed that he witnessed Mintz deliver "typed" papers to the academic advisor in her office.

The second witness, a former coach, testified that the academic advisor gave him an envelope to give to Mintz, though he did not know what was in it. Mintz claimed there was money in the envelope to pay for the papers he had just written for the players.

After the investigator's 30-minute presentation, Danny presented his father's case. In all likelihood, Mintz wrote, helped write or typed 16 papers for two players whose eligibility had expired. Regardless, there was no involvement by the basketball department!

First, there was no motivation on behalf of the academic advisor or the basketball program to commit academic fraud because the 16 papers were written during the last month of the players' senior season and, therefore, did not contribute to them being eligible. Never in the history of the NCAA has a program been charged with academic fraud for schoolwork not relevant to a student-athlete's eligibility.

Second, Mintz had a history of writing papers for students on his own initiative. He admitted to the enforcement staff that he had written at least 10 papers for students who were not athletes.

Third, Mintz enlisted his best friend, Chris Lavagnino, to lie for him. Lavagnino told the investigators he accompanied Mintz to the academic adviser's office on at least two occasions and remembered him "handing white paper, you know, uh, stapled together finished reports."

In contradiction, Mintz told the enforcement staff that he never brought the academic adviser printed paper, that all of the reports he gave her were on a "floppy" disc. Lavagnino admitted he had talked with Mintz the night before his interview. It was obvious Mintz decided to enlist his friend's help to bolster his credibility.

Finally, the envelope the former coach gave Mintz, which Mintz claimed was payment for papers he had written for the players in 2000, was actually given to Mintz during the 1998-99 school year, ***more than a year before*** the alleged academic fraud. The envelope could not possibly have been related to the papers.

The only two corroborating witnesses presented by the NCAA investigators essentially showed Mintz lied. At this point, a hush come over the room, a subtle tension coming from the university's side.

All the evidence Danny presented came from the transcripts he reviewed in Evrard and Glazier's office. The obvious question was: why didn't they address these lies? They were paid hundreds of thousands of dollars from the university to investigate these claims. They participated in the interviews. They had free and open access to the transcripts. How could they miss something so obvious?

After disproving the only real evidence the investigators presented, Danny provided a lengthy list of additional contradictions in Mintz' story. For four hours, Danny presented evidence showing Mintz' charges were false.

After, the NCAA investigators were asked to respond. Danny waited to see what evidence they would present to limit the damage done to their case. They had to have something.

Investigator Dan Matheson stood up and stated, "We just don't believe the testimony of the academic adviser. We don't believe she is truthful."

Danny almost fell out of his chair. Was he kidding? He didn't respond to any of the undisputed facts which showed *his* witness was not truthful, had a motive to lie and enticed his friends to lie. He simply sat down.

The hearing broke for lunch. On the way out of the room, Fresno State's compliance officer told Danny, "I can't believe it. We may actually win this case."

President Welty told Jerry, "Your son missed his calling. He should have been a trial attorney." Jerry congratulated his son and told him he had done a great job. Danny never felt prouder.

Jerry summed it up best by saying, "Isn't it amazing. The university is paying Glazier and Evrard all that money, and yet they missed all the evidence supporting the basketball program."

The problem Fresno State faced was that the university had already admitted the violation based upon Evrard and Glazier's recommendation.

When the hearing resumed, the chairman asked for closing statements. Investigator Matheson gave a brief statement, adding nothing to his case.

Glazier stated that the university changed its position on guilt. It now took the position that it didn't know one way or the other if a violation occurred.

The university was trying to cover its butt. It didn't want to be out on a limb if the infractions committee actually cleared the basketball program.

Danny was the last person to speak. He rose from his seat and stated: "Fourteen years ago, having just graduated from law school, I sat in the United States Supreme Court building listening to *Tarkanian v. the NCAA*. The NCAA attorney argued that the organization should not be bound by the Due Process Clause of the 14th Amendment because the NCAA was a private organization that provided due process under its own charter. They didn't need court supervision to assure due process." Danny averred, "This is a great opportunity to prove that statement true."

He closed by saying, despite the NCAA's differences with his father, the infractions committee should rule on the evidence presented at the hearing, and it wasn't a close call.

When the hearing ended, several of the committee members thanked Danny for coming and said they respected the way he defended his father.

Danny felt optimistic. The committee members were intelligent. They asked good questions and several of them appeared understanding. He could not see how they would rule against them. Still, in the back of his mind, he harbored doubts. He was certain his father had felt the same way after his previous hearings.

Jerry didn't show much emotion. He probably knew they would lose despite everything that had transpired that day.

A couple months later, the NCAA issued its decision finding Fresno State guilty of academic fraud.

Danny thought back to that fateful 5-4 decision by the United States Supreme Court. If one more justice understood the damage an NCAA decision can cause to so many lives, if one more justice understood how unfair the NCAA hearings are, his father's career and his legacy would have been much different.

CHAPTER 47:
THE HALL FINALLY CALLS!

By Lois Tarkanian

"It took way too long, way too long."

—Larry Bird, on Jerry's induction into the Hall of Fame

Jerry's grandsons, Jerry and John King, helping him up the stairs to the Hall of Fame ceremony

IN THE INTENSE white glow of stage lights, the elderly man slowly pushed his walker across the stage, head down and thrust forward, shoulders slumping. He was oblivious to the obvious: his weakness, age and poor health were in direct contrast with other honorees surrounding him.

Earlier in the Mass Mutual Center, the man had sat quietly in a chair as others came up to see him. Former players, friends and greats in the world of basketball, including Moses Malone, Larry Bird, Grant Hill, Ralph Sampson, Gary Payton and Dick Vitale.

They talked animatedly to the man, even though he could barely whisper back. Each showed him great respect. He seemed to understand what they said, and they continued laughing and talking. Delight covered his entire face.

Larry Bird leaned over and spoke into the man's ear. "It took way too long, way too long." He was right.

First nominated for the Hall of Fame in 1995, it was now almost two decades later. No wonder his age and health were in such direct contrast with the other honorees.

He used his walker to cover the block from the Mass Mutual Center to the Symphony Hall auditorium. Offered a ride, he preferred to walk the same path as the others had followed.

It wasn't easy, as there were several rough spots in the road. He continued on, and it was as if he were walking a loosely strung gauntlet of well-wishers on either side.

People waved, shouted congratulations and stopped him to take pictures. He took time with each one, savoring the moment.

Halfway there, Tom Thibodeau, coach of the Chicago Bulls, ran up to him, talking excitedly. It was obvious the two men cared deeply about each other. Thibodeau kissed the man's bald head before he left.

As he approached the high steps covered with red carpet, the man was urged to take the side entrance to avoid the stairs. He refused. Again, he wanted to follow the same path as the others, not wanting to miss a single part of the ceremony.

Two of his strong, immaculately dressed grandsons each took a side and navigated him up the stairs. The strain of doing so clearly showed on his face. He made it to the top, gave a large smile and continued on his way. Twenty minutes later he was on stage.

As he was handed his award, signifying entrance into the Naismith Basketball Hall of Fame, a strong luminous smile broke out on his face. Pure joy from within shown through, and youth returned to his features and stance.

The entire audience rose to their feet. Even those in the balcony, giving him a standing ovation.

The applause lasted far longer than that given any other honoree that day. They knew how unfair the long wait had been, knew why Rick Pitino could accept his award with articulate, energetic speech, while he could barely whisper, "Thank you."

As those present showed their respect and love for him, my mind traveled back 58 years to a summer night in Fresno, California, and one of my first dates with a fellow Fresno State student, Jerry Tarkanian.

I remember that night quite clearly. We had returned from seeing a movie and were parked in front of my family's small farmhouse. The car windows were down and the air was warm and heavy, laden with the sweet smell of grapes ripening on the vine. The night was still, almost without movement.

We talked about future plans. I told him how I had wanted to be a teacher since my earliest memory. He told me that he had wanted to be a basketball coach ever since he could remember, and that he had even slept with a basketball when he was a young boy.

Then it was quiet. He didn't say a word.

Finally, he turned to me with a voice husky with emotion. The words, at times, caught in his throat.

"I'll never be a good coach" he said. "I know I won't. I can't do it the way they tell me. And they must know what the right way is. They're the coaches. They're the ones who write the books. They're the professors."

"You can't get close to your players, they say," he said, continuing on. "Don't become personally involved with them. You are their leader, not their friend. You are the general; they are the soldiers. But

I can't do it that way. All I've ever wanted to do is coach, but I have to be close to my players. I have to be involved with them."

My mind then shifted back to the stage. "You became one of the greatest coaches ever Jerry," I thought. "Not just a good one. And you did it your own way, enfolding your players non-judgmentally and helping hundreds of young men with hope and love. And those people applauding today know that. It might have cost you dearly. That's why this honor has come so late."

When they talk about the biggest upsets in all of history, the top of the list must include a first generation Armenian, whose family survived the Genocide and the Great Depression, who endured the early death of his father, had little money and less education, but somehow made such an impact in his life that media outlets all over the world, including *The New York Times*, the *Washington Post*, the *London Times*, CNN, ESPN, even Hong Kong, Israel and Madrid reported on his life. The Las Vegas Strip, the most famous street in the world, dimmed its lights in his honor.

Despite all of the adversity Jerry faced, in death, as he had done his entire life, he won.

"I am so proud of you. And I'm sure your mother, Rose, is too. Against all odds, you carried on your family's Armenian tradition of passion, persistence and achievement."

JT with Pete Carril

*Tarkanian family
at the Naismith
HOF ceremony*

EPILOGUE

JERRY TARKANIAN WAGED a 30-year battle against the most powerful and vindictive organization in sports, the National Collegiate Athletic Association. He never backed down and he never quit. It was a David-versus-Goliath battle that cost him dearly.

The NCAA not only crippled Jerry's fabulous career, but ended it prematurely, and with venom. He was branded a crook, a cheat and, on occasion, far worse.

His character and ethics were challenged in newspapers across the nation. His reputation was sullied throughout his community and profession.

Top television shows ridiculed his basketball program. National magazines questioned his ethics and mocked his life's work.

His players were harassed and disparaged. He was forced out of the job he loved, and from the program he built from scratch. His final team was completely dismantled by the NCAA.

These battle scars remained with him in retirement. Nevertheless, Jerry can stand proud, as the uncompromising coach who stood up to a nearly invincible institution—one drunk with power, flush with money and driven by often inexplicable motivations.

While every other coach and administrator in the country shuddered at their power and complied in the most obsequious fashion with their every dictate—even when they knew the process was grossly unfair—Jerry was there, fighting to make their abuses known.

He always worked to empower athletes, coaches and institutions. He tried to ensure that due process and a fair hearing—the right of anyone accused—was honored.

Until recently, the NCAA was perceived as the white knight of intercollegiate sports, exposing and punishing corrupt individuals and institutions. Anyone who complained about its wrongdoing was just crying sour grapes because they got caught.

For decades, Jerry was the poster-boy of these supposedly corrupt individuals. Over the years, perceptions changed and gradually closed the gap back to reality.

Many of the most successful college coaches started to emulate Jerry's programs. They recruited poor inner-city black kids from broken families who couldn't afford college. Many of these kids were junior college players or four-year transfers.

These coaches implemented a pressure defense, run and gun style of play and openly paid tribute to Coach Tarkanian and what he brought to the game of basketball.

And eventually, the NCAA actions Jerry complained of for so long, actions taken to run him out of coaching, actions that the national media discarded as pure fiction from a dishonest cheat who got caught, resurfaced in recent enforcement cases.

In 2012, a NCAA investigator was overheard bragging how she was going to nail the number one ranked high school player, Shabazz Muhammad, for rules violations, promising that he would never play college basketball.

She made these statements more than a month and a half *before* any documents were turned over to the NCAA concerning the investigation, and two months *before* key witnesses were interviewed. A day after the story was published, the NCAA reinstated Muhammad and fired the investigator.

In a 2013 case involving the University of Miami, it was disclosed that NCAA investigators broke the organizations own rules in an effort to improperly obtain information and that they provided a star witness thousands of dollars while he was in jail. NCAA President Mark Emmert called the conduct of the investigators "shocking and stunning."

More recently, a Los Angeles superior court judge ruled that the NCAA was "malicious" in its investigation of former USC Assistant Coach Todd McNair, and that the NCAA tended to show "ill will or hatred" towards him.

These revelations may have shocked the national media, and maybe even the general public, but it didn't shock Jerry or anyone close to him during his 31 years of collegiate coaching.

While Jerry was ridiculed and scorned for making similar allegations decades ago, people now realize he was right.

Towards the end of his life, the perception of Jerry and what he accomplished started to change. He received an amazing number of accolades, topped off by his induction into the Naismith Hall of Fame.

Coach Tarkanian is now often mentioned as one of the best coaches of his time. It could also be argued he is the *best* coach of all-time.

This is not because of his outstanding numbers. These numbers would have been much better had it not been for the gross intrusion by the NCAA.

This is not because he accomplished what he did at schools that had few resources and no prior success. And it's not because of what he accomplished by coaching two different styles of play, to better adapt to his players.

What made Jerry such a great coach and a great man, perhaps more than any single aspect, was the way he treated his players.

During an era when racial division was rife, when inner-city kids were discriminated against because of their socio-economic backgrounds and judged incapable of performing in college academics, Tarkanian, the rebel, was there to insist differently.

When players from troubled childhoods and broken homes— thought by most to be unwelcome embarrassments to any university— Coach was there to give them a second chance. Because of him, they got a chance at redemption, a chance at success and a chance to escape the cycle of poverty and desperation in which they lived.

While some people looked upon his players and thought of 'thugs' and 'gangsters,' Coach Tarkanian looked at each one as individuals, as athletes and as human beings. To him, they all deserved dignity, respect and love.

On one particular drive home, Jerry and Lois Tarkanian explained how they viewed their lives. It was not the moments of glory that they cherished, nor the glowing lights of fame or the grasping of the championship trophy. It was not the brief moment when they stood at the pinnacle of coaching success.

Rather, it was always about the journey, the cause.

Jerry spoke glowingly of his time at Riverside City College. He and his wife referred to it as the "golden years" of their lives.

They recalled, with passion and pride, the success of so many of those junior college players and their children, and the memorable experiences they had along the way.

He reflected upon their astonishing success at Long Beach State, a success he regarded as highly unlikely and remarkable given their lack of resources, the institutional history and the nearby presence of the mightiest college basketball program in history.

"We should have never won there," he mused, adding that his troubled time in Fresno was perhaps karmic retribution for his good fortune at Long Beach.

As they drove on, their son, Danny Tarkanian, glanced at the glittering lights of the mega-resorts dotting the Las Vegas Strip. He recalled those wonderful days at UNLV, the excitement that permeated the city, the support and loyalty of so many wonderful people. And the games, the unimaginable spectacle of the games.

He recalled the red carpet, the fireworks show, the "Walk Like a Tarkanian" music video and even the shark mascot. It was perhaps the only time in college sports history that a school paraded a mascot designed after its coach.

It was a special time and a special place and, over the years, many people, friends and many more strangers alike, have stopped him to express how much Runnin' Rebel basketball meant to them. With a twinkle in their eye, they always managed to recall a certain special moment, a favorite player or a crucial game.

Memories that will never be forgotten!

Tark with Jerry King and Jerry Tarkanian, Jr. at Tark statue at UNLV (JT with two grandkids named after him)

ABOUT THE AUTHOR

DANNY TARKANIAN is a proud Nevadan and former UNLV basketball star who once led his team to 24 straight wins and the school's first ever number one NCAA ranking. At UNLV Danny graduated with high honors and was the school's first Rhodes Scholar candidate. Danny also received the prestigious NCAA post-graduate award, given to the student-athletes that most excel in both the classroom and in athletics.

Upon graduating Danny attended law school at the University of San Diego. Danny graduated 3rd in his class, magna cum laude, and was named to the Law Review. He practiced law in Nevada for seven years, including three as the founder of his own law firm. During those years his father Jerry Tarkanian, one of the winningest coaches in college basketball history at UNLV, led the UNLV Rebels to three Final Four appearances and the National Championship in 1990.

Danny co-founded the Tarkanian Basketball Academy in 2003, which teaches over 350 Clark County kids basketball skills and life skills such as work ethic, overcoming adversity, teamwork and sportsmanship. He is husband to Amy Tarkanian and the father of four. Together they are involved in a number of charities in Nevada, including Hope for Prisoners (helps newly-released prisoners return to society), Team Focus (helps fatherless boys) and the Tark Toy Drive (pediatric stroke awareness). Danny is a successful real estate developer and small businessman.

Steeped in the family traditions of education, Danny Tarkanian decided to seek public service. In 2006, Danny earned 230,000 votes in the race for Nevada Secretary of State.

Jerry and Lois

JT as student at PCC

Jerry Tarkanian

August 8, 1930 ~ February 11, 2015

CPSIA information can be obtained
at www.ICGtesting.com
Printed in the USA
BVHW060809200720
584113BV00012B/393

9 781946 875556